PENGUIN BOOKS
BBC BOOKS

The New Woman's Hour Book of Short Stories

Di Speirs was born and brought up in Scotland. She was educated in Edinburgh and at the University of St Andrews. She worked in the theatre for five years before becoming a radio journalist with the Australian Broadcasting Corporation in London and Melbourne. She joined Woman's Hour in 1990 and has been the Serials Producer for the past four years. She lives in London with her husband and their two young daughters.

Di Speirs also edited the *Woman's Hour 50th Anniversary Short Story Collection*, published by Penguin/BBC in 1996. Both are available as BBC Radio Collection Cassettes. She has also produced a number of original Woman's Hour serials on tape, including *Anna Karenina*, read by Juliet Stevenson, and *The Portrait of a Lady*, read by Miriam Margolyes. In 1996 she edited and produced 'Shirley Williams, Snakes and Ladders − A Political Diary', for radio and cassette.

The New Woman's Hour Book of Short Stories

EDITED BY DI SPEIRS

PENGUIN BOOKS
BBC BOOKS

PENGUIN BOOKS
BBC BOOKS

Published by the Penguin Group and BBC Worldwide Ltd
Penguin Books Ltd, 27 Wrights Lane, London w8 5tz, England
Penguin Putnam Inc., 375 Hudson Street, New York, New York 10014, USA
Penguin Books Australia Ltd, Ringwood, Victoria, Australia
Penguin Books Canada Ltd, 10 Alcorn Avenue, Toronto, Ontario, Canada m4v 3b2
Penguin Books (NZ) Ltd, Private Bag 102902, NSMC, Auckland, New Zealand

Penguin Books Ltd, Registered Offices: Harmondsworth, Middlesex, England

This selection first published by Penguin Books and BBC Books, a division of
BBC Worldwide Ltd 1997
10 9 8

Selection and Introduction copyright © Di Speirs, 1997
The acknowledgements on p. xiii constitute an extension of this copyright page
All rights reserved.

The moral right of the editor has been asserted

▣▣▣™ BBC used under licence

Set in 10.5/13pt Monotype Bembo
Typeset by Rowland Phototypesetting Ltd, Bury St Edmunds, Suffolk
Printed in England by Clays Ltd, St Ives plc

Contents

Introduction

Alice Munro, the distinguished Canadian short-story writer, whose work has been frequently broadcast on Woman's Hour, has described the short story as 'a world seen in a quick, glancing light'. Her description captures the essence of the successful short story. That in its very brevity and economy it conveys so much more than it covers.

To cut a story to fit a twelve-minute serial slot on radio is fraught with danger. Discarding swathe after swathe of perfectly honed prose can feel akin to butchery. The trick is to ensure the essence survives, enhanced by the reading of course. Nonetheless it is a great pleasure to re-present here a selection of stories by the very best of today's writers returned to their full and unadulterated glory; as the abiding popularity of short stories proves it works.

As with the previous three Woman's Hour collections the eighteen stories here are linked by a loose theme. Having explored 'aspects of love', 'the younger generation', and for Woman's Hour's fiftieth anniversary in 1996, a 'celebration of women', I decided this time to turn the spotlight on the opposite sex. 'Women on men' offered a broad sweep. Women writers are sometimes accused of either disregarding men altogether or of being only negative about them. Very often where men do appear they are only bit players. But, trawling through my favourite recordings from the past few years, I found a wealth of stories in which men are or share centre stage. In most cases the men are seen through the eyes of the women who encounter them. Others – notably Beryl Bainbridge and Rose Tremain – have crossed the floor to inhabit the minds of their protagonists.

In the opening story, 'Gods and Slaves', Clare Boylan's three unwise and unworldly virgins ask their mother, 'What is a man like?' Amongst the male protagonists – lovers, husbands, cooks and cads, a thief, a scientist, Mr Right and Mr Wrong and Mr 'Will-do' – you will find as many views on and of men as there are authors. There is no common line, and no stereotyping. On the whole fathers come out better than lovers. Some of the best men emerge when women choose to take on a male guise – but then perhaps it's not surprising that few women would relish stepping into the role of the dirty rat! There *are* men behaving badly: but there are also the broken-hearted, the beloved and the boys next door.

The heroes of the first three stories all leave a little to be desired. Clare Boylan is a fine Irish writer with a wicked sense of humour and an acute eye. Phelim Hartigan, the man with whom all three of her teenage singing trio are smitten, is as phlegmatic as his name suggests. His effect on them is clear: 'He began in a voice that was low and sweet but carried strongly and they, without any direction, followed in, as a woman is led by a skilled dance partner. Their voices, which had been bland and thin, at once improved, for the exciting male presence injected their singing with a tremolo of yearning. They knew every time they opened their mouths that life had begun.' Ah, the perils of youthful infatuation.

In 'Hairball', the Canadian writer Margaret Atwood's heroine is fighting for survival. Her battle is against both the male establishment – in her case the prejudices and sexism of the members of the board – and her lover – a man whose very self she has fashioned. 'He'd been Gerald when they first met. It was she who transformed him, first to Gerry, then to Ger. (Rhymed with *flair*, rhymed with *dare*.) She made him get rid of those sucky pursed-mouth ties, told him what shoes to wear, got him to buy a loose-cut Italian suit, redid his hair. A lot of his current tastes – in food, in drink, in recreational drugs, in women's entertainment underwear – were once hers . . . he is her creation.' Sadly, he is no longer behaving like perfect specimen should.

Nadine Gordimer's taut story also encompasses prejudice. It paints a portrait of a grave, enigmatic young man, Rad, who is equally hard for the reader and his lover Vera to fathom. The boot is on the other foot in Rose Tremain's delightful and thought-provoking 'The Crossing of Herald Montjoy'. Switching between the field before Agincourt and a day some three years previous when her young hero goes to propose to his love, Tremain captures that sense of *joie de vivre* when anything is possible. 'He gasped. There were days in a life so momentous they seemed to alter the size of the world. His heart felt as colossal as a cuckoo bird . . . He sat down on the grass . . . There *are* splendid lives, he thought. There *is* bravery and there is luck. There is ingenuity. A woman's shoe can be yellow . . .'

The women in the next two stories are both looking for Mr Right. Elizabeth Jolley, the distinguished Australian author who so often has an eye for the quirky and bizarre, has written a wonderful account of a middle-aged babysitter and her night spent parrying with an equally eccentric kidnapper – an altogether bad sort who nonetheless leaves her 'wishing for a happy ending'. Dawn, in 'The Immaculate Bridegroom', is far more pragmatic about her lack of a suitor – and perhaps finds the perfect solution to a common problem.

Janice Galloway is one of Scotland's most exciting writers. In 'Sonata Form' she describes Danny, a musician, and his life with Mona. Amidst the adulation of his female fans, Mona watches and waits for him in an evocative portrayal of the flaws and familiarities of a long-term relationship. 'He was close now . . . She reached for the plate from his hand without asking, took it over to the buffet . . . Danny wasn't looking in her direction but he didn't need to. His smile changed. It stayed in place for the woman Mona could only see the back of but it knew she was coming over.'

'Polaris' is almost of novella length – and was broadcast in two parts. It too examines a relationship – in this case between a newly married naval officer and Meg, left at home for three months with nothing but his dog for company – but I have included it here mostly because of Fay Weldon's wonderfully witty decision to make her three submariners – the Attack Team – into thwarted *cordon bleu* chefs who spend their time beneath the waves cooking up glorious dishes whilst potentially about to annihilate the world. At the final moment, as the 'banana and rum fritters' sizzle in the pan, the captain even remarks 'You know, if a Routine came through to push those buttons, I wouldn't! What, and lose all this?' Polaris is gone, but the peculiar and very male ethos of service life lives on and Weldon treats it with her own distinctive humour.

In 'The First Wife', Penelope Lively picks up a theme she examined in her last novel, 'Heatwave', that of a man facing the stark realities of aging. Here her fallen hero meets his first wife at a family wedding. He had, you may have guessed, previously rejected her for a younger model in an attempt to hold back time. But 'now was his chance – not to make amends but to initiate a new, rewarding relationship. That was so very much what he needed, he suddenly realized. Not some transitory flirtation with an agreeable newcomer, but a dependable, mutually supportive liaison with the person he had once known best in the world. It need not affect his marriage in any way.' Hmmm . . .

Beryl Bainbridge was eight when she began writing stories – if she worked for more than two hours her mother would say 'Run into the garden, pet. All authors need to play.' Such a regime certainly proved beneficial. She is another regular contributor not just to this book but to the serial slot over the years. Here she comes up with the type of character at which she excels, slightly sad, down on his luck, left by his wife for 'a career woman with a villa in Spain'. Now Norman is trying to build up his life again. 'In spite of every effort, he had not yet adjusted to being on his own. He had read that single men were in demand at dinner parties and things, but though he had casually let drop, in conversations with colleagues at the office, that he was on the loose, in a manner of speaking, no one had ever taken him up on it, not even to the extent of asking him round for a cup of tea.' Salvation appears in the unlikely guise of a street carnival and a crystal ball – classic Bainbridge territory.

The territory couldn't be more different in the story from the unique pen of the American author E. Annie Proulx. She, more than any other woman writer here, inhabits a male world, populated by hunters, red-necks and rough-hewn farmers and, in this case riven by the petty rivalries and hatreds between two old men who have known each other since boyhood. The futility of Hawkheel's struggle against Bill Stong is told in language which is superbly evocative of the man and the place. 'In late May he followed the trout up the narrow, sun-warmed streams, his rod thrusting skillfully through the alders, crushing underfoot ferns whose broken stems released an elusive bitter scent. In October, mists came down on him as he waded through drenched goldenrod meadows, alert for grouse. And in the numb silence of November Hawkheel was a deer hunter up on the shoulder of Antler Mountain, his back against a beech while frozen threads of ice formed on the rifle's blue metal.'

Man's weddedness to place appears in the following two stories too. Ali Smith's subject is again a man in crisis – in this case a classic mid-life one for a television producer. His solution is to flee north to his roots. By contrast the leading man in 'Tuataras' by the New Zealand author Barbara Anderson never leaves his. His crisis – though perhaps that's too strong a word for a character who is unruffled by life and whose biggest thrill is the hatching out of a scaly reptile – comes with the return of his sister after years in England and the consequent disruption of his solitary existence. This is a perfect portrait of the quintessential bachelor.

I make no apologies for including 'Silver Water' here, although in a sense the two men within it are not central. Nonetheless they constitute two of the most sympathetic men in the whole book. Written with the warmth typical of their author, the American psychiatrist Amy Bloom, they are an integral part of a story that, judging by the letters I received when it was broadcast, touched listeners, particularly men, more than any other in the past year. It is a tender, heart-rending gem.

Love and a tender empathy flow through 'Walker Brothers Cowboy' too. It is another masterpiece from one of the doyennes of the short story, Alice Munro – a writer who began with the form as a young mother who didn't have time to write anything longer and now would not choose to. Here she recounts a visit one sultry summer afternoon in the depression to a farm house outside a Canadian hick town. Perfectly crafted as always, there couldn't be a better example of a whole world seen in a glancing light as a child glimpses her father's past. ' "Here's luck!" ' says Nora. 'She and my father drink and I know what it is. Whisky. One of the things my mother has told me in our talks together is that my father never drinks whisky. But I see he does. He drinks whisky and he talks of people whose names I have never heard before.'

Two other stories also examine fathers through the eyes of their children. Mary Morrissy is an Irish journalist whose first novel *Mother of Pearl* was received – and serialized – to great acclaim. In her pithy and often lyrical writing she has the ability to fathom actions and reactions that are undeniably human but not always honourable. Helen Dunmore, winner of the first Orange Prize for fiction, is well known as a poet and a novelist. Always adept at writing with a child's eye, here she describes the fear engendered by an autocratic father and counterpoints it beautifully.

Deborah Moggach is a firm Woman's Hour favourite and the only author to have graced all four short-story collections! A brilliant commentator on our times her stories are often funny, always skilfully perceptive. 'Stopping at the Lights' is a gentler tale than some; her hero, if such he is, a quiet man named Jim. 'Jim believed he worked on the Wall of Death even though he only drove the equipment lorry. His real name was Arnold, in fact, but he re-christened himself after Jim Reeves, another of his heroes. I only learnt this near the end. With all the harm in the world, what's the harm in that?'

Heroes, villains, sweethearts and sweet talkers. Of course not one of these eighteen exceptional writers claims to be giving a definitive answer to the singing sisters' question, 'What is a man like?' But I hope that the characters you encounter here – entertaining, infuriating, charming even – will give the lie to those who claim women don't or won't write about men well.

Di Speirs
Serials Producer, Woman's Hour
May 1997

Acknowledgements

The short stories in this selection are taken from the following books and magazines, to whose publishers acknowledgement is made:

That Bad Woman, copyright © Clare Boylan, 1995 (reproduced by permission of the author, c/o Rogers, Coleridge & White Ltd, 20 Powis Mews, London W11 1JN), Little, Brown and Company (UK); *Wilderness Tips*, copyright © Margaret Atwood, 1991, Bloomsbury (published at £14.99); *Jump and Other Stories*, copyright © Nadine Gordimer, 1991, Bloomsbury (published at £13.99); *Evangelista's Fan*, copyright © Rose Tremain, 1994, Sinclair-Stevenson ('The Crossing of Herald Montjoy' first appeared in *The Independent*, 1993); *Cosmopolitan* 1992, copyright © Elizabeth Jolley, 1992; *Dear George & Other Stories*, copyright © Helen Simpson, 1995, William Heinemann Ltd; *Where You Find It*, copyright © Janice Galloway, 1996, Jonathan Cape; *Polaris and Other Stories*, copyright © Fay Weldon, 1985, Hodder and Stoughton; *Beyond the Blue Mountains*, copyright © Penelope Lively, 1994, Viking ('The First Wife' was previously published in *Living*, 1994); *Collected Stories*, copyright © Beryl Bainbridge, 1985, Penguin Books Ltd ('Through a Glass Brightly' was first published by Gerald Duckworth & Co. in *Mum and Mr Armitage*); *Heart Songs*, copyright © E. Annie Proulx, 1995, Fourth Estate Limited ('On the Antler' appeared in somewhat different form in *Harrowsmith*, 1983); *Free Love*, copyright © Ali Smith, 1995, Virago Press; *I Think We Should Go into the Jungle*, copyright © Barbara Anderson, 1989 (reprinted by permission of The Peters Fraser & Dunlop Group Limited on behalf of the author), Martin Secker & Warburg Limited; *Come to Me*, copyright © Amy

Bloom, 1991, 1993 (reproduced by permission of Curtis Brown Group Ltd, London), HarperCollins Publishers, Inc. ('Silver Water' appeared in a slightly different form in *Story* (Autumn 1991)); *Selected Stories*, copyright © Alice Munro, 1996, Chatto & Windus Ltd; *A Lazy Eye*, copyright © Mary Morrissy, 1993, Jonathan Cape; *Love of Fat Men*, copyright © Helen Dunmore, 1997 (reprinted by permission of A. P. Watt Ltd on behalf of the author), Viking; *Changing Babies and Other Stories*, copyright © Deborah Moggach, 1995, William Heinemann Ltd.

Gods and Slaves

CLARE BOYLAN

Their mother always said that if any of the girls got pregnant their father would throw her out in the street. This warning acted more effectively than any threat to their own security, keeping them in a state of grace for longer than was necessary or appealing. Modesty flowed around them like a moat and there was no brother who might act as drawbridge. They wondered about men a great deal and sometimes begged their mother, 'What is a man like?' and she replied that if they wanted to know what men were like they had only to look at the picture in the hall. The picture was a framed photograph of Roman statuary, gods or slaves, but the chiselled unmentionables had crumbled into dust long before the camera was invented and they had to ply their fervid imaginations to vague porous whorls, not very large, they suspected, even before air pollution had attacked their finer points.

It is likely that they would have continued gazing vexedly at this faded image until middle age dimmed their eyesight had not Phelim Hartigan appeared. From that moment it became clear that at least one female in the household was going to be seduced and each one was alert to the event. The mother wore high heels and hid her hair net. The girls washed their long blonde hair in camomile flowers and did special exercises that promised bosoms as big as melons. Phelim Hartigan was not a tall man but was of a forceful structure. Other men looked like suits filled with cushions or coat hangers, but he was all muscle, sprung from a root of generation. He had thick black curly hair and green eyes and when he sang in *basso profundo* it sent vibrations right up through the furniture and through the person who was sitting on it too. From the moment he entered the house his prerogative was established. The black cat, Mrs Danvers, flung herself on his knee and picked impatiently at the weave of his trousers, Even the father, when he opened the door, appeared to be handing him a menu.

They got Phelim through an advertisement. The sisters sang in close harmony in the manner of the Andrews Sisters for the entertainment or endurance of visitors at Christmas. As they came into their teens the notion presented itself that this talent might transport them into the larger world, where men were. Their mother was very proud of them and relaxed her normal vigilance to see their gifts admired. They were paid ten shillings a week to sing in variety concerts for which she sewed up an assortment of costumes, depending on her mood. Sometimes they were chaste white frocks in cotton piqué and on other occasions they were scarlet satin shifts through which the unfulfilled peaks of their whirlpool bras pointed like the horns of minor pantomime devils.

The theatres were in the poor suburbs of Dublin and had been first cinemas and then bingo halls. Cinerama was dragooned in as a final bid to save the cinemas. Trains apparently came off their rails and hurtled into the audience or rivers were seen to burst their banks and explode through the screen. Stereophonic systems surrounded the audience with noises of disaster, but neither miracles nor disaster can compensate a loss of faith. With the start of the sixties people had jobs and money. They wanted real life. This fad was short-lived. Later on the picture houses would be pool halls or carpet warehouses but for a few years variety became popular, with clamorous rock groups imitating the Crickets or the Comets and male comedians who dressed as women, stuffing cabbages inside their jumpers.

The girls stood rigid upon the stage, one day perky as the models in Persil ads, the next sleekly gleaming like women in motor oil commercials. They made uniform swipes at the air with their hands, and their voices, tonally perfect, flowed about them like a cloud of summer flies. But they got no further. People in the nearest rows looked bewildered. 'We can't hear you.' When they moved close to the microphone it whistled. 'Get them off ya!' yelled the gurriers from the back. Within a few weeks everyone got used to the silent girl performers, as they had once accepted silent films, and they continued to appear weekly, but neither their careers nor their lives progressed. In the dressing area, with the smell of cold sweat and beer, they were timidly pawed by midget pop performers. A squint-eyed comedian in his forties invited Kay, who was thirteen, to dinner. She asked could her sisters come too and he, gazing soulfully askew, declared, 'There are times when a man likes to be alone with a woman.' They decided that they must look for more sophisticated outlets, nightclubs or television. They auditioned for television, where the volume could be adjusted with knobs, but were turned down on the basis that they were lacking in 'oomph'.

For two shillings you could place a card in the window of a music shop on the quays and it was like purchasing a magic spell. 'All-girl professional singing group seeks male backing,' the notice read. A stream of young men arrived at the house, where once it had seemed that no man would ever come. They travelled on foot, by bicycle, on throbbing motorbikes, with guitars, mouth organs, accordions. Most of them were wan and spotty, no adepts in oomph. The sisters had lived too long on a diet of pure romance to accommodate any imperfection. They entertained a good-looking country boy until a dispute arose about the division of their fee. 'What do ye care about cash?' he had said bitterly. 'Youse birds are sittin' on a fortune.' After a series of disappointments they took to stationing themselves within the folds of the drawing-room curtains, and there they lived, quiet as the cat. When a fresh applicant pushed the creaky gate they would signal one another and make a swift appraisal before informing the youth that the position had been filled.

The notice in the music shop must have grown sallow and flyblown by the time Phelim Hartigan found it, for several years had passed and the girls had all but given up singing for more useful pursuits, such as typing and dressmaking. Kay came home from school one day and found him sitting in the dining-room strumming his guitar and singing in his beautiful deep voice. He fixed his eye on her and sang on, and she grew very pale and then very red, and fled to the kitchen. Mother was thrashing pastry with a rolling pin. 'That is Mr Hartigan. He is to accompany you girls,' she said and then, surprising her youngest daughter beyond all measure, 'I have invited him to tea.'

They never knew where Phelim came from. He was much older than the other young men, being about twenty-nine. They had no idea why he answered the advertisement, for he was a good musician as well as a good singer. They questioned him but he rarely made conversation. He would strum a few pulsating chords and name a song. He began in a voice that was low and sweet but carried strongly and they, without any direction, followed in, as a woman is led by a skilled dance partner. Their voices, which had been bland and thin, at once improved, for the exciting male presence injected their singing with a tremolo of yearning. They knew every time they opened their mouths that life had begun. That fundamental tremor was akin to a biblical upheaval that could breathe life into dust, roll back the stones from caves, rend their clothing, make them free to do anything. Yet they had been brought up as spinsters. They had no idea how to persuade. 'Rehearsals twice a week,' they told Phelim sharply. (They had always been once a week.) On the days between they silently examined their noses for blackheads and blew on their palms to test their breath.

'Stand up straight,' he commanded Maeve. 'Of the four of us, you are the only one with breasts. Little breasts, but let them be seen.' The girls eyed him suspiciously. No one said breasts. Bosoms were all right, being a joke word, but breasts were a portion of the anatomy not openly acknowledged between the sexes. 'Let down your hair,' he told Cecilia. He unpinned her plaits and raked them loose with his fingers. An electrified cornfield fled over her shoulders. 'You girls cannot hold your breath for the whole of your lives.' He inhaled deeply, allowing the air to go all the way down his body. 'You must sing from . . . here.' And before their very eyes he touched himself. There. They had stopped breathing completely, their eyes riveted to that part of his clothing that had a restless, lumpy look, like a boy's pocket where a mouse was hidden.

Two weeks later the restructured group made its first appearance at the Apollo in Sundrive. The girls had begun to change. Released from the petrifying spell of innocence, they were less gawky, less astonished. Touches of colour appeared in their cheeks. They no longer carried their bodies as the mortifying baggage of looming fecundity, but with a swish, like the net slips, stiffened with sugar, they introduced beneath their skirts accentuated with Waspee belts. Toenails, hitherto the yellow torment of an older generation (hewn into a V when ingrown), became pearly lozenges, winking through peep-toe shoes. The sisters were in white. He wore black – black shirt, black leather jacket and jeans. The audience looked rebellious. They remembered the silent girl trio fondly. Phelim began to mumble something unrecognizable in a little Woody Guthrie voice, making the audience strain to listen. When they were lulled he made a mighty twang on his guitar, gyrated the middle portion of his anatomy and the song became recognizable as 'Jailhouse Rock'. The girls clapped their hands and bent into the microphone for the chorus. Phelim thrust his guitar floorward as if to tango, bent backwards with angled knees, projected his hips at unsuspecting housewives and filled the cold little theatre with his great warm voice. The women in the audience did something that no Dublin audience had ever done before. They screamed. That night their weekly earnings were promoted to thirty shillings a week.

For a moment, poised before the baying housewives, the sisters had felt afraid. Then melodic whistles interposed the soughing dirge and this was pulsed with the crisp percussion of applause. Phelim was laughing as he gathered them forward to share the praise. The wall of discord that swept around them like Cinerama became a jubilee march. The scuffed stage was a triumphal platform. Acid stage lights on twisted wires rained down dazzling splinters that dusted their hair and their white dresses with gold. Oh, they understood they were not fit for worship, they were ordinary women who knew better than to rise above their station, but they were the brides of an idol. Phelim their creature. The sisters exchanged sated glances. They felt fulfilled, accomplished. They had achieved the primary object of mating, which is to make other women jealous.

The idyll that followed this conquest was of short duration. The notion crept in on them that each of the sisters was another woman. A man could not be jointly claimed. Possession was a singular objective. The enchantment of his appearance in their life was soured by the need to clarify his position in it. All their lives they had been fused by curiosity. Now they were sundered by the more powerful force of rivalry. When Phelim gave Cecilia a lift on the pillion of his motorcycle, Maeve stormed out of the house and came back with a startled boy, whom she called a boyfriend. Kay wore a dress so short that her mother said she would be ashamed to have it hanging on her clothesline, let alone on her daughter.

The brides were stymied. All their efforts to claim his attention appeared only to cultivate his indifference. One day he did not appear for rehearsal. 'And I had bought crinkle chips for tea,' the mother said disconsolately. It was not to be a solo occurrence. He told the girls he had other things on his mind, there was a difficult decision he had to make. Delight deserted them. They grew anxious, inert, waiting for him to make the difficult choice between them. 'Of course,' the mother crushingly mused, 'a man like that would have other women.' Had they not been so uncomfortably tethered by the baffling hex they might have taken pleasure in the success of their singing. The group had been offered a fee of three pounds by a rival theatre. They were invited once again to audition for television.

All week the mother laboured on their new costumes, cream art silk with gold coin spots. All day they steamed their skin, singed their hair and scraped tiny golden strands from their legs, tautly humming choruses and harmonies. They had been stiffly poised in the drawing-room for half an hour awaiting Phelim when the doorbell rang. Their mother went to answer it so that their attention had fled with her to the hall even as they listened to the news on the wireless that President John Kennedy had been assassinated. The mother came back and leaned in the doorway. She seemed shaken, as if she had received the same terrible bulletin at the door. 'That was a boy,' she said. 'He was sent by Phelim. Phelim will not be coming. He will not be coming back at all.'

The girls sang alone at the audition. They were turned down, as they knew they would be. When this was out of the way they found themselves husbands as quickly as possible. Even Kay, shrugging off her school bag, broke her mother's heart by riling a boy with her short skirt and struggling up the aisle as a teenage bride and mother-to-be.

They talked about Phelim only once after his disappearance.

'He is dead,' Maeve decided. 'Mother would not tell us.'

'An accident with his motorbike,' Cecilia agreed.

And Kay proposed that if not dead, then he had certainly been called to the priesthood. Any other possibilities were too painful to contemplate, but even this resolution brought no relief. It only turned them into women. That the Lord should claim two such prizes on a single day! After all, there was no contest, only sport for the gods.

They settled down to marriage with that look of bewilderment and resignation that young wives had before the Beatles. They never again regained the closeness of their childhood for they had been healed of curiosity and, naturally, they no longer had recourse to the question, 'What is a man like?'

Hairball

MARGARET ATWOOD

On the thirteenth of November, day of unluck, month of the dead, Kat went into the Toronto General Hospital for an operation. It was for an ovarian cyst, a large one.

Many women had them, the doctor told her. Nobody knew why. There wasn't any way of finding out whether the thing was malignant, whether it contained, already, the spores of death. Not before they went in. He spoke of 'going in' the way she'd heard old veterans in TV documentaries speak of assaults on enemy territory. There was the same tensing of the jaw, the same fierce gritting of the teeth, the same grim enjoyment. Except that what he would be going into was her body. Counting down, waiting for the anaesthetic, Kat too gritted her teeth fiercely. She was terrified, but also she was curious. Curiosity has got her through a lot.

She'd made the doctor promise to save the thing for her, whatever it was, so she could have a look. She was intensely interested in her own body, in anything it might choose to do or produce; although when flaky Dania, who did layout at the magazine, told her this growth was a message to her from her body and she ought to sleep with an amethyst under her pillow to calm her vibrations, Kat told her to stuff it.

The cyst turned out to be a benign tumour. Kat liked that use of *benign*, as if the thing had a soul and wished her well. It was big as a grapefruit, the doctor said. 'Big as a coconut,' said Kat. Other people had grapefruits. 'Coconut' was better. It conveyed the hardness of it, and the hairiness, too.

The hair in it was red – long strands of it wound round and round inside, like a ball of wet wool gone berserk or like the guck you pulled out of a clogged bathroom-sink drain. There were little bones in it too, or fragments of bone; bird bones, the bones of a sparrow crushed by a car. There was a scattering of nails, toe or finger. There were five perfectly formed teeth.

'Is this abnormal?' Kat asked the doctor, who smiled. Now that he had gone in and come out again, unscathed, he was less clenched.

'Abnormal? No,' he said carefully, as if breaking the news to a mother about a freakish accident to her newborn. 'Let's say it's fairly common.' Kat was a little disappointed. She would have preferred uniqueness.

She asked for a bottle of formaldehyde, and put the cut-open tumour into it. It was hers, it was benign, it did not deserve to be thrown away. She took it back to her apartment and stuck it on the mantelpiece. She named it Hairball. It isn't that different from having a stuffed bear's head or a preserved ex-pet or anything else with fur and teeth looming over your fireplace; or she pretends it isn't. Anyway, it certainly makes an impression.

Ger doesn't like it. Despite his supposed yen for the new and outré, he is a squeamish man. The first time he comes around (sneaks around, creeps around) after the operation, he tells Kat to throw Hairball out. He calls it 'disgusting'. Kat refuses point-blank, and says she'd rather have Hairball in a bottle on her mantelpiece than the soppy dead flowers he's brought her, which will anyway rot a lot sooner than Hairball will. As a mantelpiece ornament, Hairball is far superior. Ger says Kat has a tendency to push things to extremes, to go over the edge, merely from a juvenile desire to shock, which is hardly a substitute for wit. One of these days, he says, she will go way too far. Too far for him, is what he means.

'That's why you hired me, isn't it?' she says. 'Because I go way too far.' But he's in one of his analysing moods. He can see these tendencies of hers reflected in her work on the magazine, he says. All that leather and those grotesque and tortured-looking poses are heading down a track he and others are not at all sure they should continue to follow. Does she see what he means, does she take his point? It's a point that's been made before. She shakes her head slightly, says nothing. She knows how that translates: there have been complaints from the advertisers. *Too bizarre, too kinky.* Tough.

'Want to see my scar?' she says. 'Don't make me laugh, though, you'll crack it open.' Stuff like that makes him dizzy: anything with a hint of blood, anything gynaecological. He almost threw up in the delivery room when his wife had a baby two years ago. He'd told her that with pride. Kat thinks about sticking a cigarette into the side of her mouth, as in a black-and-white movie of the forties. She thinks about blowing the smoke into his face.

Her insolence used to excite him, during their arguments. Then there would be a grab of her upper arms, a smouldering, violent kiss. He kisses her as if he thinks someone else is watching him, judging the image they make together. Kissing the latest thing, hard and shiny, purple-mouthed, crop-headed; kissing a girl, a woman, a girl, in a little crotch-hugger skirt and skin-tight leggings. He likes mirrors.

But he isn't excited now. And she can't decoy him into bed; she isn't ready for that yet, she isn't healed. He has a drink, which he doesn't finish, holds her hand as an afterthought, gives her a couple of avuncular pats on the off-white outsized alpaca shoulder, leaves too quickly.

'Goodbye, Gerald,' she says. She pronounces the name with mockery. It's a negation of him, an abolishment of him, like ripping a medal off his chest. It's a warning.

He'd been Gerald when they first met. It was she who transformed him, first to Gerry, then to Ger. (Rhymed with *flair*, rhymed with *dare*.) She made him get rid of those sucky pursed-mouth ties, told him what shoes to wear, got him to buy a loose-cut Italian suit, redid his hair. A lot of his current tastes – in food, in drink, in recreational drugs, in women's entertainment underwear – were once hers. In his new phase, with his new, hard, stripped-down name ending on the sharpened note of *r*, he is her creation.

As she is her own. During her childhood she was a romanticized

Katherine, dressed by her misty-eyed, fussy mother in dresses that looked like ruffled pillowcases. By high school she'd shed the frills and emerged as a bouncy, round-faced Kathy, with gleaming freshly washed hair and enviable teeth, eager to please and no more interesting than a health-food ad. At university she was Kath, blunt and no-bullshit in her Take-Back-the-Night jeans and checked shirt and her bricklayer-style striped-denim peaked hat. When she ran away to England, she sliced herself down to Kat. It was economical, street-feline, and pointed as a nail. It was also unusual. In England you had to do something to get their attention, especially if you weren't English. Safe in this incarnation, she Ramboed through the eighties.

It was the name, she still thinks, that got her the interview and then the job. The job with an avant-garde magazine, the kind that was printed on matte stock in black and white, with overexposed close-ups of women with hair blowing over their eyes, one nostril prominent: *the razor's edge*, it was called. Haircuts as art, some real art, film reviews, a little stardust, wardrobes of ideas that were clothes and of clothes that were ideas – the metaphysical shoulder pad. She learned her trade well, hands-on. She learned what worked.

She made her way up the ladder, from layout to design, then to the supervision of whole spreads, and then whole issues. It wasn't easy, but it was worth it. She had become a creator; she created total looks. After a while she could walk down the street in Soho or stand in the lobby at openings and witness her handiwork incarnate, strolling around in outfits she'd put together, spouting her warmed-over pronouncements. It was like being God, only God had never got around to off-the-rack lines.

By that time her face had lost its roundness, though the teeth of course remained: there was something to be said for North American dentistry. She'd shaved off most of her hair, worked on the drop-dead stare, perfected a certain turn of the neck that conveyed an aloof inner authority. What you had to make them believe was that you knew something they didn't know yet. What you also had to make them believe was that they too could know this thing, this thing that would give them eminence and power and sexual allure, that would attract envy to them – but for a price. The price of the magazine. What they could never get through their heads was that it was done entirely with cameras. Frozen light, frozen time. Given the angle, she could make any woman look ugly. Any man as well. She could make anyone look beautiful, or at least interesting. It was all photography, it was all iconography. It was all in the choosing eye. This was the thing that could never be bought, no matter how much of your pitiful monthly wage you blew on snakeskin.

Despite the status, *the razor's edge* was fairly low-paying. Kat herself could not afford many of the things she contextualized so well. The grottiness and expense of London began to get to her; she got tired of gorging on the canapés at literary launches in order to scrimp on groceries, tired of the fuggy smell of cigarettes ground into the red-and-maroon carpeting of pubs, tired of the pipes bursting every time it froze in winter, and of the Clarissas and Melissas and Penelopes at the magazine rabbiting on about how they had been literally, absolutely, totally freezing all night, and how it literally, absolutely, totally, usually never got that cold. It always got that cold. The pipes always burst. Nobody thought of putting in real pipes, ones that would not burst next time. Burst pipes were an English tradition, like so many others.

Like, for instance, English men. Charm the knickers off you with their mellow vowels and frivolous verbiage, and then, once they'd got them off, panic and run. Or else stay and whinge. The English called it *whingeing* instead of whining. It was better, really. Like a creaking hinge. It was a traditional compliment to be whinged at by an Englishman. It was his way of saying he trusted you, he was conferring upon you the privilege of getting to know the real him. The inner, whinging him. That was how they thought of women, secretly: whinge receptacles. Kat could play it, but that didn't mean she liked it.

She had an advantage over the English women, though: she was of no class. She had no class. She was in a class of her own. She could roll around among the English men, all different kinds of them, secure in the knowledge that she was not being measured against the class yardsticks and accent-detectors they carried around in their back pockets, was not subject to the petty snobberies and resentments that lent such richness to their inner lives. The flip side of this freedom was that she was beyond the pale. She was a colonial – how fresh, how vital, how anonymous, how finally of no consequence. Like a hole in the wall, she could be told all secrets and then be abandoned with no guilt.

She was too smart, of course. The English men were very competitive; they liked to win. Several times it hurt. Twice she had abortions, because the men in question were not up for the alternative. She learned to say that she didn't want children anyway, that if she longed for a rug-rat she would buy a gerbil. Her life began to seem long. Her adrenalin was running out. Soon she would be thirty, and all she could see ahead was more of the same.

This was how things were when Gerald turned up. 'You're terrific,' he said, and she was ready to hear it, even from him, even though *terrific* was a word that had probably gone out with fifties' crew-cuts. She was ready for his voice by that time too: the flat, metallic nasal tone of the Great Lakes, with its clear hard *r*s and its absence of theatricality. Dull normal. The speech of her people. It came to her suddenly that she was an exile.

Gerald was scouting, Gerald was recruiting. He'd heard about her, looked at her work, sought her out. One of the big companies back in Toronto was launching a new fashion-oriented magazine, he said: up-market, international in its coverage, of course, but with some Canadian fashion in it too, and with lists of stores where the items portrayed could actually be bought. In that respect they felt they'd have it all over the competition, those American magazines that assumed you could only get Gucci in New York or Los Angeles. Heck, times had changed, you could get it in Edmonton! You could get it in Winnipeg!

Kat had been away too long. There was Canadian fashion now? The English quip would be to say that 'Canadian fashion' was an oxymoron. She refrained from making it, lit a cigarette with her cyanide-green Covent Garden-boutique leather-covered lighter (as featured in the May issue of *the razor's edge*), looked Gerald in the eye. 'London is a lot to give up,' she said levelly. She glanced around the see-me-here Mayfair restaurant where they were finishing lunch, a restaurant she'd chosen because she'd known he was paying. She'd never spend that kind of money on food otherwise. 'Where would I eat?'

Gerald assured her that Toronto was now the restaurant capital of Canada. He himself would be happy to be her guide. There was a great Chinatown, there was world-class Italian. Then he paused, took a breath. 'I've been meaning to ask you,' he said. 'About the name. Is that Kat as in Krazy?' He thought this was suggestive. She'd heard it before.

'No,' she said. 'It's Kat as in KitKat. That's a chocolate bar. Melts in your mouth.' She gave him her stare, quirked her mouth, just a twitch.

Gerald became flustered, but he pushed on. They wanted her, they needed her, they loved her, he said in essence. Someone with her fresh, innovative approach and her experience would be worth a lot of money to them, relatively speaking. But there were rewards other than the money. She would be in on the initial concept, she would have a formative influence, she would have a free hand. He named a sum that made her gasp, inaudibly of course. By now she knew better than to betray desire.

So she made the journey back, did her three months of culture shock, tried the world-class Italian and the great Chinese, and seduced Gerald at the first opportunity, right in his junior vice-presidential office. It was the first time Gerald had been seduced in such a location, or perhaps ever. Even though it was after hours, the danger frenzied him. It was the idea of it. The daring. The image of Kat kneeling on the broadloom, in a legendary bra that until now he'd seen only in the lingerie ads of the Sunday *New York Times*, unzipping him in full view of the silver-framed engagement portrait of his wife that complemented the impossible ballpoint pen set on his desk. At that time he was so straight he felt compelled to take off his wedding ring and place it carefully in the ashtray first. The next day he brought her a box of David Wood Food Shop chocolate truffles. They were the best, he told her, anxious that she should recognize their quality. She found the gesture banal, but also sweet. The banality, the sweetness, the hunger to impress: that was Gerald.

Gerald was the kind of man she wouldn't have bothered with in London. He was not funny, he was not knowledgeable, he had little verbal charm. But he was eager, he was tractable, he was blank paper. Although he was eight years older than she was, he seemed much younger. She took pleasure from his furtive, boyish delight in his own wickedness. And he was so grateful. 'I can hardly believe this is happening,' he said, more frequently than was necessary and usually in bed.

His wife, whom Kat encountered (and still encounters) at many tedious company events, helped to explain his gratitude. The wife was a priss. Her name was Cheryl. Her hair looked as if she still used big rollers and embalm-your-hairdo spray; her mind was room-by-room Laura Ashley wallpaper: tiny, unopened pastel buds arranged in straight rows. She probably put on rubber gloves to make love, and checked it off on a list afterwards. One more messy household chore. She looked at Kat as if she'd like to spritz her with air deodorizer. Kat revenged herself by picturing Cheryl's bathrooms: hand towels embroidered with lilies, fuzzy covers on the toilet seats.

The magazine itself got off to a rocky start. Although Kat had lots of lovely money to play with, and although it was a challenge to be working in colour, she did not have the free hand Gerald had promised her. She had to contend with the company board of directors, who were all men, who were all accountants or indistinguishable from them, who were cautious and slow as moles.

'It's simple,' Kat told them. 'You bombard them with images of what they ought to be, and you make them feel grotty for being the way they are. You're working with the gap between reality and perception. That's why you have to hit them with something new, something they've never seen before, something they aren't. Nothing sells like anxiety.'

The board, on the other hand, felt that the readership should simply be offered more of what they already had. More fur, more sumptuous leather, more cashmere. More established names. The board had no sense of improvisation, no wish to take risks; no sporting instincts, no desire to put one over on the readers just for the hell of it. 'Fashion is like hunting,' Kat told them, hoping to appeal to their male hormones, if any. 'It's playful, it's intense, it's predatory. It's blood and guts. It's erotic.' But to them it was about good taste. They wanted Dress-for-Success. Kat wanted scattergun ambush.

Everything became a compromise. Kat had wanted to call the magazine *All the Rage*, but the board was put off by the vibrations of anger in the word 'rage'. They thought it was too feminist, of all things. 'It's a *forties* sound,' Kat said. 'Forties is *back*. Don't you get it?' But they didn't. They wanted to call it *Or*. French for *gold*, and blatant enough in its values, but without any base note, as Kat told them. They sawed off at *Felice*, which had qualities each side wanted. It was vaguely French-sounding, it meant 'happy' (so much less threatening than rage), and, although you couldn't expect the others to notice, for Kat it had a feline bouquet which counteracted the laciness. She had it done in hot-pink lipstick-scrawl, which helped some. She could live with it, but it had not been her first love.

This battle has been fought and refought over every innovation in design, every new angle Kat has tried to bring in, every innocuous bit of semi-kink. There was a big row over a spread that did lingerie, half pulled off and with broken glass perfume bottles strewn on the floor. There was an uproar over the two nouveau-stockinged legs, one tied to a chair with a third, different-coloured stocking. They had not understood the man's three-hundred-dollar leather gloves positioned ambiguously around a neck.

And so it has gone on, for five years.

After Gerald has left, Kat paces her living-room. Pace, pace. Her stitches pull. She's not looking forward to her solitary dinner of microwaved leftovers. She's not sure now why she came back here, to this flat burg beside the polluted inland sea. Was it Ger? Ludicrous thought but no longer out of the question. Is he the reason she stays, despite her growing impatience with him?

He's no longer fully rewarding. They've learned each other too well, they take short-cuts now; their time together has shrunk from whole stolen rolling and sensuous afternoons to a few hours snatched between work and dinner-time. She no longer knows what she wants from him. She tells herself she's worth more, she should branch out; but she doesn't see other men, she can't, somehow. She's tried once or twice but it didn't work. Sometimes she goes out to dinner or a flick with one of the gay designers. She likes the gossip.

Maybe she misses London. She feels caged, in this country, in this city, in this room. She could start with the room, she could open a window. It's too stuffy in here. There's an undertone of formaldehyde, from Hairball's bottle. The flowers she got for the operation are mostly wilted, all except Gerald's from today. Come to think of it, why didn't he send her any at the hospital? Did he forget, or was it a message?

'Hairball,' she says, 'I wish you could talk. I could have a more intelligent conversation with you than with most of the losers in this turkey farm.' Hairball's baby teeth glint in the light; it looks as if it's about to speak.

Kat feels her own forehead. She wonders if she's running a temperature. Something ominous is going on, behind her back. There haven't been enough phone calls from the magazine; they've been able to muddle on without her, which is bad news. Reigning queens should never go on vacation, or have operations either. Uneasy lies the head. She has a sixth sense about these things, she's been involved in enough palace coups to know the signs, she has sensitive antennae for the footfalls of impending treachery.

The next morning she pulls herself together, downs an espresso from her mini-machine, picks out an aggressive touch-me-if-you-dare suede outfit in armour grey, and drags herself to the office, although she isn't due in till next week. Surprise, surprise. Whispering knots break up in the corridors, greet her with false welcome as she limps past. She settles herself at her minimalist desk, checks her mail. Her head is pounding, her stitches hurt. Ger gets wind of her arrival; he wants to see her a.s.a.p., and not for lunch.

He awaits her in his newly done wheat-on-white office, with the eighteenth-century desk they chose together, the Victorian inkstand, the framed blow-ups from the magazine, the hands in maroon leather, wrists manacled with pearls, the Hermès scarf twisted into a blindfold, the model's mouth blossoming lusciously beneath it. Some of her best stuff. He's beautifully done up, in a lick-my-neck silk shirt open at the throat, an eat-your-heart-out Italian silk-and-wool loose-knit sweater. Oh, cool insouciance. Oh, eyebrow language. He's a money man who lusted after art, and now he's got some, now he is some. Body art. Her art. She's done her job well; he's finally sexy.

He's smooth as lacquer. 'I didn't want to break this to you until next week,' he says. He breaks it to her. It's the board of directors. They think she's too bizarre, they think she goes way too far. Nothing he could do about it, although naturally he tried.

Naturally. Betrayal. The monster has turned on its own mad scientist. 'I gave you life!' she wants to scream at him.

She isn't in good shape. She can hardly stand. She stands, despite his offer of a chair. She sees now what she's wanted, what she's been missing. Gerald is what she's been missing – the stable, unfashionable, previous, tight-assed Gerald. Not Ger, not the one she's made in her own image. The other one, before he got ruined. The Gerald with a house and a small child and a picture of his wife in a silver frame on his desk. She wants to be in that silver frame. She wants the child. She's been robbed.

'And who is my lucky replacement?' she says. She needs a cigarette, but does not want to reveal her shaking hands.

'Actually, it's me,' he says, trying for modesty.

This is too absurd. Gerald couldn't edit a phone book. 'You?' she says faintly. She has the good sense not to laugh.

'I've always wanted to get out of the money end of things here,' he says, 'into the creative area. I knew you'd understand, since it can't be you at any rate. I knew you'd prefer someone who could, well, sort of build on your foundations.' Pompous asshole. She looks at his neck. She longs for him, hates herself for it, and is powerless.

The room wavers. He slides towards her across the wheat-coloured broadloom, takes her by the grey suede upper arms. 'I'll write you a good reference,' he says. 'Don't worry about that. Of course, we can still see one another. I'd miss our afternoons.'

'Of course,' she says. He kisses her, a voluptuous kiss, or it would look like one to a third party, and she lets him. *In a pig's ear.*

She makes it home in a taxi. The driver is rude to her and gets away with it; she doesn't have the energy. In her mailbox is an engraved invitation: Ger and Cheryl are having a drinks party, tomorrow evening. Post-marked five days ago. Cheryl is behind the times.

Kat undresses, runs a shallow bath. There's not much to drink around here, there's nothing to sniff or smoke. What an oversight; she's stuck with herself. There are other jobs. There are other men, or that's the theory. Still, something's been ripped out of her. How could this have happened, to her? When knives were slated for backs, she'd always done the stabbing. Any headed her way she's seen coming in time, and thwarted. Maybe she's losing her edge.

She stares into the bathroom mirror, assesses her face in the misted glass. A face of the eighties, a mask face, a bottom-line face; push the weak to the wall and grab what you can. But now it's the nineties. Is she out of style, so soon? She's only thirty-five, and she's already losing track of what people ten years younger are thinking. That could be fatal. As time goes by she'll have to race faster and faster to keep up, and for what? Part of the life she should have had is just a gap, it isn't there, it's nothing. What can be salvaged from it, what can be redone, what can be done at all?

When she climbs out of the tub after her sponge bath, she almost falls. She has a fever, no doubt about it. Inside her something is leaking, or else festering; she can hear it, like a dripping tap. A running sore, a sore from running so hard. She should go to the emergency ward at some hospital, get herself shot up with antibiotics. Instead she lurches into the living-room, takes Hairball down from the mantelpiece in its bottle, places it on the coffee table. She sits cross-legged, listens. Filaments wave. She can hear a kind of buzz, like bees at work.

She'd asked the doctor if it could have started as a child, a fertilized egg that escaped somehow and got into the wrong place. No, said the doctor. Some people thought this kind of tumour was present in seedling form from birth, or before it. It might be the woman's undeveloped twin. What they really were was unknown. They had many kinds of tissue, though. Even brain tissue. Though of course all of these tissues lack structure.

Still, sitting here on the rug looking in at it, she pictures it as a child. It has come out of her, after all. It is flesh of her flesh. Her child with Gerald, her thwarted child, not allowed to grow normally. Her warped child, taking its revenge.

'Hairball,' she says. 'You're so ugly. Only a mother could love you.' She feels sorry for it. She feels loss. Tears run down her face. Crying is not something she does, not normally, not lately.

Hairball speaks to her, without words. It is irreducible, it has the texture of reality, it is not an image. What it tells her is everything she's never wanted to hear about herself. This is new knowledge, dark and precious and necessary. It cuts.

She shakes her head. What are you doing, sitting on the floor and talking to a hairball? You are sick, she tells herself. Take a Tylenol and go to bed.

The next day she feels a little better. Dania from layout calls her and makes dove-like, sympathetic coos at her, and wants to drop by during lunch hour to take a look at her aura. Kat tells her to come off it. Dania gets huffy, and says that Kat's losing her job is a price for immoral behaviour in a previous life. Kat tells her to stuff it; anyway, she's done enough immoral behaviour in this life to account for the whole thing. 'Why are you so full of hate?' asks Dania. She doesn't say it like a point she's making, she sounds truly baffled.

'I don't know,' says Kat. It's a straight answer.

After she hangs up she paces the floor. She's crackling inside, like hot fat under the broiler. What she's thinking about is Cheryl, bustling about her cosy house, preparing for the party. Cheryl fiddles with her freeze-framed hair, positions an overloaded vase of flowers, fusses about the caterers. Gerald comes in, kisses her lightly on the cheek. A connubial scene. His conscience is nicely washed. The witch is dead, his foot is on the body, the trophy; he's had his dirty fling, he's ready now for the rest of his life.

Kat takes a taxi to the David Wood Food Shop and buys two dozen chocolate truffles. She has them put into an oversized box, then into an oversized bag with the store logo on it. Then she goes home and takes Hairball out of its bottle. She drains it in the kitchen strainer and pats it damp-dry, tenderly, with paper towels. She sprinkles it with powdered cocoa, which forms a brown pasty crust. It still smells like formaldehyde, so she wraps it in Saran Wrap and then in tinfoil, and then in pink tissue paper, which she ties with a mauve bow. She places it in the David Wood box in a bed of shredded tissue, with the truffles nestled around. She closes the box, tapes it, puts it into the bag, stuffs several sheets of pink paper on top. It's her gift, valuable and dangerous. It's her messenger, but the message it will deliver is its own. It will tell the truth, to whoever asks. It's right that Gerald should have it; after all, it's his child too.

She prints on the card, 'Gerald, Sorry I couldn't be with you. This is all the rage. Love, K.'

When evening has fallen and the party must be in full swing, she calls a delivery taxi. Cheryl will not distrust anything that arrives in such an expensive bag. She will open it in public, in front of everyone. There will be distress, there will be questions. Secrets will be unearthed. There will be pain. After that, everything will go way too far.

She is not well; her heart is pounding, space is wavering once more. But outside the window it's snowing, the soft, damp, windless flakes of her childhood. She puts on her coat and goes out, foolishly. She intends to walk just to the corner, but when she reaches the corner she goes on. The snow melts against her face like small fingers touching. She has done an outrageous thing, but she doesn't feel guilty. She feels light and peaceful and filled with charity, and temporarily without a name.

Some Are Born to Sweet Delight

NADINE GORDIMER

Some are Born to sweet delight,
Some are Born to Endless Night.

WILLIAM BLAKE, *Auguries of Innocence*

They took him in. Since their son had got himself signed up at sea for eighteen months on an oil rig, the boy's cubbyhole of a room was vacant; and the rent money was a help. There had rubbed off on the braid of the commissionaire father's uniform, through the contact of club members' coats and briefcases he relieved them of, loyal consciousness of the danger of bombs affixed under the cars of members of parliament and financiers. The father said 'I've no quarrel with that' when the owners of the house whose basement flat the family occupied stipulated 'No Irish'. But to discriminate against any other foreigners from the old Empire was against the principles of the house owners, who were also the mother's employers – cleaning three times a week and baby-sitting through the childhood of three boys she thought of as her own. So it was a way of pleasing Upstairs to let the room to this young man, a foreigner who likely had been turned away from other vacancies posted on a board at the supermarket. He was clean and tidy enough; and he didn't hang around the kitchen, hoping to be asked to eat with the family, the way one of their own kind would. He didn't eye Vera.

Vera was seventeen, and a filing clerk with prospects of advancement; her father had got her started in an important firm through the kindness of one of his gentlemen at the club. A word in the right place; and now it was up to her to become a secretary, maybe one day even a private secretary to someone like the members of the club, and travel to the Continent, America — anywhere.

'You have to dress decently for a firm like that. Let others show their backsides.'

'Dad!' The flat was small, the walls thin — suppose the lodger heard him. Her pupils dilated with a blush, half shyness, half annoyance. On Friday and Saturday nights she wore T-shirts with spangled graffiti across her breasts and went with girl-friends to the discothèque, although she'd had to let the pink side of her hair grow out. On Sundays they sat on wooden benches outside the pub with teasing local boys, drinking beer shandies. Once it was straight beer laced with something and they made her drunk, but her father had been engaged as doorman for a private party and her mother had taken the Upstairs children to the zoo, so nobody heard her vomiting in the bathroom.

So she thought.

He was in the kitchen when she went, wiping the slime from her panting mouth, to drink water. He always addressed her as 'miss' — 'Good afternoon, miss'. He was himself filling a glass.

She stopped where she was; sourness was in her mouth and nose, oozing towards the foreign stranger, she mustn't go a step nearer. Shame tingled over nausea and tears. Shame heaved in her stomach, her throat opened, and she just reached the sink in time to disgorge the final remains of a pizza minced by her teeth and digestive juices, floating in beer. 'Go away. Go away!' her hand flung in rejection behind her. She opened both taps to blast her shame down the drain. 'Get out!'

He was there beside her, in the disgusting stink of her, and he had wetted a dish-towel and was wiping her face, her dirty mouth, her tears. He was steadying her by the arm and sitting her down at the kitchen table. And she knew that his kind didn't even drink, he probably never had smelled alcohol before. If it had been one of her own crowd it would have been different.

She began to cry again. Very quietly, slowly, he put his hand on hers, taking charge of the wrist like a doctor preparing to follow the measure of a heart in a pulse-beat. Slowly – the pace was his – she quietened; she looked down, without moving her head, at the hand. Slowly, she drew her own hand from underneath, in parting.

As she left the kitchen a few meaningless echoes of what had happened to her went back and forth – are you all right yes I'm all right are you sure yes I'm all right.

She slept through her parents' return and next morning said she'd had flu.

He could no longer be an unnoticed presence in the house, outside her occupation with her work and the friends she made among the other junior employees, and her preoccupation, in her leisure, with the discothèque and cinema where the hand-holding and sex-tussles with local boys took place. He said, 'Good afternoon,' as they saw each other approaching in the passage between the family's quarters and his room, or couldn't avoid coinciding at the gate of the tiny area garden where her mother's geraniums bloomed and the empty milk bottles were set out. He didn't say 'miss'; it was as if the omission were assuring, Don't worry, I won't tell anyone, *although I know all about what you do*, everything, I won't talk about you among my friends – did he even have any friends? Her mother told her he worked in the kitchens of a smart restaurant – her mother had to be sure a lodger had steady pay before he could be let into the house. Vera saw other foreigners like him about, gathered loosely as if they didn't know where to go; of course, they didn't come to the disco and they were not part of the crowd of familiars at the cinema. They were together but looked alone. It was something noticed the way she might notice, without expecting to fathom, the strange expression of a caged animal, far from wherever it belonged.

She owed him a signal in return for his trustworthiness. Next time they happened to meet in the house she said 'I'm Vera.'

As if he didn't know, hadn't heard her mother and father call her. Again he did the right thing, merely nodded politely.

'I've never really caught your name.'

'Our names are hard for you here. Just call me Rad.' His English was stiff, pronounced syllable by syllable in a soft voice.

'So it's short for something?'

'What is that?'

'A nickname. Bob for Robert.'

'Something like that.'

She ended this first meeting on a new footing the only way she knew how: 'Well, see you later, then' – the vague dismissal used casually among her friends when no such commitment existed. But on a Sunday when she was leaving the house to wander down to see who was gathered at the pub she went up the basement steps and saw that he was in the area garden. He was reading newspapers – three or four of them stacked on the mud-plastered grass at his side. She picked up his name and used it for the first time, easily as a key turning in a greased lock. 'Hullo, Rad.'

He rose from the chair he had brought out from his room. 'I hope your mother won't mind? I wanted to ask, but she's not at home.'

'Oh no, not Ma, we've had that old chair for ages, a bit of fresh air won't crack it up more than it is already.'

She stood on the short path, he stood beside the old rattan chair; then sat down again so that she could walk off without giving offence – she left to her friends, he left to his reading.

She said 'I won't tell.'

And so it was out, what was between them alone, in the family house. And they laughed, smiled, both of them. She walked over to where he sat. 'Got the day off? You work in some restaurant, don't you, what's it like?'

'I'm on the evening shift today.' He stayed himself a moment, head on one side, with aloof boredom. 'It's something. Just a job. What you can get.'

'I know. But I suppose working in a restaurant at least the food's thrown in, as well.'

He looked out over the railings a moment, away from her. 'I don't eat that food.'

She began to be overcome by a strong reluctance to go through the gate, round the corner, down the road to The Mitre and the whistles and appreciative pinches which would greet her in her new flowered Bermudas, his black eyes following her all the way, although he'd be reading his papers with her forgotten. To gain time she looked at the papers. The one in his hand was English. On the others, lying there, she was confronted with a flowing script of tails and gliding flourishes, the secret of somebody else's language. She could not go to the pub; she could not let him know that was where she was going. The deceptions that did for parents were not for him. But the fact was there was no deception: she *wasn't* going to the pub, she suddenly wasn't going.

She sat down on the motoring section of the English newspaper he'd discarded and crossed her legs in an X from the bare round knees. 'Good news from home?'

He gestured with his foot towards the papers in his secret language; his naked foot was an intimate object, another secret.

'From my home, no good news.'

She understood this must be some business about politics, over there – she was in awe and ignorance of politics, nothing to do with her. 'So that's why you went away.'

He didn't need to answer.

'You know, I can't imagine going away.'

'You don't want to leave your friends.'

She caught the allusion, pulled a childish face, dismissing them. 'Mum and Dad . . . everything.'

He nodded, as if in sympathy for her imagined loss, but made no admission of what must be his own.

'Though I'm mad keen to travel. I mean, that's my idea, taking this job. Seeing other places – just visiting, you know. If I make myself capable and that, I might get the chance. There's one secretary in our offices who goes everywhere with her boss, she brings us all back souvenirs, she's very generous.'

'You want to see the world. But now your friends are waiting for you.'

She shook off the insistence with a laugh. 'And you want to go home!'

'No.' He looked at her with the distant expression of an adult before the innocence of a child. 'Not yet.'

The authority of his mood over hers, that had been established in the kitchen that time, was there. She was hesitant and humble rather than flirtatious when she changed the subject. 'Shall we have – will you have some tea if I make it? Is it all right?' He'd never eaten in the house; perhaps the family's food and drink were taboo for him in his religion, like the stuff he could have eaten free in the restaurant.

He smiled. 'Yes it's all right.' And he got up and padded along behind her on his slim feet to the kitchen. As with a wipe over the clean surfaces of her mother's sink and table, the other time in the kitchen was cleared by ordinary business about brewing tea, putting out cups. She set him to cut the gingerbread: 'Go on, try it, it's my mother's homemade.' She watched with an anxious smile, curiosity, while his beautiful teeth broke into its crumbling softness. He nodded, granting grave approval with a full mouth. She mimicked him, nodding and smiling; and, like a doe approaching a leaf, she took from his hand the fragrant slice with the semicircle marked by his teeth, and took a bite out of it.

Vera didn't go to the pub any more. At first they came to look for her – her chums, her mates – and nobody believed her excuses when she wouldn't come along with them. She hung about the house on Sundays, helping her mother. 'Have you had a tiff or something?'

As she always told her bosom friends, she was lucky with her kind of mother, not strict and suspicious like some. 'No, Ma. They're okay, but it's always the same thing, same things to say, every weekend.'

'Well . . . shows you're growing up, moving on – it's natural. You'll find new friends, more interesting, more your type.'

Vera listened to hear if he was in his room or had had to go to work – his shifts at the restaurant, she had learnt from timing his presence and absences, were irregular. He was very quiet, didn't play a radio or cassettes but she always could feel if he was there, in his room. That summer was a real summer for once; if he was off shift he would bring the old rattan chair into the garden and read, or stretch out his legs and lie back with his face lifted to the humid sun. He must be thinking of where he came from; very hot, she imagined it, desert and thickly-white cubes of houses with palm trees. She went out with a rug – nothing unusual about wanting to sunbathe in your own area garden – and chatted to him as if just because he happened to be there. She watched his eyes travelling from right to left along the scrolling print of his newspapers, and when he paused, yawned, rested his head and closed his lids against the light, could ask him about home – his home. He described streets and cities and cafés and bazaars – it wasn't at all like her idea of desert and oases. 'But there are palm trees?'

'Yes, nightclubs, rich people's palaces to show tourists,' but there are also factories and prison camps and poor people living on a handful of beans a day.'

She picked at the grass: 'I see. Were you – were your family – do you like beans?'

He was not to be drawn; he was never to be drawn.

'If you know how to make them, they are good.'

'If we get some, will you tell us how they're cooked?'

'I'll make them for you.'

So one Sunday Vera told her mother Rad, the lodger, wanted to prepare a meal for the family. Her parents were rather touched; nice, here was a delicate mark of gratitude, such a glum character, he'd never shown any sign before. Her father was prepared to put up with something that probably wouldn't agree with him. 'Different people, different ways. Maybe it's a custom with them, when they're taken in, like bringing a bunch of flowers.' The meal went off well. The dish was delicious and not too spicy; after all, gingerbread was spiced, too. When her father opened a bottle of beer and put it down at Rad's place, Vera quickly lifted it away. 'He doesn't drink, Dad.'

Graciousness called forth graciousness; Vera's mother issued a reciprocal invitation. 'You must come and have our Sunday dinner one day – my chicken with apple pie to follow.'

But the invitation was in the same code as 'See you later'. It was not mentioned again. One Sunday Vera shook the grass from her rug. 'I'm going for a walk.' And the lodger slowly got up from his chair, put his newspaper aside, and they went through the gate. The neighbours must have seen her with him. The pair went where she led, although they were side by side, loosely, the way she'd seen young men of his kind together. They went on walking a long way, down streets and then into a park. She loved to watch people flying kites; now he was the one who watched her as she watched. It seemed to be his way of getting to know her; to know anything. It wasn't the way of other boys – her kind – but then he was a foreigner here, there must be so much he needed to find out. Another weekend she had the idea to take a picnic. That meant an outing for the whole day. She packed apples and bread and cheese – remembering no ham – under the eyes of her mother. There was a silence between them. In it was her mother's recognition of the accusation she, Vera, knew she ought to bring against herself: Vera was 'chasing' a man; this man. All her mother said was 'Are you joining other friends?' She didn't lie. 'No. He's never been up the river. I thought we'd take a boat trip.'

In time she began to miss the cinema. Without guile she asked him if he had seen this film or that; she presumed that when he was heard going out for the evening the cinema would be where he went, with friends of his – his kind – she never saw. What did they do if they didn't go to a movie? It wouldn't be bars, and she knew instinctively he wouldn't be found in a disco, she couldn't see him shaking and stomping under twitching coloured lights.

He hadn't seen any film she mentioned. 'Won't you come?' It happened like the first walk. He looked at her again as he had then. 'D'you think so?'

'Why ever not. Everybody goes to movies.'

But she knew why not. She sat beside him in the theatre with solemnity. It was unlike any other time, in that familiar place of pleasure. He did not hold her hand; only that time, that time in the kitchen. They went together to the cinema regularly. The silence between her and her parents grew; her mother was like a cheerful bird whose cage had been covered. Whatever her mother and father thought, whatever they feared – nothing had happened, nothing happened until one public holiday when Vera and the lodger were both off work and they went on one of their long walks into the country (that was all they could do, he didn't play sport, there wasn't any activity with other young people he knew how to enjoy). On that day celebrated for a royal birthday or religious anniversary that couldn't mean anything to him, in deep grass under profound trees he made love to Vera for the first time. He had never so much as kissed her before, not on any evening walking home from the cinema, not when they were alone in the house and the opportunity was obvious as the discretion of the kitchen clock sounding through the empty passage, and the blind eye of the television set in the sitting-room. All that he had never done with her was begun and accomplished with unstoppable passion, summoned up as if at a mere command to himself; between this and the placing of his hand on hers in the kitchen, months before, there was nothing. Now she had the lips from which, like a doe, she had taken a morsel touched with his saliva, she had the naked body promised by the first glimpse of the naked feet. She had lost her virginity, like all her sister schoolgirls, at fourteen or fifteen, she had been fucked, half-struggling, by some awkward local in a car or a back room, once or twice. But now she was overcome, amazed, engulfed by a sensuality she had no idea was inside her, a bounty of talent unexpected and unknown as a burst of song would have been welling from one who knew she had no voice. She wept with love for this man who might never, never have come to her, never have found her from so far away. She wept because she was so afraid it might so nearly never have happened. He wiped her tears, he dressed her with the comforting resignation to her emotion a mother shows with an over-excited child.

She didn't hope to conceal from her mother what they were doing; she knew her mother knew. Her mother felt her gliding silently from her room down the passage to the lodger's room, the room that still smelt of her brother, late at night, and returning very early in the morning. In the dark Vera knew every floorboard that creaked, how to avoid the swish of her pyjamas touching past a wall; at dawn saw the squinting beam of the rising sun sloped through a window that she had never known was so placed it could let in any phase of the sun's passage across the sky. Everything was changed.

What could her mother have said? Maybe he had different words in his language; the only ones she and her mother had wouldn't do, weren't meant for a situation not provided for in their lives. *Do you know what you're doing? Do you know what he is? We don't have any objection to them, but all the same. What about your life? What about the good firm your father's got you into? What'll it look like, there?*

The innocent release of sensuality in the girl gave her an authority that prevailed in the house. She brought him to the table for meals, now; he ate what he could. Her parents knew this presence, in the code of their kind, only as the signal by which an 'engaged' daughter would bring home her intended. But outwardly between Vera and her father and mother the form was kept up that his position was still that of a lodger, a lodger who had somehow become part of the household in that capacity. There was no need for him to pretend or assume any role; he never showed any kind of presumption towards their daughter, spoke to her with the same reserve that he, a stranger, showed to them. When he and the girl rose from the table to go out together it was always as if he accompanied her, without interest, at her volition.

Because her father was a man, even if an old one and her father, he recognized the power of sensuality in a female and was defeated, intimidated by its obstinacy. *He* couldn't take the whole business up with her; her mother must do that. He quarrelled with his wife over it. So she confronted their daughter. *Where will it end?* Both she and the girl understood: he'll go back where he comes from, and where'll you be? He'll drop you when he's had enough of what he wanted from you.

Where would it end? Rad occasionally acknowledged her among his friends, now – it turned out he did have some friends, yes, young men like him, from his home. He and she encountered them on the street and instead of excusing himself and leaving her waiting obediently like one of those pet dogs tied up outside the supermarket, as he usually had done when he went over to speak to his friends, he took her with him and, as if remembering her presence after a minute or two of talk, interrupted himself: 'She's Vera.' Their greetings, the way they looked at her, made her feel that he had told them about her, after all, and she was happy. They made remarks in their own language she was sure referred to her. If she had moved on, from the pub, the disco, the parents, she was accepted, belonged somewhere else.

And then she found she was pregnant. She had no girlfriend to turn to who could be trusted not to say those things: he'll go back where he comes from, he'll drop you when he's had enough or what he wanted from you. After the second month she bought a kit from the pharmacy and tested her urine. Then she went to a doctor because that do-it-yourself thing might be mistaken.

'I thought you said you would be all right.'

That was all he said, after thinking for a moment, when she told him.

'Don't worry, I'll find something. I'll do something about it. I'm sorry, Rad. Just forget it.' She was afraid he would stop loving her – her term for love-making.

When she went to him tentatively that night he caressed her more beautifully and earnestly than ever while possessing her.

She remembered reading in some women's magazine that it was dangerous to do anything to get rid of 'it' (she gave her pregnancy no other identity) after three months. Through roundabout enquiries she found a doctor who did abortions, and booked an appointment, taking an advance on her holiday bonus to meet the fee asked.

'By the way, it'll be all over next Saturday. I've found someone.' Timidly, that week, she brought up the subject she had avoided between them.

He looked at her as if thinking very carefully before he spoke, thinking apart from her, in his own language, as she was often sure he was doing. Perhaps he had forgotten – it was really her business, her fault, she knew. Then he pronounced what neither had: 'The baby?'

'Well . . .' She waited, granting this.

He did not take her in his arms, he did not touch her. 'You will have the baby. We will marry.'

It flew from her awkward, unbelieving, aghast with joy: 'You want to marry me!'

'Yes, you're going to be my wife.'

'Because of this? – a baby?'

He was gazing at her intensely, wandering over the sight of her. 'Because I've chosen you.'

Of course, being a foreigner, he didn't come out with things the way an English speaker would express them.

'And I love *you*,' she said, 'I love you, I love you,' babbling through vows and tears. He put a hand on one of hers, as he had done in the kitchen of her mother's house; once, and never since.

She saw a couple in a mini-series standing hand-in-hand, telling them: 'We're getting married' – hugs and laughter.

But she told her parents alone, without him there. It was safer that way, she thought, for him. And she phrased it in proof of his good intentions as a triumphant answer to her mother's warnings, spoken and unspoken. 'Rad's going to marry me.'

'He wants to marry you?' Her mother corrected. The burst of a high-pitched cry. The father twitched an angry look at his wife.

Now it was time for the scene to conform to the TV family announcement. 'We're going to get married.'

Her father's head flew up and sank slowly, he turned away.

'You want to be married to him?' Her mother's palm spread on her breast to cover the blow.

The girl was brimming feeling, reaching for them.

Her father was shaking his head like a sick dog.

'And I'm pregnant and he's glad.'

Her mother turned to her father but there was no help coming from him. She spoke impatiently flatly. 'So that's it.'

'No, that's not it. It's not it at all.' She would not say to them 'I love him', she would not let them spoil that by trying to make her feel ashamed. 'It's what I want.'

'It's what she wants.' Her mother was addressing her father.

He had to speak. He gestured towards his daughter's body, where there was no sign yet to show life growing there. 'Nothing to be done then.'

When the girl had left the room he glared at his wife. 'Bloody bastard.'

'Hush. Hush.' There was a baby to be born, poor innocent.

And it was, indeed, the new life the father had gestured at in Vera's belly that changed everything. The foreigner, the lodger – had to think of him now as the future son-in-law, Vera's intended – told Vera and her parents he was sending her to his home for his parents to meet her. 'To your country?'

He answered with the gravity with which, they realized, marriage was regarded where he came from. 'The bride must meet the parents. They must know her as I know hers.'

If anyone had doubted the seriousness of his intentions – well, they could be ashamed of those doubts, now; he was sending her home, openly and proudly, his foreigner, to be accepted by his parents. 'But have you told them about the baby, Rad?' She didn't express this embarrassment in front of her mother and father. 'What do you think? That is why you are going.' He slowed, then spoke again. 'It's a child of our family.'

So she was going to travel at last! In addition to every other joy! In a state of continual excitement between desire for Rad – now openly sharing her room with her – and the pride of telling her work-mates why she was taking her annual leave just then, she went out of her way to encounter former friends whom she had avoided. To say she was travelling to meet her fiancé's family; she was getting married in a few months, she was having a baby – yes – proof of this now in the rounding under the flowered jumpsuit she wore to show it off. For her mother, too, a son-in-law who was not one of their kind became a distinction rather than a shame. 'Our Vera's a girl who's always known her own mind. It's a changing world, she's not one just to go on repeating the same life as we've had.' The only thing that hadn't changed in the world was joy over a little one coming. Vera was thrilled, they were all thrilled at the idea of a baby, a first grandchild. Oh that one was going to be spoilt all right! The prospective grandmother was knitting, although Vera laughed and said babies weren't dressed in that sort of thing any more, hers was going to wear those little unisex frog suits in bright colours. There was a deposit down on a pram fit for an infant prince or princess.

It was understood that if the intended could afford to send his girl all the way home just to meet his parents before the wedding, he had advanced himself in the restaurant business, despite the disadvantages young men like him had in an unwelcoming country. Upstairs was pleased with the news; Upstairs came down one evening and brought a bottle of champagne as a gift to toast Vera, whom they'd known since she was a child, and her boy – much pleasant laughter when the prospective husband filled everyone's glass and then served himself with orange juice. Even the commissionaire felt confident enough to tell one of his gentlemen at the club that his daughter was getting married but first about to go abroad to meet the young man's parents. His gentlemen's children were always travelling; in his ears every day were overheard snatches of destinations – 'by bicycle in China, can you believe it' . . . 'two months in Peru, rather nice . . .' . . . 'snorkeling on the Barrier Reef, last I heard'. *Visiting her future parents-in-law where there is desert and palm trees*; not bad!

The parents wanted to have a little party, before she left, a combined engagement party and farewell. Vera had in mind a few of her old friends brought together with those friends of his she'd been introduced to and with whom she knew he still spent some time – she didn't expect to go along with him, it wasn't their custom for women, and she couldn't understand their language, anyway. But he didn't seem to think a party would work. She had her holiday bonus (to remember what she had drawn it for, originally, was something that, feeling the baby tapping its presence softly inside her, she couldn't believe of herself) and she kept asking him what she could buy as presents for his family – his parents, his sisters and brothers, she had learnt all their names. He said he would buy things, he knew what to get. As the day for her departure approached, he still had not done so. 'But I want to pack! I want to know how much room to leave, Rad!' He brought some men's clothing she couldn't judge and some dresses and scarves she didn't like but didn't dare say so – she supposed the clothes his sisters liked were quite different from what she enjoyed wearing – a good thing she hadn't done the choosing.

She didn't want her mother to come to the airport; they'd both be too emotional. Leaving Rad was strangely different; it was not leaving Rad but going, carrying his baby, to the mystery that was Rad, that was in Rad's silences, his blind love-making, the way he watched her, thinking in his own language so that she could not follow anything in his eyes. It would all be revealed when she arrived where he came from.

He had to work, the day she left, until it was time to take her to the airport. Two of his friends, whom she could scarcely recognize from the others in the group she had met occasionally, came with him to fetch her in the taxi one of them drove. She held Rad's hand, making a tight double fist on his thigh, while the men talked in their language. At the airport the others left him to go in alone with her. He gave her another, last-minute gift for home. 'Oh Rad – where'm I going to put it? The ticket says one handbaggage!' But she squeezed his arm in happy recognition of his thoughts for his family. 'It can go in – easy, easy.' He unzipped her carryall as they stood in the queue at the check-in counter. She knelt with her knees spread to accommodate her belly, and helped him. 'What is it, anyway – I hope not something that's going to break?' He was making a bed for the package. 'Just toys for my sister's kid. Plastic.' 'I could have put them in the suitcase – oh Rad . . . what room'll I have for duty-free!' In her excitement, she was addressing the queue for the American airline's flight which would take her on the first leg of her journey. These fellow passengers were another kind of foreigner, Americans, but she felt she knew them all; they were going to be travelling in her happiness, she was taking them with her.

She held him with all her strength and he kept her pressed against his body; she could not see his face. He stood and watched her as she went through passport control and she stopped again and again to wave but she saw Rad could not wave, could not wave. Only watch her until he could not see her any longer. And she saw him in her mind still looking at her, as she had done at the beginning when she had imagined herself as still under his eyes if she had gone to the pub on a Sunday morning.

Over the sea, the airliner blew up in midair. Everyone on board died. The black box was recovered from the bed of the sea and revealed that there had been an explosion in the tourist-class cabin followed by a fire; and there the messages ended; silence, the disintegration of the plane. No one knows if all were killed outright or if some survived to drown. An inquiry into the disaster continued for a year. The background of every passenger was traced, and the circumstances that led to the journey of each. There were some arrests; people detained for questioning and then released. They were innocent – but they were foreigners, of course. Then there was another disaster of the same nature, and a statement from a group with an apocalyptic name representing a faction of the world's wronged, claiming the destruction of both planes in some complication of vengeance for holy wars, land annexation, invasions, imprisonments, cross-border raids, territorial disputes, bombings, sinkings, kidnappings no one outside the initiated could understand. A member of the group, a young man known as Rad among many other aliases, had placed in the handbaggage of the daughter of the family with whom he lodged, and who was pregnant by him, an explosive device. Plastic. A bomb of a plastic type undetectable by the usual procedures of airport security.

Vera was chosen.

Vera had taken them all, taken the baby inside her; down, along with her happiness.

The Crossing of Herald Montjoy

ROSE TREMAIN

A piece of ground near Agincourt
October 1415

He does not have far to ride.

The distance between the two encamped armies is little more than a mile. They are so close that at night-time, in the cold stillness, each can hear the laughter of the other, and the swearing and the cries. They're like neighbouring farmers, eavesdropping in the moonlight.

The French are noisier than the English. There are far more of them, they have more liquor and they seem to know more songs.

Herald Montjoy walks out from the French camp, through the wood on the right towards Maisoncelles, and stands among the trees and listens to the English. He can hear a lot of hammering. He thinks the exhausted soldiers may be trying to make cabins out of elm. He remembers his little nephew, Roland, who has made a tree-house. He loves Roland. Having no children of his own, he's tried to describe what he is to Roland. He has told him: 'A herald is a watcher. It's important to understand this. He oversees the conduct of armies, but doesn't really belong to them. He's not a man-at-arms, but a man apart.'

Then, a morning comes, salt-white with frost, when Herald Montjoy is summoned to the Dauphin's tent. The Dauphin instructs him to ride out across the fields to the English camp and enquire whether the English King is ready to ransom himself, to save his ragged army from certain defeat. The Dauphin's tent is sumptuous with blue and gold hangings. The Dauphin is doing body-building exercises all the while he is talking. As Montjoy leaves the tent, he hears him say to the Duke of Alençon: 'God, I'm fit.'

Herald Montjoy gets on his horse. The land he must cross has been ploughed and he's worried that the horse is going to stumble on the icy ridges of earth. A mist hangs on the fields, milky and dense, and the herald wishes that this, too, wasn't there. This and the hard frost give the day such strange singularity.

A piece of ground near the Manor of La Vallée.
April 1412

He did not have far to ride.

The distance between his parents' house and the manor where Cecile lived was little more than two miles. He and his horse knew every step by heart. It was mostly downhill. And he would see the house long before he reached it. And always his thoughts flew ahead of him and landed, gentle as birds, on Cecile's head and on her shoulders and on her feet in coloured shoes.

She was so . . . *exceptional.* He tried, on these journeys to and from her house, to decide what, if anything, she resembled – in nature, or in man's inventions. He wondered whether he could compare her to a lake of water lilies where silvery fish glimmered deep down. Or was she like a sundial, unerring, yet always speaking, in her adoration of ephemeral things, of time's passing?

He decided there was nothing and no one as strangely beautiful as her. Not even the landscape through which he and his horse had to pass, with its flowering meadows, its clear stream, its silent woods and its perfumed air. Not even his dreams, in which he sometimes gave himself wings and flew up into the sky and floated above France.

No. Cecile was more to him than any of these things. She kept honey bees in tall hives in her father's orchard. Her beekeeping hat had a gossamer veil that fell to earth all round her, and whenever Herald Montjoy dreamed of flying above France, there below him walked Cecile in her bee-veil with nothing on underneath.

He knew he had to marry Cecile. He had to possess her: her body, her soul, her petticoats, her bees, her shoe cupboard. He couldn't wait much longer.

He was a handsome man, with dark soft hair and a curling lip, and he had no doubt that when he proposed to Cecile he would be accepted. He would say to her father: 'Sir, in two or three years' time, I aim to become Chief Herald of France. I do not think that is an unrealistic boast.'

Agincourt.
October 1415

His hat is a strange confection, indigo blue with loops of velvet that fall just above his left eye and bounce up and down as the horse canters.

This bouncing of his blue hat as he advances into the icy mist makes him fret. It's as if everything is conspiring to blind him on this frozen day. He finds himself wishing it were night, with a round moon to light the field and the songs and the hammering of the English to guide him on. He feels that, under these conditions, he would see and think much more clearly; whereas, in this fog, with the forest petrified and silent close by, he feels confused and half-afraid.

He reins in his horse and turns him into the wood and dismounts. He sets down the weighty standard by an oak tree.

He ties the horse to the tree. He takes off his hat, runs a hand through his curly hair. All around him is the tracery of the night's frost, fingering every spine. He asks himself: Why afraid, Montjoy?

He is thirty years old, three years older than Henry of England.

Is everyone on this piece of earth afraid of the battle that is there and not there in every mind? Of the future battle that is coming or may never happen – there and not there, departing like a lover, returning like a fever?

The Dauphin isn't afraid. 'Afraid? Bunk!' And then he admires his leg. 'The English won't last more than half an hour. If that.'

His instructions reveal his nonchalance: 'Just tell the King to give himself up for ransom, all right, Montjoy? Then that sack of bones he calls an army can go home and litter up Southampton.'

He's been told to ride fast, to return quickly. The Dauphin's getting impatient with all the waiting. Montjoy has never disobeyed an order in his life, yet now he's in the wood, scratching his head, standing still, staring at the trees. He feels as if he can't make this crossing, but he doesn't know why.

La Vallée.
April 1412

He felt weightless on that April morning. He felt as if he could swing himself up off his horse and into the air. He was wearing a sky-blue tunic. The sun shone on those soft curls of his.

He was riding to La Vallée to ask for Cecile's hand. His mother and father had waved and grinned as he'd set off: 'Such a *beautiful* girl, son. So striking! We wish you joy and success.'

His thoughts, as always, had already landed on Cecile. They caressed her shoulder. They lay trapped like butterflies under her lavender-coloured cloak as she put it on and walked out of the house carrying a basket.

What was she going to put in the basket? Branches of blossom?

A thought is seldom trapped for long. It can travel anywhere. It can make decisions.

Montjoy's thoughts escaped from under the cloak. They walked with Cecile through the damp grass. They hid in the shadow of her skirts, high up in the darkness between her legs. They were touched in a caressing way as she took each step.

So then he had to slow his horse, dismount, walk to a stream, try to clear his head. 'You're running too fast,' he told himself. 'You're not her bridegroom yet.'

He knelt over the stream and cupped icy spring water and splashed his face. He gasped. There were days in a life so momentous they seemed to alter the size of the world. His heart felt as colossal as a cuckoo bird. The sky above his kneeling figure expanded and expanded, wider, fatter, closer to heaven than it had ever been.

He sat down on the grass. His horse grazed and flicked his tail at the spring flies. There *are* splendid lives, he thought. There *is* bravery and there is luck. There is ingenuity. A woman's shoe can be yellow . . .

There were yellow flowers at the stream's edge. Montjoy wasn't good at the names of flowers, but he sat there for a long while, admiring these particular ones.

Agincourt.
October 1415

In this desolate wood, Montjoy looks for something green, something that will be soft to the touch.

This fear that he can't name has seeped from his mind, down and down all through him and touched his heart like a ghost and then his sphincter, and now he's crouching down and defecating onto the dry bracken.

He can see nothing green, nothing soft to the touch to wipe his arse with. He has to scrape up handfuls of harsh bracken and fallen leaves and clean himself with these. As he pulls up his stockings, he feels like weeping.

The wood oppresses him. He'd come into the wood to find a moment's peace before he has to complete his ride to the English camp. But the wood feels dead.

Leaving his horse tied up and the standard leaning against the tree, he makes his way back towards the ploughed field under its curtain of mist.

He walks forward, his feet unsteady on the frosted ridges. He can sense, now, that the mist is going to clear and that the day may after all be fine. Already, there's more light on the field.

He looks down at the earth. He wonders who works this land, what crop he has in mind for the year to come. The loops of Montjoy's indigo hat fall over his eyes. He is standing now on the place where the very centre of the battle will be. Here, where his feet are, an English soldier will fall, his lungs pierced with a lance, blood bursting from his throat. All around him will lie his doomed compatriots, souls vanished into the air. This is the crop to come: in an ecstasy of death, this land will be seeded with the English. And it will be his task to count them – his and the English heralds' – to make an orderly tally, even if limbs or heads are severed and fall some way from the torsos. All heralds must be precise. They mustn't look away. Afterwards, he will say to his nephew, Roland: 'I saw it. It took place near the castle of Agincourt. But you couldn't call it a great battle. It was too one-sided.'

He is aware, suddenly, that a lot of time has passed since he set out. Far ahead, he can hear the English resume their pathetic hammering. And this comforts him, somehow. His fear has lessened.

He strides back into the wood and unties his horse. The horse is trembling with cold. He slaps it gently to warm it.

He mounts and takes up his standard. He faces his horse towards the light soaking through the rising mist and rides on.

La Vallée.
April 1412

Sitting by the stream with the sun warm on his nose, Montjoy rehearsed his declaration of love and his offer of marriage.

He imagined Cecile standing with her back towards him, looking out of a window. He went down on one knee, but she hadn't noticed this. Her shoulders were very still. He said: 'Cecile, I think it must have been apparent to you for some time that I consider you to be the centre of my universe . . .'

He imagined her smiling – *so now he's going to propose to me!* – but trying to conceal the smile.

He said: 'And really so it is. Or rather, it's more than this: you have actually altered the way I see the world. Before I met you, my life seemed so small, so circumscribed. But together, you and I could become masters – or rather, I mean, master and mistress – of a fine destiny!'

He decided it was wise, or at least diplomatic, to ask Cecile at this point whether she, too, felt the earth transformed by *his* presence at her side. And he imagined that she turned from the window and came running to him and pulled him to his feet and said: 'Yes, Montjoy! Yes. I feel the earth transformed!' And then he kissed her.

The kiss was so heavenly that Montjoy, alone by the stream, let it last for several minutes. His eyes were fixed on some vacant spot, unseeing. Above him flew thrushes and finches. Fleets of minnows sailed by him in the water.

When the kiss was over, Montjoy looked around him. At dusk, he would ride back this way with Cecile's promise to be his wife locked inside him like money locked in a box. And always, after today, when he rode this way, he would feel that this was hallowed ground – the spongy grass, the yellow flowers, the icy stream – because it was here that his future came to meet him.

A bee buzzed by him.

He got to his feet. He and the bee were moving to the same enchanted, perfumed destination.

Agincourt.
October 1415

One of their scavenge-parties, sent out to gather nuts and berries and firewood, sees him coming with his flying banner from far off. Two of the party stand and gape at him; two others start running back to the English camp.

They make him feel smart, these bedraggled English, carrying bundles of sticks. His blue hat no longer feels ridiculous, but slightly stylish. He bounces high in the saddle.

He is memorizing the Dauphin's instructions: 'Look, Montjoy, the thing is perfectly simple. The English can't possibly win. We outnumber them five to one. If they can't understand this simple arithmetic, do a demonstration with pebbles or coins or any damn thing that happens to be at hand. They are about to be overwhelmed. What a marvellous word! *Overwhelmed.* I love it. Right?'

And now, as the mist disperses, he can begin to see the English camp. It huddles in among some thin trees. Just as he'd envisaged, the men have made themselves hovels from sticks and bracken. There are a few threadbare tents. Smoke rises from a dozen small fires. He can see soldiers grouped around them, trying to warm themselves. They turn their white faces towards him.

Montjoy has never been to England. He has been told that one corner of it lies under water, but that elsewhere there are great forests, older than time. And these men that he sees look half drowned to him, or else, with this pallor they have, appear like people who live perpetually in a wooded darkness.

He slows his horse. Like grey ghosts, English soldiers have crept out of the trees and stand staring at him. What honour for France can there possibly be in slaughtering people already half dead? What honour for the heralds to oversee such a massacre? He thinks of Roland. In the tender privacy of the boy's tree-house, Montjoy had once said to him: 'Roland, there are two things that have counted with me in my life and one of them is honour . . .'

But his thoughts are interrupted, because now he realizes that a group of men-at-arms is approaching him. They have formed themselves into a square. In the middle of the square, Montjoy can glimpse something bright. It is the crown on the King's head.

Montjoy takes off his hat. He dismounts. Carrying the standard and leading his horse, he moves forward on foot. And in this moment (he can't say why) a fragment of his earlier fear lodges in his heart and he sees coming towards him, as if in a dream or a vision, not Henry of England but his beloved Cecile, wearing a garland of yellow flowers round her hair.

He falters. Then he urges himself on. He is aware, now, that hundreds of the English ghosts have come out of the trees and are gazing at him.

He bows to the King. When he looks up, he sees a squarish, bony face and a complexion less pale than those around him. The regard is soft and the voice, when he hears it, is gentle.

'Well, herald?'

'Sir,' says Montjoy, 'I've come from the Dauphin. He and all the nobles with him urge you to consider your position. They estimate that your army is outnumbered by five to one and they feel that, to save your men from certain death, the best course you can follow is to give yourself up for ransom . . .'

Montjoy sees one of the men-at-arms belch silently. He decides that two things keep these people from fleeing back to Calais: drink and the presence of their King.

'What is your name, herald?' asks the King.

'Montjoy, sir.'

The King smiles. The men-at-arms appear to stare through Montjoy at the piece of ground over which he has just travelled.

Still smiling, the King says: 'Montjoy, say this to Prince Dauphin. We would like to remind him that there are very few certainties on earth. Extraordinarily few. When I was a boy, I kept a stag beetle in an ivory box. I used to speak to it. And one evening, it spoke back to me. Until that time, I'd been absolutely certain that a stag beetle was unable to talk.'

The King laughs. The men-at-arms turn their anxious eyes from the field and look at their monarch.

'So you see,' says the King, 'one never knows.'

'What did the beetle say, sir?' asks Montjoy.

'Oh, I don't remember. Just a word or two. It was the unexpectedness that struck me. So there you are, herald. Your Dauphin can believe in his certainty or not as he pleases. It makes no difference to us. We will not be ransomed.'

The ghostly faces have clustered near to the King and are trying to listen to what he's saying. They stare and blink in the sunlight so foreign to them. They scratch their bodies through their clothing.

'God go with you, Montjoy,' says the King.

Montjoy bows. The King and his men-at arms turn round and walk away. Montjoy replaces his blue hat on his dark head.

La Vallée.
April 1412

There was the house. There were the doves, like winged thoughts, on the roof. Smoke drifted up from one of the stone chimneys.

Montjoy was still rehearsing his proposal as he dismounted and handed the reins of his horse to a servant. Then the servant informed him that Mademoiselle Cecile and her parents had gone to visit a cousin struck down by a tumbling weathercock. They were not expected back until late afternoon.

In the tableau Montjoy had seen in his mind, there had been *morning* light at the window where Cecile stood while he told her about the alteration to his world. And he liked things to proceed as he'd imagined them. So now he hesitated: should he leave or should he wait?

He decided to wait. The servant led his horse away. He sat on a stone wall and stared up at the sky. Then, he walked to the orchard where the apple blossom was in flower and stood near to Cecile's beehives. The traffic of bees to and from them absorbed his attention for a long time. He kept picturing the honeyed world inside. He decided that the thing in nature Cecile most closely resembled was a cluster of bees. She moved in ways that he couldn't fully understand and yet all the while there was purpose in her.

Cecile discovered him in the orchard. He'd fallen asleep in the sun and was dreaming of the sea. When he woke and found Cecile standing above him, he believed, for a fragment of a second, that she was a ship in sail, moving past him and on.

She was laughing. Montjoy realized how ridiculous he must look, asleep in the grass like a peasant boy. He scrambled to his feet, straightening his tunic, running a hand through his hair. Desperately, he searched for words.

Before he found any, Cecile held out her hands for him to take. He noticed then that her face was very pink and her eyes wide. She was wearing a white dress.

'My friend!' she said, 'I'm so glad to find you here! So happy! That you should be here – and sleeping like a child – is somehow perfectly right. Because I'm in such a state! You can tell just by looking at me, can't you? I'm in such a state of pure joy!'

'Are you, Cecile?'

'Yes! And you are just the person I want to share it with. You've been such a sweet friend to me and now I can tell you my wonderful news! What day is it? I'll always remember this day. Always and always. Now ask me why!'

'Why, Cecile?'

'Because Monsieur de Granvilliers proposed to me this afternoon. I'm going to be married! I'm going to have a wonderful life!'

Cecile let go of Montjoy's hands and went dancing off round the orchard, twirling her arms above her head. Montjoy saw that the shoes she was wearing that day were also white and it occurred to him that the grass would soon stain them. The grass appeared dry, but it wasn't. He could feel its dampness on his buttocks and against his shoulder blades and all down his spine.

> *Agincourt.*
> *October 1415*

Returning at a canter, Montjoy soon leaves the smells and sounds of the English camp behind. He doesn't stop to look at the field or the wood. He isn't thinking about the battle to come, but about the kind of voice a stag beetle might possess. Up in his tree-house, Roland makes up different voices for the wind and the stars. Some of the stars don't speak, only yawn.

The Dauphin is at lunch with his favourite counts and dukes. They're eating blackbirds.

'God, Montjoy,' says the Dauphin, 'you've been an age. What happened?'

Montjoy is very hot after his ride. He can feel sweat in his hair.

'I'm sorry, sir,' he says. 'I explained to the King how far he's outnumbered, but –'

'But what?'

'He refuses to be ransomed. He seems willing to fight.'

The Dauphin picks up a blackbird and bites it in half, crunching the little bones. He speaks with his mouth full. 'Did you explain it properly? Five to *one*. Did you show him?'

'There wasn't an opportunity to show him, sir. His mind is made up.'

'Well then, he's a fool,' says the Dauphin. 'A bumptious fool. It means that he's now going to die. Simple as that. Every single one of them is going to die.'

The Dauphin eats the second half of his blackbird. He spits out a piece of bone and wipes his mouth. 'Get me the Constable of France, Montjoy,' he says. 'We'll get all this over with tomorrow. I'm tired of being here. And the food's ghastly. Off you go.'

Montjoy backs out of the Dauphin's tent. He feels tired. He feels he could lie down anywhere and sleep.

La Vallée.
April 1412

Out of politeness, he had to pay his respects to Cecile's parents before he could leave. They told him that Monsieur de Granvilliers had hinted at his intention to marry Cecile back in January. Cecile's mother said: 'We're very flattered. This is a very good match.'

Montjoy wanted to say: I love her better than Granvilliers. She alters my earth. I'd sleep with her in my arms. I'd buy her any number of pairs of shoes.

But he kept silent and only nodded.

Then he rode back along the way he had come. The sun was going down and glinted red in the fast-running stream. He tried not to think of anything at all. When he got to the clump of yellow flowers, he looked the other way. His horse stumbled on a stone and he wished he could become that stone and feel nothing.

Montjoy's parents were eating dinner when he arrived back at the house. They looked up expectantly from their soup and put down their spoons.

Montjoy stood in the doorway and looked at them. For the first time in his life, he envied them with an aching, fathomless envy. They had lived side by side contentedly for thirty-one years. They still shared their bed.

He put a fist up to his mouth. Through the clenched fist, he said: 'Cecile's not in my life any more. So please don't mention her again. She's in the past and I don't want to speak about it. It or her. I don't want to talk about any of it. Ever.'

He turned and left the room before either his mother or his father could say a word.

Agincourt.
October 1415

He has been summoned by the English King, three years his junior.

It's getting dark. The rain that came in the early morning has stopped and a white moon is rising. And under the white moon lie the French dead.

He and his horse have to pick their way among corpses. There's a shine on them and on the fouled earth where they lie.

For the second time in Montjoy's life, he asks himself, as he rides on into a gathering dusk: 'Why was something as terrible as this not foreseen by me?'

He remembers the Dauphin's mockery: 'They won't last half an hour!' He remembers his own imaginary words to Roland: 'You couldn't call it a great battle. It was too one-sided.'

He's a herald. Heralds ride in the vanguard of events, they announce. They watch and assess. They bring the expected after them. But not him. Despite his eminence, despite his optimistic name, the unimaginable follows him like a shadow.

He doesn't know precisely how this day was lost. He tried to follow what was occurring. He kept weaving in and out of the wood, trying to see, trying to get a picture. He heard the English arrows fly. He saw a cloud of arrows fall on the first line of cavalry, heard them clatter on helmets and backplates, like hailstones on an army kitchen. He saw some horses go down and their riders fall, helpless as saucepans in their armour, kicked or trampled by hooves.

Then he saw, as the first line rode on, the English men-at-arms fall back. They fell back in a ghostly way, just as, before, they emerged from the wood – one moment there and the next moment not there. And where they'd been standing, facing the French cavalry, on the very place where they'd been, now there was a line of stakes, newly sharpened, pointing out of the ground. There was a thick fence of them, a thousand or more, three or four deep with room in between them for only the most insubstantial men.

He knew the horses would rear, would try to turn, would do all that they could not to be thrown onto the stakes. But many of them couldn't turn because in their massed charge, flank to flank, they were coming on too fast and so they exploded onto the fence and their riders were pitched forward into the enemy's arms.

One of the other heralds had told him at dawn: 'The English are eating handfuls of earth. This means they accept their coming death and burial.' And he'd felt pity for them, as violent as love. Now, Montjoy's horse carries him awkwardly, slipping and staggering in the mud, through the field of the French dead. The dead appear fat with this white moon up, casting bulky shadows. Montjoy covers his mouth with his blue glove and tips his head back and looks for stars. There is one in the west, yawning, and he thinks again of Roland in his tree-house and then of all the souls of the French struggling to cross the chasm of the sky.

He won't give an account of the battle to Roland because then he would have to answer too many unanswerable questions. Why did the first line of French cavalry turn round and collide with the men-at-arms coming forward? Does this mean that some of the French foot soldiers died before they even reached the English line? And then, when they reached the line, what happened that so many died so quickly? Were they packed together so tightly in a mass that they couldn't fight properly? Was the mass, shouting and pushing and afraid and confused, soon walled up behind its own dead?

It had rained so hard all through the battle, the heralds' task of seeing had been impeded.

All Montjoy can hope now, as he nears the English camp and hears voices singing, is that time will bring him understanding.

He rides on. He must make a formal acknowledgement of defeat to King Henry. He hopes that his voice is going to be strong, but fears that it may sound weak and small, like the voice of a stag beetle in an ivory box.

He feels exhausted. In his exhaustion, he aches to be no longer a man apart, but a man going home to his wife with a gift of crimson shoes.

Little Lewis Has Had a Lovely Sleep

ELIZABETH JOLLEY

There's blood showing under the door of the bathroom. Under the door of the room they call the little bathroom. Part of the nursery suite in this house. I'm babysitting. This isn't the only place I go to but Mrs Porter at the agency mostly sends me here. There's never been blood here or in any place before. The sight of blood upsets me. It isn't anything you expect when you're babysitting, is it?

This has been a long night. It is a long night I should say. It isn't over yet. I keep hoping Little Lewis is all right. He's Little Lewis because of his father being called Lewis. Big Lewis. I don't call any of the family by their first names except for Little Lewis, naturally. Dr Barnett I always say, and Mrs Barnett. They are both very nice people and that's why what's happened is so much worse. Mrs Barnett is against nuclear war and she's all for animal rights. She's in favour of subsidized sterilization but it worries her, she says, because animals aren't in a position to choose. That's a bit like I am now. I've got no choice just now about sitting here on this chair out here on the balcony when just inside the playroom is the nice bed Mrs Barnett made for me on the divan. From here I can see Little Lewis's bedroom door and I can see the door of the little bathroom and the blood.

I'd rather be in bed. Before they went out Dr Barnett

wheeled the TV in from their own bedroom across the passage.

'Some culture for you, Miss Vales,' he said smiling down at me. He brought in a whole pile of magazines too. New glossies, they cost a fortune. I've hardly had a chance to look at them because of what's happened. Just before they went downstairs Mrs Barnett suddenly remembered the calamine.

'Little Lewis,' she said to me, 'Little Lewis has a touch of prickly heat. Could you dab his rash before he goes to bed. It's medicated,' she said, 'and soothing.' Mrs Barnett has a lovely smile especially when she's happy about going out.

I'm to be here all night. It's an all-night party they've gone to. A slumber party, they call it. Mrs Barnett laughed about it. She said she'd always thought slumber parties are what schoolgirls have. It's not my business but I can't help wondering what those well-off people will get up to during the night. It's drugs as well as sex and alcohol Mrs Porter at the agency always says. These days she says things is different from what they were. Little Lewis, in my opinion, is well out of it here with me. Or should I say *was* to all intents and purposes well out of it.

'Shall you be nervous, Miss Vales, dear?' Mrs Barnett asked when she said they would be out all night. 'Suburbs aren't the quiet places they used to be,' she said. I told her I wouldn't be at all nervous. I told her I always felt very safe in her house.

'I'm afraid the main road is terribly noisy,' she says then. She always apologizes and I always tell her that I like the main road. The sound of the traffic is company, I tell her.

The people next door,' Mrs Barnett said, 'are away – so you are very much on your own tonight.' She made me promise to phone her if I felt nervous. The house, she said, was well locked up. She said she had put a phone number on a bit of paper for me.

Mrs Barnett and Dr Barnett are two such nice people and Little Lewis, though I never tell him this of course, is the sweetest little boy I ever knew. When Mrs Porter at the agency first sent me to babysit here she said that Little Lewis might be a trouble.

'Don't you take no nonsense, Emily Vales,' Mrs Porter said to me that first time. 'Where you're going is one of the wealthiest houses this side of Christendom, and rich people's children is used to having their own way. It's a big house, right on the main road. It's got trees all along in front and there's a brass plate set in the wall. A doctor plate. You'll find it easy. That child,' Mrs Porter said, 'that child's used to having everything he wants. As you know, he's *gifted*! Just you don't take no nonsense!' 'I won't Mrs Porter, dear, never you worry,' I told her.

I've been pretending that Dr Barnett's a bone surgeon on account of bone surgeons having muscles. I do hope they'll be home soon. It's getting lighter every minute. They should be home soon.

I suppose the little bathroom's all spoilt. There must be blood all over it. But that's the least of it all. Mrs Porter says some people put all their money into their bathrooms. You know, His and Hers. A nice bathroom's a nice bathroom, but when all's said and done you don't live in the bathroom, that's what Mrs Porter says, though I will say this, matching towels do give a bit of class. At the agency, where I live, the bathroom's really old. It's got a wood floor and there's a tree outside growing in at the window even though it's upstairs. Mrs Porter says there's better things to do with money than put it in the bathroom. I mean, she *likes* her old brass and porcelain.

I wish I could tell Mrs Barnett and Dr Barnett that there's a gun on the piano downstairs. They'll be surprised. I'd like them to get it, the gun, before someone else does. I know this seems silly of me but I did think for a while that Mr Right had come around the corner for me at last. Mrs Porter always says that for every pot there's always a lid. She reads the tea leaves. She's always seeing a tall dark handsome stranger, Mr Right, in my cup. I've been at the agency, living there I mean, boarding for some years. Mrs Porter says the pension cheques help cover the rents and the rates. She's helping Mr Treadaway, the new gentleman, put in his application. Mr Treadaway's an old man. A bit of a giggle. Not Mr *Right*. No way!

It's like this. After Dr Barnett and Mrs Barnett have gone downstairs Lewis and I go out on the balcony to wave as the car comes down the drive and into the street. It's a wide leafy avenue leading into Perth. The houses here cost a fortune.

'Wave, Lewis,' I say, 'there's Mother's hand. See Mother's hand, Lewis? Wave to Mother, Lewis. That's a good boy!' We lean over the parapet to watch the big shiny car glide away. 'Your mother's a lovely person,' I tell Lewis. I tell him that I'd do anything in the whole world for her. 'Did you see her hand,' I ask him, 'and her beautiful lacy glove?'

'Yes,' he says. 'Now let's play the game,' he says as soon as the car has disappeared down there in the long line of cars heading for the city. 'It's too hot for bed.'

We're right up high in the tops of the street trees. Lovely and cool. While Little Lewis finds the things we need for the game I listen to the parrots. They squabble, hidden in the trees, and the cicadas keep on and on. I don't mind them. They're good company. It's the mosquitoes I don't like, so I have a smoke to keep them away. Gorgeous up here. Really nice.

'Here's your paper and pencil.' Lewis pulls one of the chairs up to the parapet.

'No leaning over!' I say. 'I don't want you falling over.' He is an obedient little boy so I haven't any worries really. 'Right,' I say. 'I'll take everything from the left and you do the right. Okay! Here's a taxi coming my side. A taxi. It's gone in next door. How many points for a taxi?'

'Two,' Lewis says. 'You've a bus your side, that's four plus two gives you six.'

'There's a bike your side,' I tell him. 'You don't get many bikes on this road. Six for a bike, isn't it?'

'Six all!' Lewis says. He's so grown-up sometimes. 'Look!' he says. 'There's a man *walking*!'

'Where? Don't often see anyone walking these days. Not along here you don't.'

'There he is. He's got red hair. You'll see him in a minute, down there under the trees. He's yours. You get ten for him. Look! There he is. He walks in a funny way.'

'That makes me sixteen,' I say. I ask if there are extra points for a limp. Lewis really laughs at that. He doesn't laugh often, being a serious child and dedicated to his music. Mrs Porter and I watched him on TV not so long ago playing his little violin. Ever so nicely dressed, and the way he bowed! Ever so sweet he was. I'll never forget it.

'He's turning back! He's coming back.' Lewis is excited. 'I'll get ten points as well if he keeps coming back.'

'Mind you don't go over the edge! Sit down!' I have another smoke. Keeps the mossies away.

'He *is* coming all the way back. Thanks, Mr Man, for my ten points. Sixteen all!' Lewis prints his score.

'Listen! A police siren. And an ambulance.' We listen.

'They're yours.' Lewis sounds disappointed. 'They're yours,' he says with perfect manners, just like his mother and father. I can't help seeing him, in my mind, in his little velvet suit with the white ruffles round his neck. 'Five points each,' he says, 'makes you twenty-six.'

'They'll be back,' I say. 'The hospital's this way. You'll get them on the way back.'

'Look! Look!' he shouts. 'That man's coming back. You've got him your side, that's thirty-six for you. He's looking at the houses. P'raps he's lost. He's really staring at our house!'

'Sit back, Lewis.' I'm uneasy. 'We don't want to be stared at as if we're in the zoo.'

'He's looking straight up here now. He's got funny eyes.' Lewis is laughing.

'Forget him!' I say. 'Here's a car my side. Must say you've got good eyesight. That's two for the car, for me.'

'Makes you thirty-eight, Miss Vales,' Lewis says. 'You're winning.'

I'm thinking about the taxi. It's still next door. I feel indignant. Why should anyone keep a taxi waiting that long? 'The driver must be a relative,' I say.

'Girls,' Lewis says, 'girls live there. Schoolgirls.'

'Ah, well,' I say, 'perhaps the driver's their uncle. An uncle would

wait.' It's just like this well-to-do posh neighbourhood. I can't help
thinking that schoolgirls these days have everything their own way.
Like Mrs Porter at the agency says, all they think about is sex,
food and money. 'Mind you!' she says, pointing her pencil at Mr
Treadaway and me. 'Mind you! Not always in that order. I'd say
money then sex and food more often than not.' Miss Mallow, the
retired lady teacher who has Mrs Porter's downstairs front room,
comes in just then and is quite upset and says that not all schoolgirls
are as Mrs Porter is saying they are. And Mrs Porter says to Miss
Mallow, 'And how would you know, dear, you having been shut
away such a long time?' That really makes me wonder about Miss
Mallow.

'When that taxi comes out,' Lewis says, 'I might get the points.
They've all gone away next door, he's sure to realize his mistake
and come out soon.'

I'm wondering now if it was a taxi that went in there. And then
I see the man, he's still down there, looking up.

'There he is. Our man.' I try to laugh as if he's funny. 'What a
mop of red hair!' I feel uneasy again. My mother used to say
something about red-headed men. What was it, beware red hair –
something about a limp and a squint.

'Miss Vales! Miss Vales!' Lewis is excited. 'The sirens. They are
coming back. You said they would. My side. Ten points. That
makes me twenty-six and ten, thirty-six, but you get two for the
taxi and ten makes – you got two for the car . . .'

'There's the clock striking seven, Lewis,' I say, 'and you yawning
fit to swallow the whole street!'

I usually sing him to sleep. Even though he's quite big now,
going on seven, I always hold him on my lap while I sing.

I think at first it's the east wind. I left the balcony doors open because
of the heat. I think it must be the east wind raising the curtain and
knocking a potted plant down. When the curtain lifts again I see a
leg over the parapet and a hand grasping the back of one of the little
wrought-iron chairs out there. I'm sitting here in bed with the TV
really soft and I'm scared stiff. Whoever's out there is swearing to

himself, keeping his voice very low. He knocks another plant over. I'm wishing I'd closed the balcony doors and locked them.

'Who are you?' I say, hardly able to make my voice sound. 'What d'you want? How did you get up here? You can't come in here. Get out!' He's saying something but I can't hear him because he's got a knitted cardigan wrapped round his head.

'I can't hear a word of what you're saying,' I say. 'Take that thing off your head.'

'Where's the boy?' He moves the jumper a bit to free his mouth. His eyeholes move then and he has to pull the jumper back.

'In bed of course,' I say, 'where everyone should be this time of night. Fancy you cutting into that lovely cable stitch! A flour bag with holes for the eyes would have been better. Look out!' I say. 'You're going to crash straight into the TV.'

'Where's the boy?' He stumbles over the furniture. 'The boy, the kid. I've come for the kid.'

'I've just told you, you stupid robot,' I tell him, 'Lewis is in his bed,' and I tell him he's the very devil if he's woken up in the night. 'He screams for hours,' I say, 'and what's more, he *bites*.'

I'm shaking all over wondering if it's safer in bed or out of bed. I mean for rape, you see. 'Dr Barnett'll be home any minute now,' I say. I tell him I wouldn't like to be in his shoes when Dr Barnett comes in, and then I see he's got bare feet. Isn't that just like the thing!

I try to laugh off the bare feet. But he keeps insisting that he wants the boy. And I tell him about Lewis's daddy being called Big Lewis and that he made all the furniture because he's an orthopaedic surgeon, a bone doctor who saws and chops through bones. 'He'll just twist you into a little knot,' I say. 'He'll knock you into next week.'

It's then he tells me, would you believe, that he's the uncle and that Lewis loves him very much.

'No one said anything about a relative,' I say. 'What sort of relative? Uncle monkey,' I say, 'coming up the street and over the balcony?' He says he's full of surprises. He can't help it, he says.

Jokes and surprises. He's hidden the car next door, he says. So that's it, I say, the taxi, we saw it. 'Uncle, I *don't* think!'

'All you gotta do,' he says, 'is get the kiddie ready. I don't want no nonsense. Haven't all day.'

'You mean night,' I quip, but he doesn't get the joke. He keeps on that he's seen the TV show and the pictures in the paper. 'I want that little egghead,' he says. 'He's a wonder child. A prodigy. Just what I need. And here's the ransom letter.' With that he slaps an envelope on the table.

'You'll not touch him.' I'm really angry. 'Not put one finger on him and that's final. Get out! And take that filthy envelope with you. It's disgusting!'

'It'll be the worse for you if you don't cooperate.'

'Oh my! We do use big words!' I tell him his cardigan's slipping.

Then he tells me to get dressed and to get Lewis up and dressed. 'You're no dumb blonde!' he says. 'Get dressed. I won't look. And pack his little duds. You'll have to come too. He can bite you 'stead of me. Bring some of his toys,' he says, 'make him more at home.' He goes on about Little Lewis being spoilt rotten and tells me to put his toothbrush in as he might be stopping for a few days.

I tell him I'm not coming and neither is Little Lewis. I tell him to just wait till Mrs Porter at the agency hears about this, and the police. I tell him I'd know his red hair any place and the old woolly is not hiding a thing. 'Mrs Porter'll get the police on to you straight away.'

'Listen,' he says, 'any trouble and I'll shoot!' He says he doesn't like violence and I'm not to think for one minute that he likes doing what he's doing. Then he goes on about what he calls inequality, about the rich getting richer and the poor getting nothing at all, getting poorer.

'Lady!' he says, changing his voice, just like in a movie, could be right out of *Gone with the Wind*. 'Lady,' he says, 'dissyeah's ain't no chile lover. Ah doan dig chillun, not one bit, specially eggheads. Ah doan dig but Ah gotta hev dis lid chile.' And then, believe you me, he's all fruitcake just like Mr Treadaway. Robin Hood here, talking just like Mr Treadaway does because he can't help it, says, 'I'd prefer, actually, to do this whole thing without violence of any kind.' And then he goes on telling me he's very tenderhearted.

'Oh my! Little Red Robin Hood! Robin Readhead!' I try to work up a bit of a giggle and I tell him straight he'd frighten the pants off any child. I mean, can he be *serious*!

He says then he'll have a mosey round and see if there's anything he ought to get his mitts on.

'That's my bag, if you don't mind, my handbag.' I try to get the bag off him but he holds it up high. I tell him that if he goes away, right now, he can have my purse, my pension cheque, library cards and all.

'Great!' he says and smashes Little Lewis's piggy bank, carrying on about one-cent bits, and grannies and aunties too mean to fill the pig with decent money. 'Pore lil honey chile!' he says. 'Ahm disgusted, Ah reelly em!'

I'm thinking of slipping into the Barnetts' bedroom to the phone but he's wise to this and puts himself in the doorway. I tell him it's so hot and I feel faint and why doesn't he take that woolly right off his head and why don't we both go and get ourselves a nice cool drink.

'Too right!' he says. And all this time the traffic is pouring along down there on the main road unconcerned. There's no way I can cooee a car or anything.

'*À votre* Sandy – oops! I made a boo-boo.' I correct myself. 'Should be *à votre santé.*'

'Come again?' He's got the hiccups. He's got a nice laugh I tell him.

'Ditto,' he says, very gracious for all he's an intruder.

'Oops. You drink too fast. Your very good health.' I make my voice posh. 'Down the hatch!' Just like Mr Treadaway.

He doesn't drink, he tells me. Neither do I, I tell him, but this is an occasion, isn't it? He's very particular about not drinking, he says. But he says what I am pouring for him is very refreshing.

'A pleasant combination,' he says. 'Never had it before,' he says. 'Gin, vodka and orange, you say?'

'There's a first time for everything,' I tell him. 'Have a drop more,' I say. 'You haven't tried the port and lemon yet.'

We're getting a bit noisy, the two of us. It's lucky Lewis sleeps sound. We've been down to the kitchen and fetched up apple pie and cheese and mustard pickle. Mrs Barnett, I tell him, always says to help myself if I'm hungry. That's the kind of person she is. I show him the lovely magazines and I nearly let on that Dr Barnett is a sweet kind man but catch myself in time. My nerves are shot to pieces, practically.

'He's a real wolf in sheep's clothing,' I say. 'He's a terrible man. His family and his friends are scared stiff of him.'

'Come again? I beg yours?' His mouth's full.

'Let me top you up.' I tell him that Dr Barnett appears to be gentle but he is really very violent and quick-tempered. 'He killed a man at a party once, would you believe, so Mrs Barnett told me.' I explain that the reason he's not put away for the crime was because of self-defence. 'It was an intruder,' I tell him. 'A bit like yourself, if you don't mind my saying so. Dr Barnett, quick as a flash, lost his temper, grabbed him, and pressed him in all the fatal places – being a doctor he knows the human body very well – and killed him in seconds. Mrs Porter says that kind of death is more painful than any other.'

He's not all that impressed so I offer him more food and drink. 'There's plenty more pie,' I say.

'Lady,' he says, 'lady, I never pass up a piece of pie.' I tell him his accent is perfect and that he should be in a movie. He agrees with that. I tell him about Mrs Barnett and how when Little Lewis had earache one night she had me round for ten minutes to sing him to sleep and then paid me the four hours' flat rate and for taxis each way. 'That's what Mrs Barnett's like,' I tell him. 'The only song I know is "Short'nin' Bread", perhaps you know it?' I explain that Little Lewis likes me to sing it as if I was a black mammy, 'Mama's little baby loves short'nin' bread – I only know that line of the song,' I say, 'but it's enough for Little Lewis. Though he's going on seven he just loves to sit on my lap while I sing.' When I've finished telling, he's crying, would you believe, so I change the subject.

'When's your birthday?' I ask him. 'Don't tell me,' I say. 'Let me guess. It's at Christmas. I bet you came like little Baby Jesus on Christmas Eve . . .'

He doesn't seem to hear me. He's busy with his gun. Tapping it and holding it up. I'm dead scared, I can tell you.

'Having trouble with your gun?' My voice is all silly and shaky. 'I'd put it away if it's for real.'

'June,' he says, 'beginning of June. It's for real, this gun.' He taps it some more and holds it level with my head.

I grab at the June birthday and carry on quick as I can about us being Gemini. 'Join the club,' I say. I tell him we're the youngest of the zodiac. I tell him that we really liked being children and never wanted to grow up. I tell him that Mrs Porter at the agency has told me that Gemini people are supposed to be devious and that a Gemini should, if possible, marry a Leo and that us both being Gemini was bad luck because two Geminis should not marry. 'Little Lewis,' I say, 'is Virgo, makes him pernickety, a bit pernickety. Nothing too bad. He does have to have special food. Mrs Porter,' I go on, 'makes a point of knowing the birth signs of the children. She won't let us babysit when there's a full moon. Only in pairs. The pay's the same. The clients pay double. Mrs Porter says it's better to be safe than sorry.' He's still messing about with the gun. I try to think of something else to say.

'Gemini men are really nice,' I say, 'even when they're putting on an act. Did you know,' I ask him, 'did you know you're supposed to be agile and lively *and* amusing in bed? I hope you don't mind my saying that.'

'I can't sit here all night,' he says suddenly, his voice all rough. 'I've listened to enough nonsense. Now get the kid up like I told you before.'

'Don't point that thing at me,' I say, 'it's dangerous to point a gun like that.' Then I have the idea of taking him in to have a teeny peek at Little Lewis to see if he really has a fancy for him.

'Doesn't matter if I like him or not,' he shouts. 'He's only the means to an end. So shut up, will ya! Belt up! Dress up and pack up!'

I start on then about Little Lewis's pyjamas. 'You should just see his little pyjamas,' I say. 'Paisley pattern, all colours, he's got tartan ones too, the Gordons and the Hunting Stewarts and one with little racing cars all over, bows and arrows too –'

'Who cares?' he yells and he tells me it's the boy he wants and not his pyjamas. He starts on then telling me that Lewis has everything. Every child should have the same advantages. 'Look at all those expensive toys, that train set and those remote-control trucks and that cubby-house and the chiming musical clock,' he says, his voice going towards a scream. 'You name it, he's got it. This whole house full, all of it, represents food and shelter for other people who need both. The kid's coming with me!'

I tell him to keep his voice down. I tell him I'm every inch of the way with him. I couldn't agree more. 'That's how the world is,' I say. 'Ask Mrs Porter,' I say. 'She knows some families who only think of getting bigger and bigger houses. Their daughters – still at school, mind you! – all have their own cars and new clothes and shoes every day of the week. As for their weddings, Mrs Porter says she's never seen so much waste. You name it, she says, they'll have it. But,' I say, 'your taking Little Lewis isn't going to help. Scaring Little Lewis to death and killing his mommy and daddy with grief won't solve anything. You'll get caught,' I say. 'Red hair, a limp, and a squint. You'll get picked up straight off. Anyway, I don't believe you!' Suddenly I'm saying things I never thought I would say. 'You want money for *stuff*, don't you,' I say. 'Mrs Porter says thousands of people steal to get *stuff*. And we just don't know about it.'

'Oh, shut up and rack off,' he says. 'You shouldn't criticize a person for something he can't help. I'm an educated man and I'm into doing something for my fellow human beings, I . . .'

'Listen Little Red Hood,' I say. 'Admit you're *hooked*. Admit you want a fix. If you're really educated, you'll know that if you didn't have a grievance you'd have no reason to exist.'

'Oh la-di-da!' He's really angry. 'Where'd you get that from?'

'I can read you like a book,' I say. 'I'm Gemini same as you are. P'raps you don't know this but you and I have this gift of changing,' and here I change to Mr Treadaway's voice. Mr Treadaway, before his misfortune, Mrs Porter told me, was one of *them*, a pansy ironmonger with a flair for the arts. He wore loose English shorts, body shirts, all colours, and had his hair permed. He wore spectacles and still does. I change to Mr Treadaway's voice. 'You and I,' I say, 'have this gift of changing our flexible personalities to suit all occasions.'

'Another of Mrs Porter's earth-shattering gems,' he says. And before he can say anything else I remember Lewis's calamine lotion. I'm remembering, that is, something I forgot.

I give a great gasp. 'Come on, lover boy!' I say. 'Come and hold the torch and the bottle. I've forgotten to do Little Lewis's chest.'

'What the matter with the kid?' He's worried.

I peel down the sheet. 'Shine the light,' I say in a whisper and I unbutton Lewis's ducky little pyjamas.

'What's that? What's that on his chest?' He backs off still holding the torch and the bottle. I'm dabbing Lewis lightly with the cotton wool. Of course I explain it's a terrible infection he has and it comes out worse in adults.

Back in the playroom he's mad. He starts smashing things, the clock and the chairs. 'Temper! Temper!' I say, pulling Lewis's door closed quickly.

'You've made me waste my whole night.' He's practically weeping with rage.

'What about *my* night?' I say. 'I've lost my beauty sleep.'

Downstairs I show him the knives and forks. 'There's little tiny knives too,' I say, 'with porcelain handles, very old and valuable. There's pure silver spoons and all these really nice arntray dishes, all silver.' I tell him I'll help him load his car. There's famous paintings, I tell him, in Dr Barnett's collection and I suggest he have a pick over Mrs Barnett's rings and jewels. 'She's got some lovely things,' I say. 'I hate to see you disappointed,' I say. 'You'll need a wall.'

'Come again?'

'A wall, you *know*,' I say, 'a fence I should say.'

'Oh!' he says. 'I'm not that kind. This isn't my line at all. As a matter of fact, if you must know, if you must know . . .' His voice is thick with all the spirits he's had and he's near tears. He's shivering too. 'If you must know,' he says, 'all I've got to go home to is a dark house and a wife I detest, well, no – it's she who detests me. Perhaps that explains things a bit. I don't know.'

I feel sorry for him. I don't know why because he's awful really. And feeling sorry for him is my big mistake, or nearly is.

'We'll toss,' he says. 'All this or him. Heads I get him. Tails, all this stuff and the paintings, the Hans Heysens and the Tom Robertses. And any others we can get in the car,' he says.

'All righty then,' I say. 'But I'm warning you Little Lewis is a terrible crybaby. Temperamental. You'll have no end of trouble!'

'I know. I know,' he says, 'seen him on TV. You don't have to tell me.' He's strolling zigzag in the gallery like he owns the place. 'Not bad,' he says as he pauses in front of the pictures. 'That a grand piano over there in the alcove?' He's over there like a shot. Smart aleck, I'm thinking, doesn't miss a trick. Drop dead! I'm wishing.

'Yes, it is, yes,' I say all friendly and chatty, 'and next to it, covered up, is the harp. Pure gold.' I'm talking too fast. 'Harps,' I say, 'are so delicate, aren't they? *I took my harp to a party, but nobody asked me to play.*' I keep on humming and laughing. 'Remember Gracie Fields?' I say. He doesn't. But who would now? Only from a record on the radio. I sing some more. Humming, laughing, chatting and laughing, I'm getting on my own nerves. 'You like the piano?' I say.

'Oh yes.' Nonchalantly he runs his fingers over the keys. 'It's in very good condition,' he says. He plays some chords.

'That's nice,' I say. 'Why don't you have a go? Be my guest. I thought you had nice hands. Mrs Porter would say with hands like those you'd have to be a piano player or a thief. Sit down to it,' I say. 'I'll not run away. You can pop your gun up here, out of the way.'

★

We're dancing. I don't think I've ever enjoyed myself as much as I am just now. He plays really well and is a beautiful dancer. When he's dancing he doesn't seem to limp at all. I've never been held like this before. It's heaven!

'The floor's perfect,' he says. Before we started to dance we had *Drink to Me Only with Thine Eyes*. I told him it was my mother's favourite song, 'and Mrs Porter loves it,' I said. He played a piano piece, a sort of march. And then I found the records. A samba with vocals, the old 'Tango Bolero' and 'Jealousy' and heaps of others. We're dancing and laughing our heads off. Up the gallery and back.

'Wonderful!' I say. 'Makes me forget I'm the wrong side of forty.' I've hardly any breath left.

'You're not exactly Helen of Troy,' he says to me then, 'but has anyone ever told you you're beautiful?' He's purring close to my ear, taking me once more round the floor after the record's finished. I always feel this is the sign of a true gentleman. To go on with the dance.

'Mrs Porter always says,' I say, 'that true beauty can only be revealed – wait for it,' I say, laughing, 'in an X-ray!' I'm laughing that much I can hardly speak. 'Mrs Porter,' I say, 'can see into the future. She says Mr Right is just around the corner and will turn up for me *unexpectedly* . . .' I can see at once I've done what I always do. I always say too much. I've put my foot right in it. Saying too much. I've no head for drink. That's part of the trouble.

'Yeah?' His voice suddenly changes. 'Now,' he says, 'what about that toss? Thought I'd forgotten it, did you? I'm not leaving without the kid. Get that straight!'

'You haven't won yet,' I say. To be perfectly honest I'm shocked at the sudden change in him. Perhaps in a stupid way I actually was thinking we were on the way to a happy ending with Little Lewis safely asleep in his bed till the morning. Me! Wishing for a happy ending. What a laugh! As if anyone would ever come my way!

'Yeah?' he says again. 'Get him up. Have yourselves dressed and ready to leave right away.'

★

Up in the playroom he sits down on the one good chair and kicks a broken one. He groans and puts his head down. 'My head, it's splitting,' he says.

'I'll go for some aspirin,' I say, thinking of the phone.

'You'll not go anywhere.' He groans again. 'I'm sick.'

'I'll make a nice cup of tea,' I tell him, 'here in the playroom. You go into Mrs Barnett's little cupboard, her side of the bed. She's got everything in there. You go and get some tablets, pick your choice.' He doesn't move. I try once more. God! I'm trying. I don't know how, but I'm trying.

He groans, terrible groaning it is. 'My bloody head! Shit! You've poisoned me. Bloody hell you'll pay for this!'

'Language!' I say. 'Temper! Watch your language in the presence of a lady. Listen,' I say, 'come on out and get some air on the balcony. You'll feel better directly. Look! I'll pull the curtains back. It's getting light.'

All he does is groan and hold his head.

'Listen,' I tell him, 'Mrs Porter always says never mix your drinks. We've made a little mistake, that's all.' I try to be as soothing as I can. 'You'll be better soon.'

For a while he ferrets around in Mrs Barnett's cupboard. He makes me go there with him and he chooses a whole heap of pills and all the time I'm telling him about the game and how it's better than the toss. He swallows his pills. I'm too scared to see what they are.

'Not too many,' I say. I'm anxious, suppose he dies, it'll be my fault.

'Shut your face!' he says.

I'm a dill. That's what I am. Why am I such a dill! I've taken the wrong side. He's stacking up the points, he's up to eighty-seven already. He's got the side with everything heading for the city, all the cars and buses in the early-morning rat race. I could kill myself for being the biggest dill there ever was. First to get a hundred wins and he's up to eighty-seven and what have I got? Twelve. I've got twelve. Nothing's coming my way. I'm praying for a cycling club or some bush walkers. They would be leaving town early, on my side.

'No one walks these days,' he says just as if he can read my mind. But I tell him earlier that there's more points for people walking. 'I'm winning.' He pauses, letting the stream of traffic below go uncounted. 'I'll have the kid, like I said, like we arranged. Once I've got the money I'll have a place in the country. Open space and trees, paddocks, a little house not too far from the road, an orchard, a few sheep, banks of grass by a quiet river, the smell of hay . . .' He stops talking and in a leisurely way adds six to his eighty-seven.

'Ninety-four,' he says dreamily. 'I like this game.'

'Ninety-three,' I say. He's looking uneasy. 'You made a mistake,' I say, 'gave yourself one too many.'

'Er, I'll have to use the bathroom,' he says.

'Be my guest,' I say. 'We'll suspend play at ninety-three to twelve.'

'I'll have to tie you up,' he says. 'Ninety-four.'

'Feel free,' I say. I'm desperate. 'Any rope?' I say. 'Ninety-*three* it is. Suspended.'

He's got the rope he came up on. He says he left it for when he makes his getaway.

'Stupid,' I say. 'If you're in the house, you can leave by the front door. How stupid can you be!'

I tell him the rope's dirty and he's to put it round some newspaper. 'I don't want that filthy thing next to my skin,' I say. 'And not too tight either. I bruise easy. And I've told you I'll not go anywhere. I promise I'll just sit here.'

I tell him where the little bathroom is. 'If you want to be more deluxe,' I call after him, 'the en sooitt's off the master bedroom across the passage.'

He goes. That's the last I see of him. I call out now and then. I think he's taken a tumble in there. I did hear a noise like someone falling and now there's this blood showing under the door. The sight of blood upsets me. I feel sick. There's more blood. He must have hit his head, perhaps on the corner of the basin. I'm wishing the Barnetts, Dr Barnett and Mrs Barnett, would come home now, this very minute, even though it's early. I wish they would walk in right now so that I could tell them Little Lewis has had a lovely sleep and there's a gentleman bleeding in the bathroom.

The Immaculate Bridegroom

HELEN SIMPSON

Dawn climbed smiling up from her warm white dream, magnolia petal slippers whispering in the cathedral hush beneath wild silk underskirts, enormously hooped, and bud-studded gypsophila like a mystic cloud of gnats: then reached the top, real life again, and felt her face drop, along with her heart, and stomach, and the corners of her mouth.

'It's not fair,' she said. She turned her head on the pillow and stared at the wallpaper. This was a tangled but repetitious pattern of tiny briar roses she had seized on for her boudoir twenty years ago, a rare choice allowed by her parents at the onset of adolescence, and never regretted.

'What's wrong, darling?' said her mother, Sylvia, appearing with the tea.

'Oh, the usual,' grunted Dawn, heaving herself up and jutting out her underlip like a thwarted baby. 'I'm fed up. I want everything to be different.'

'It does seem so unfair,' tutted Sylvia.

'It is,' Dawn agreed.

'Sometimes I curse Roger,' said Sylvia.

Dawn gave a soft scream and rounded on her.

'I *told* you, Mum!' she hissed. 'If you mention his name again, I'll.'

'Sorry dear,' said Sylvia. 'I can't help thinking of all those years.'

'Well, *don't*,' said Dawn, heaving herself out of bed and over to the dressing table. She scowled into its triple mirror, her profile aping the hard-nosed sullenness of a Quattrocento Gonzaga.

'Who knows what might turn up,' said her mother hopelessly.

'Nothing ever does, though, turn up, does it,' said Dawn in injured tones. 'I'll tell you what, Mum, I don't see why the likes of Sandra Bailey who was never anything special, and great fat legs, why she should have her big day and not me.'

'It does seem cruel,' Sylvia agreed. 'We'd manage it much better than Sandra Bailey and her mother.'

'I don't see why I should be done out of it.'

'No, *I* don't see why you should be done out of it.'

'The most important day of my life.'

'I *don't* see why,' said Sylvia. 'And I'm being done out of it too, your big day. The bride's mother. It's obviously completely unfair.'

Dawn got up and started prowling round the bedroom, abstractedly brushing her hair, which crackled with static under the bristles.

'You're a modern girl,' said her mother admiringly. 'You don't have to put up with things.'

'No,' said Dawn. 'I don't.'

'Don't make the mistakes I did,' said Sylvia. 'Too passive. Putting up with things.'

'You're absolutely right, Mum!' said Dawn, pausing by the Rossetti poster of Beata Beatrix, taut with the bright-eyed rapture of one to whom the truth has been revealed. Then she sagged. 'But. Even so. It would be awfully difficult . . .'

Sylvia leant forward urgently across the tea tray.

'Nothing worth having's ever easy, Dawn,' she enunciated.

'So you think . . . ?'

'Follow your heart's desire.'

'You're right!' breathed Dawn. 'Oh, Mum. I will!'

Dawn's father Harry was less than delighted at her news.

'Do you know what weddings cost?' he grunted. '*Do* you?'

'Oh, you old killjoy,' Sylvia twitted him.

'Anyway, when did Roger decide to do the decent thing?' said

Harry. 'First I've heard of it. Thought he disappeared off the scene years ago.'

'It's not Roger,' said Dawn, pink-cheeked, her eyes starting to brim.

'Then who the hell is it?' said Harry.

'Trust you to be difficult,' snapped Sylvia. 'Can't you see you're upsetting the girl, Harry? Marriages are made in Heaven. Killjoy. You have to *work* at a marriage. You wouldn't deny that, I suppose!' She paused for a bitter laugh. 'You wouldn't deny I've had to work at our marriage like some poor devil of a pit pony while you've suited yourself. No. You wouldn't have the nerve!'

'What?' said Harry.

'Come on, darling,' said Sylvia. 'Let's ring your aunts. Your cousins. Tell them the good news. He's thrilled for you really, he just needs time to get used to the idea.'

Once Dawn had found two friends willing to act as bridesmaids, they convened in a winebar to chew over past weddings and plan this one.

'Amethysts like little mauve raindrops,' sighed Milly. 'A sort of pomander affair made of stephanotis and love-in-a-mist looped round her wrist on a ribbon. You can imagine. With *her* hair.'

'Sort of fluffy, her hair,' said Dawn thoughtfully.

'Yes, not exactly everyday hair,' said Milly. 'But perfect under tulle, that shade of yellow, like a baby chick. Oh, I do love weddings! They're my absolute favourite thing.'

Milly sat on the other side of the corridor from Dawn at work. Dawn hadn't known her for very long but she seemed quite kind and posh and would know what's what. Also, while she wasn't risibly spotty or funny looking, neither was she particularly pretty, which was ideal. The same went for Christine on the looks front, though Dawn had known her much longer, since school-days.

'So tell us about him,' said Christine, draining her second glass and stuffing in a handful of dry roast. 'Mr Right. Where did you meet him?'

'Yes, we don't even know his name!' said Milly. 'So mysterious!'

'Rochester,' said Dawn.

'Rochester?' said Christine. 'What on earth were you doing in Rochester?'

'No,' said Dawn. 'That's his name. Mr Rochester.' She paused. 'Tony.'

'And is he tall, dark and handsome?' inquired Christine sharply.

'Yes,' said Dawn. 'At least, I think so.'

'I should hope so!' said Milly. 'That you do, I mean. That's all that matters, isn't it.'

'Yes,' said Dawn.

'Unlike Patrick,' said Christine violently, pouring herself another glass. 'He's a first-class shit.'

'Patrick's her boyfriend,' Dawn explained to Milly.

The talk turned to the unsatisfactory nature of modern men, the way they seemed to flit around now more than they ever used to, never building anything up, never tying themselves down, never amounting to much.

'They take eight or nine of your best years,' snarled Christine. 'Keep you hanging on and hanging on, then they bugger off when crunch time comes.'

'Patrick's not about to do that, is he?' asked Dawn shrewdly.

'Your Roger was classic, though,' said Christine, intercutting. 'Leaving you high and dry at thirty-three. Fantastic.'

They looked at each other with dislike.

'But Tony's not like that,' said Milly, brightly, at last. 'Hopefully.'

'What does Tony do?' asked Christine.

'He works in the world of finance,' said Dawn. There was a pause. '*High* finance,' she added softly.

'And how did he propose?' asked Christine in spite of herself.

'It wasn't in so many words,' said Dawn, her eyes shining out at the middle distance. 'It was more we became aware. Both of us. That we'd somehow found our other half. I feel so at home with him that it's almost like being on my own. We two are one.'

'So when can we meet him?' asked Christine. 'Your other half.'

'The thing is,' said Dawn, 'he has a very responsible job. He's rarely around.'

'Your time together is precious,' suggested Milly.

'Surely he relaxes sometimes,' said Christine.

'Well, he has his, his club,' said Dawn.

'What?' said Christine. 'Golf? How old is he?'

'He does it for his health,' said Dawn. She fiddled with her bracelet. 'He has a weak heart,' she added, with a sudden hard look.

After that, preparations for the wedding started in earnest. Sylvia bought a book on how to do it, packed with prescriptive nuptial etiquette and including a countdown list of which jobs needed doing when and by whom.

'It's good luck for you to see a sweep on the way to church,' she said distractedly. 'Or a grey horse. I don't know which would be more difficult to arrange. Which would you prefer, dear?'

'Milly's got an Edwardian sixpence for my shoe,' said Dawn with satisfaction.

'The bridegroom's function,' read Sylvia, suddenly anxious. 'He buys the ring. That's all right, you can have mine. Call it an heirloom. He provides the bride's mother's corsage, first checking the colour of her outfit to avoid colour clashes. I think I can manage that. Oh. He tips the verger.'

'What's a verger?' asked Dawn.

'It doesn't say,' said Sylvia. 'We'll have to find out.'

'Cooker hood. Nutcrackers. Stepladder,' read Dawn, turning to the list of suggested wedding presents. 'Cream jug. Wok. Skillet. What's a skillet when it's at home?'

'I wouldn't include too many little things like the nutcrackers,' said Sylvia. 'Or the cream jug. People can be very mean. Specially relatives.'

'Music in church,' Dawn went on, flicking through the pages. She started to hum. 'I quite liked that one Princess Diana had at her wedding. You know, "I vow to thee my country".'

'That was a *real* wedding,' crooned Sylvia. 'Just like a fairytale. You can't take that away, you can't say it wasn't perfect. Nothing to do with what came after.'

'No,' agreed Dawn. 'It was above all that. And I liked the wedding in *The Sound of Music* too, just before the interval. Seven stepchildren, though. Quite a handful.'

'She was the sort who was good with children, though, wasn't she,' said Sylvia. 'She went on to do Mary Poppins.'

'The Arrival of the Queen of Sheba!' said Dawn. 'I'll have that. You remember Mum, I did it for Grade V. *Dudda* dudda *dudda* dudda *dudda* dudda *dudda* dudda *da* da da da da da da da *da* dee *da* dee *da* dee *da* dee DUDDA dudda!' She ran out of breath and started laughing.

The invitations, spidered with soft silvery italics, took two days to address, owing to the invitees' complicated web of *mésalliances*, formal and otherwise, tearings asunder, impediments, third-time-roundings, and only the occasional straightforward nuclear smugness to speed things up.

'You see, look,' said Sylvia. 'Your cousin Bridget, she was born Bridget Riley, but she married George Filmer.'

'George Filmer!' snorted Harry.

'We all make mistakes,' said Sylvia. 'So they'd have been Mr and Mrs George Filmer, and if he'd died she'd still be Mrs George Filmer. But she divorced, didn't she, after the Stanley knife incident, so then she was Mrs Bridget Filmer. Not Riley again, mark you, not the name she was born with.'

'Her father's name,' said Harry. 'Now he *was* a bugger. No wonder she didn't want *his* name back.'

'But then she married again, Robert Billington, God rest his soul. So now she's Mrs Robert Billington, even though poor Bob's passed away.'

'She did all right out of that, didn't she,' said Harry. 'She's a powerful woman now. All that life insurance. No one ever mentioned seeing a Stanley knife, did they, on the scene, when Bob's body was found?'

'Harry,' said Sylvia. 'I'm warning you. One crack like that at the reception and I'll.'

'Do we *have* to have cousin Bridget?' said Dawn pensively.

'Yes,' said Sylvia. 'She's your flesh and blood. Unfortunately.'

'Mrs Dawn Rochester,' smiled Dawn.

'No,' said Harry. 'Mrs Tony Rochester. You'd have to give him the push before you could call yourself Dawn again.'

'Oh, yes,' said Dawn, looking mildly confused. 'So I would.'

There was no getting round it, said Sylvia, they would have to see the vicar. They couldn't leave it any longer, putting it off and putting it off. She had hinted at the possibility of a putative future hiccup on the phone and he had said, well, he'd have to see, but most things were not insurmountable these days, always allowing for the bishop.

Once in his front room, mother and daughter found themselves crouching forward, chins thrust out sincerely, faces reddened by the horrible realization that what they wanted might not be allowed to happen.

'The thing is, Vicar,' said Sylvia, 'Dawn's fiancé has a very responsible job. He's never there.'

'My goodness me,' said the rector. He searched their faces for existential satire, but saw nothing like that beneath the sweat of their embarrassment.

'He's in the world of finance,' Dawn chipped in.

'So we were wondering,' said Sylvia in a rush,' If by any remote chance he wasn't able to be there on the day, and we're ninety-nine-point-nine per cent sure he will be of course, well, in that event perhaps we could arrange a proxy.'

'A proxy?' said the rector, who had been expecting a double divorcee, say, or a bigamist, but not this.

'Do you remember Prince Arthur? Henry VII's eldest boy?' said Sylvia. 'Well, his father wanted a dynastic marriage with Spain, because the Tudors were new, not really supposed to be there, so he married little Arthur off to the Infanta, but the children were too young to marry really. So they sent a proxy over to Madrid, to stand in for the prince.'

Sylvia had an encyclopaedic knowledge of the various ins and outs of the British monarchy from the Plantagenets onward, acquired during forty-odd years of reading nothing much but Jean Plaidy and Anya Seton.

'On the wedding night,' she continued, 'The proxy touched the Infanta's naked skin with the heel of his bare foot, and that counted as a symbol of the,' she lowered her eyes modestly, 'the consummation of the marriage. So we were wondering, Vicar, if in the unlikely event that Dawn's intended was called away, on her big day I mean . . .'

'. . . by the world of finance . . .'

'. . . by the world of finance, yes, would a, a proxy be acceptable to you? Because the boy next door's quite willing to stand in. He's the sort who's naturally unpopular, so he'd do anything for you. We've known him years, he and Dawn used to play French skipping but she's never fancied him. In fact I think he's probably the other way if anything.'

'Oh he is,' said Dawn. 'It's a fact. He came out in January.'

'Oh?' said Sylvia. 'That's news to me.'

'It'd be news to his mother too,' said Dawn. 'He's doing it generation by generation, working back gradually. To the difficult ones. Personally, I wish him well.'

'Excuse me,' said the rector. 'May I interrupt at this point? Well, Sylvia. Well, Dawn. My turn now. I want to let you know where I stand *vis à vis* the horns of your dilemma. And that directly relates to my views on the Church of England.'

'Yes, Vicar,' said Sylvia. 'Dawn, sit up straight.'

'Strongly ecumenical though my sympathies are,' continued the rector, 'I cannot help but feel that the Church of England has a superior understanding of life's complexities. We are capable of responding to the changing needs of humanity, indeed to the passage of time itself. We shift. And we are proud to shift. When necessary. You know the story about the oak tree breaking and the reed bending? Well, that is what I love about the Church of England – its reediness. Dawn, are you listening?'

'Yes, Vicar,' said Dawn, who had been thinking she ought to do her nails tonight, it was getting urgent.

'Now, Dawn, as I see it,' said the rector, 'You are a lamb newly returned to the fold.'

'What, like the prodigal son?' said Dawn, resentfully.

'She's been a good daughter,' said Sylvia. 'A model daughter.'

'I'm sure she has. So I take it you will both agree to come to church every Sunday until Dawn's wedding and at least every other Sunday for the next five years, by which time I hope you will both be as they say "hooked". On pain of annulment of the marriage if either of you default, I'm afraid.'

'They certainly squeeze their pound of flesh out of you these days, vicars,' said Sylvia. 'I'm sure it never used to be like that.'

She had baked a cake for seven hours at Mark 2, in a tin lined with double greaseproof and protected outside by a palisade of three thicknesses of newspaper tied with string. This cake and its two smaller companions had been cooled, painted with hot jam, cooled again, marzipanned, then given a final bubble-free royal icing mantle on four consecutive evenings.

Now Sylvia attached a number two writing nozzle to the icing bag and started to inscribe in tiny cursive script, 'Let me not to the marriage of true minds.'

'It's quite long,' said Dawn anxiously. 'Are you sure you'll get it all on?'

'Fourteen lines,' said Sylvia. 'I've done it before.'

'It's just I'd hate to lose the last couplet,' fussed Dawn.

'Only one *d* in impediment,' clucked Sylvia. 'Blast. I hate that word.'

The night before, Dawn could not sleep. She sat in her little bedroom and looked round for what she imagined would be the last time at the miniature rose wallpaper, the herd of furry toys, Lizzie Siddal in a frizzy shroud of hair, the bookshelf freighted with flower fairies, Milly-Molly-Mandies and fantastical tales of princesses and boarding schools.

The trouble was, she acknowledged, she could not think what he looked like. She could imagine a looming shape in the doorway, a dark brown voice, a muscular thigh. But she could not envisage his face. After a while this bothered her so much that she called out to her mother, who was sitting up late with a fine black felt-tip stroking in a crossbar on each Order of Service sheet in the line which read: *And did those feel in ancient times.*

'If I'm honest, Mum,' she sniffed, 'I'm not sure how well I really know him.'

'That's only natural, darling,' said Sylvia. 'You're not married yet.'

'But he seems sort of shadowy.'

'Plenty of time for the solid stuff after the wedding. Things *should* be dreamy before.'

'Am I doing the right thing, though?' wept Dawn. 'What if he turns out like Roger? Or Dad?'

'Listen Dawn,' said Sylvia sharply. 'He's an altogether different class of man. He won't.'

'But am I really in love?' she wailed.

'Of course you are!' snapped Sylvia. 'Pull yourself together. What do you want to do? Give the ring back? Call it all off? It's a bit late in the day for that, you know.'

'I know,' said Dawn, trumpeting into a tissue. 'Sorry, Mum. It didn't seem quite real for a minute there. Just nerves.'

Four hours of the early part of the morning had been allowed for the preparation of the bride, and that allowance had not proved excessive. Dawn's colour had been rising steadily since she woke up; she was now very pink indeed under her heated rollers and had almost stopped breathing.

'I think I've got a temperature,' she puffed.

'Excitement,' said Milly knowledgeably, freezing her nail varnish with a fixative spray. 'Don't worry, I've got some green make-up on me. I've done this before. You'll look like an arum lily by the time I've finished with you.'

Sylvia was peeling the price tag from the sole of the bride's gentian satin courts.

'Something blue, I imagine *they're* supposed to be,' Christine sniffed.

'A bit distracting for the congregation,' said Sylvia. 'While the bride kneels for her vows, £39.99 cast up at them. They *are* blue, Christine, no "supposed" about it.'

'Don't forget to step out of the house on your right foot when you leave for church,' said Milly. 'Or it's bad luck forever.'

'Oh dear,' said Dawn. 'There's such a lot to remember.'

Milly and Christine, sugar-pink caryatids in sashed and sprigged Swiss lawn, helped Dawn, by now gasping for air like a fish, into the wedding dress. It was a square-necked seersucker gown with leg-o'-mutton sleeves and a hundred and eighty-two hand-covered buttons.

'Ooooh,' went the women, with the sigh that people make as fireworks fade.

When Dawn and her father arrived at the church, the rector hurried forward to meet them with a long face.

'I'm afraid I have something of a disappointment for you, my dear,' he said to Dawn.

She recoiled in a rustle of puckered silk.

'You promised,' she hissed, a furious swan on the path. 'You promised!'

'Never fear,' said the rector hurriedly, with a lop-sided smile. 'What I was going to say was, it looks as though our gallant proxy may be called on after all.'

Then Dawn put a hand to her thumping heart and smiled, while Harry turned and waved at the limousine parked by the lych gate. Out jumped the boy next door, spruce and shy. They shooed him into the church before them, waited a moment and then, at a sign from the rector, the opening chords of the Arrival of the Queen of Sheba cascaded down and they went slowly in.

Just as a camcorder may cause offence during a wedding ceremony, so may an authorial presence. Imagination must supply the dog-rose blushes of the bride beneath her clouding of organdie tulle, the satin slippers moving at the hem of her dress like blue-nosed mice, and the soaring and crashing of the organ music.

Some guests could not help but notice, however, that what with the bride's family seated shoulder to shoulder in the left-hand pews and only the mother of the boy next door on the right, there was something of an imbalance. The church had lolled like a clumsily ballasted ship.

There was some comment on this at the reception afterwards.

'Bit of a one-sided wedding,' said an aunt from Birkenhead.

'Bit of a one-horse affair all round,' replied Mrs Robert Billington. 'Not even a sit-down meal.'

'I mean, did you notice,' persisted the aunt. 'Our side of the church was packed, but on the other side nobody but the next door neighbour.'

'Ironic, really, after all these years, to end up with the boy next door,' sniffed Mrs Billington.

'Though someone was telling me he was only a stand-in,' puzzled the aunt.

'A stand-in?' said Mrs Billington. 'A stand-in for what?'

'That's what I said,' the aunt agreed. She shrugged. 'Dawn makes a lovely bride, though, doesn't she. Bless her.'

The bride's father's speech concentrated on anecdotes relating to his daughter's tantrums, teenage skin complaints, and disastrous sexual escapades, on her tendency to treat money like water and to cry at the drop of a hat.

'Tony had better tread carefully, that's all I can say!' he finished. 'I must admit, though, from what I've seen, he's not exactly keen to throw his weight around. It's a shame he couldn't be here with us today – these high fliers – but rest assured everyone, he will be there to meet Dawn off the plane at the honeymoon destination. More than that I'm not allowed to divulge.'

Then Dawn ran whooping through an archway of hands and a shower of rice, off out to the car and away. Sylvia stood and cried.

'There, there,' said Harry. 'He'll take good care of her.'

And he obviously did. She came back brown as a Sunday roast – radiant! It was a shame he'd had to carry on from St Lucia but it would have been foolish not to fly on to the Philippines to clinch the deal he'd been working on at the time of their wedding, and Dawn was quite happy about that.

'I'm not worried,' she said to Milly and Christine at their post-honeymoon get-together to view the wedding photographs. 'He can look after himself.'

The story should end here, happily ever after so to speak; unfortunately it is necessary to add a coda.

Such serenity, such newly wed insouciance, threw the blow, when it fell, into cruelly sharp relief. News of Tony's demise on foreign shores, a massive coronary at a vital convention, tragic though it undoubtedly was, and of course untimely, apparently trailed clouds of fiscal glory. His actions that day, just before the fatal stoppage, had saved the livelihoods of thousands of shareholders, Dawn told them (though it had left her no better off than before since, oddly enough, he had died without leaving a bean). She mopped her eyes and blew her nose with subdued grace.

Widowhood had conferred on Dawn an unexpected gravitas. It soon became apparent that she was not after all utterly bereft. This was discovered following the harrowing news of Tony's decease, when she hinted that their all-too-brief honeymoon had borne fruit.

Tony had not died without issue, it seemed, or, at least, not exactly. Dawn grew bulkier by the week and developed a sleepy smile. There was some comfort in this situation, friends and relatives remarked; she would have someone to cherish. It would be company for her. And if the child were a boy – as indeed eventually proved to be the case – then his father's name, as well as his memory, would live on.

Sonata Form

JANICE GALLOWAY

A few stands, those coffins they put cellos in, the odd coat and sports bag. The flowers were there too but not him. She checked the wee toilet, the shower cubicle. No drips, nothing. It was just one of those things about being with Danny. People came and got him. They walked by the rank and file sticking their fiddles back in cases and zeroed in, even if he hadn't had time to wash yet, to change out of his soaking shirt. She'd seen him taking off his concert trousers, unpeeling the cloth off his legs, steaming like a horse and they just came in anyway, exchanging pleasantries as if he didn't need time to do even that by himself. She'd seen him zip hairs out by the roots doing himself up blind, maintaining eye-contact and a smile rather than say anything. Tongue biting. You had to do a lot of tongue biting in dressing rooms.

Over on the practice piano, two bus tickets, a chewed pencil. His teethmarks. Mona put it in her bag with the spare she'd brought in case he needed it then draped her coat over a chair-back, the shoulder-bag out of sight beneath it. No point carrying stuff you didn't need. His coat wasn't on the stool where it usually was. She looked around, scanning. It was there in an empty box in the corner, the tails junked on top with the lining showing. Crimson lining. Everybody else had grey but not Danny. You always found them no problem: in among all the other castoffs, Danny's tails were something else. Mona looked at them, the Ribena-coloured splash and black wings falling onto the floor. At least the poor bugger had had time to change his jacket. There would be women through there very disappointed. She went over and fixed it so it wouldn't crease, smoothed the arms flat. A few hundred quids' worth lying any old how. On the way out, she shut the door carefully behind her.

After ten minutes of blind alleys and droopy paperchains it was there like you couldn't miss it. People were spilling out the door, trolleys of drink rolling in. Every so often, great baboon-howls about nothing evident would roar out of the interior then fade. The second-desk double bass and big blond guy who played the trumpet walked in, doing their bit as players' reps. Some people actually liked it, Danny said. They liked the free food, especially this time of year. Eric and Simon were there too, hovering around the open door, peering in: Simon with a bunch of something and Eric not wearing his specs. They came sometimes but seeing them was always a surprise. Simon turned then and saw her. They walked over with their arms wide, smiling the same way. She knew they knew. You could tell by looking at them. Simon rubbed his cheek against hers, gave her one of those lightweight hugs he did. You just got used to them starting when they were finished. They were good hugs anyway. She told them it was great to see them and watched them go coy.

'Well,' she said, 'you got your money's worth. Was he great or was he great?'

'Oh you,' Eric said. He rolled his eyes. Never mind him.

'No,' Simon said. 'We want to talk about you.'

'Let's have a look at you then,' Eric said. He held her out at arm's length and looked meaningfully at her belly through the black frock. They all did. There was nothing to see yet but they all did it anyway. It was pleasantly embarrassing. Simon said he thought Danny was playing great just for the record and they laughed. It helped. Another few minutes of when's it due and how well she was looking. Things were just starting to get easier when Simon braced up, looked down at his wrist. 'Sorry,' he said. They had to rush, wouldn't come in this time: too much stuff to do, she knew how it was.

'Ivor Novello for somebody's party,' Eric said. 'But we need the money.'

Simon stuck the bunch of flowers into her hand. 'Give the maestro our love,' he said. 'And tell him these aren't his.'

Mona cuddled them into the crook of an arm. Roses. Not for Danny. She didn't know what to say. They left walking backwards and blowing kisses. Mona watched them, waving, knowing they knew they wouldn't have gotten in anyway. Friends didn't. These dos weren't for musicians at all, not even the ones who'd been playing. She heard the main door batter back on its hinges, knew they were irretrievably gone. The draft made the corridor chilly. Her cardigan was back in the dressing room but she had no idea how to get back there. There was nothing else for it. She put the roses down carefully on an empty trolley, ran a hand over her stomach wishing it showed more and walked inside.

Danny was on the other side of the room holding a wine glass and an empty paper plate in the middle of a huddle of women. It was where he always was at these things, what he was always holding. She nodded to let him know not to stop what he was in the middle of and just took her time. Mona liked looking at Danny and you only got to look at somebody properly when they were distracted, not knowing you were watching. You got to read things they didn't necessarily know they were telling you. Right now, he looked that way he did when a concert was over and he thought he'd done OK. Self-conscious, shagged out and radiant. She knew that look from other places as well: it always meant something good. He was close now, close enough for familiar cosmetic smells to reach, a deodorant and aftershave cocktail. She reached for the plate from his hand without asking, took it over to the buffet table and stood in line with the men already there, loading up with fish and meat, lumps of mayonnaise-thick salad. Getting the nosh was Mona's thing: it gave her something to do. Cutlery in paper napkins, bowls, oval-shaped plates and glasses. Most of the table was glasses. The salmon had eyes in this time. It looked up at nothing, pink muscu-lature in tatters.

'Best bit eh?'

A man with a tight tie reached past for a sheet of ham. A waitress with silver-coloured prong efforts was holding a slice out for him but he didn't seem to see her.

'Best bit,' he said. 'Where they wheel out the eats.'

He rolled the ham into a tube, popped it into his mouth, offered her a plate then saw she had one already.

'That's the girl,' he said. He waved his fork in a cheery kind of way and strolled along to the next tray, chewing. The waitress still held the same bit of ham out but someone else got it first. Mona didn't want it anyway. She walked further up, found egg sandwich triangles, some cheese: the only vegetarian stuff that wasn't salad. They always had loads of salad at these things. Danny couldn't eat salad after concerts. It gave him the shits. He always had bad shits before concerts with the nerves and everything and it hung on. He probably wouldn't eat the sandwiches either but she would take a couple anyway. Just in case. She back-to-backed them on the plate, lifted a glass of something orange and picked her way back through. Danny wasn't looking in her direction but he didn't need to. His smile changed. It stayed in place for the woman Mona could only see the back of but it knew she was coming over.

Her son played, she was saying. Who knew maybe one day professionally she only wished she'd thought to let him come along you could have told him to stick in you don't mind if I call you Daniel. Then Mona got over and interrupted.

'Hi,' she said. She pushed the plate between them.

The woman with the son stepped back, followed the length of the arm to Mona's face.

'This is Mona,' Danny said.

Mona put her juice down on the table edge, offered the freed hand for shaking. The woman with the son made a very big smile.

'Lovely,' she said. 'Lovely.'

She didn't take the hand though. Some women didn't. Danny claimed his plate and looked hard at the shapes on it. Mona knew what he was thinking. He was thinking they never gave you real food at these things but not saying, pushing the triangles about with his eyes down. Mona let her arm drop, picked up the glass again. She smiled too.

'So,' she said. 'Enjoy the concert?'

'My goodness yes,' she said. 'Yes yes. Who wouldn't have?' Mona nodded.

'I was just saying to Daniel here I'm *such* an admirer.'

It was said for Danny to hear and he knew. He'd seen it coming and turned away just in time. A woman in a black strapless thing who'd been waiting for just that moment had got him as soon as he'd shifted his footing. Mona and the woman with the son looked at each other again. The woman coughed, looked at her empty glass, back at Mona.

'Sorry,' she said. 'Heather.' She almost pointed at herself, thought better of it. 'I don't know who you are.'

'Mona,' Mona said.

'Of course,' she said. 'Of course. And you're . . . are you a fan too?'

'No, no.' Mona was no good at this kind of thing. She could hear herself being no good at it. 'I just live with him.'

'Oh,' Heather said. The hand without the glass fluttered up to her neck. 'I should have known, shouldn't I?'

'No you shouldn't,' Mona said.

'I didn't even know he was married. Just didn't occur.'

'He's not,' Mona said. 'He isn't.'

'Sorry?'

'Married. We're not married.'

'Yes,' she said. A studious looked crossed over her face. 'I see. It must be lovely anyway.' She turned and smiled at someone over her shoulder. 'Jean?'

She looked behind her. Three women looked up. The two talking to Danny didn't.

'Jean?' It was louder this time. 'There's someone you have to meet here. Come over. Come and meet . . . um . . .'

'Mona,' Mona said.

'Daniel's wife,' Heather said.

All three came over. Mona held out her hand again. Two

responded this time. Mona said her name to each of them to be on the safe side. She had to ask theirs. Jean, Carolyn, Stephanie, they said. They all had lovely teeth.

'You must be very proud,' Jean said.

'I know I would be,' said Carolyn.

'Oh yes,' Mona said, 'very proud.'

'He plays so beautifully. We were just saying, weren't we girls?' Jean opened her eyes wide to take them all in. 'Just saying we could listen all night.'

'We were not,' Carolyn said. 'We were saying how good-looking he was. Tell the truth, Jean.'

'You'll get me hung,' Jean said. 'All right, I admit it. We were talking about more than the playing if I have to be brutally honest.'

'Good-looking,' Stephanie said. '*And* gifted. You're a very lucky girl.'

'I expect you know that too, Mona eh?' Carolyn winked.

'Oh yes,' Mona said. 'Certainly do.'

They laughed this time. Sort of giggled. Mona's glass was needing refilled.

'I envy you, though. All that beautiful music going on all the time under your own roof, friendly terms with Wagner and Mendelssohn, the *Moonlight Sonata* raging away next door.' Jean sighed. 'It must be marvellous.'

'Well.' Mona looked at her. 'He plays mostly contemporary these days. More Maxwell Davies then Mendelssohn. Folk who're still alive kind of thing.'

'Sorry?' Stephanie looked as if she hadn't heard right.

'Beamish, Wier,' said Mona. 'Nicholson.'

'Never mind,' said Jean.

'What's it like, though, living with that kind of creative talent? Living with it?' Carolyn's eyes got bigger. 'It must be terribly romantic.'

'Oh you get used to it,' Mona said. 'You . . . um . . . cope.'

'Maybe Mona is a musician too, though,' said Stephanie. 'Creative people often team up with other creative people, the shared sensitivities and everything. I bet you're a musician too. Am I right?'

'No, I'm not a musician,' Mona said.

She couldn't see Heather any more. Her voice was still there though, the word *sensual* rising and fading back into the continuous buzz from somewhere else.

'Shame,' Carolyn said. 'Still it's probably just as well. Somebody needs to be the practical one, able to do the organizing and things.' She took Mona's glass and put it on a passing tray, served them both another. 'Sorting out his music and concert clothes and so on.'

'Did you see his fingers?' Jean looked at Stephanie. 'They're solid! Solid muscle!'

'Really?' Stephanie looked horrified.

'They're H U G E. Literally. Bulging. People don't think about it as a physical job do they? But there you are. Literally bulging.'

'I bet he's impractical though.' Carolyn again. 'Creative people are famous for it. I bet being close to that sort of person has its downside.'

'Well,' Mona said.

'Not good with time-keeping I bet.'

'Well.' Mona wasn't sure she should be saying this but she said it anyway. 'He's doesn't dust or anything. I lift a lot of socks up.'

'It is though?' Jean was fiddling with her hair, drawing her fingers through it, separating the lacquered sheets. 'Physical, I mean. Does he train?'

Mona could hear Danny's voice close enough to whisper to. 'That's my job, after all,' he was saying. 'That's part of what people pay me to do.' Someone must have asked him how he remembered all those notes. A man laughed as though the answer was a joke of some kind and there was the sound of a hand slapping a back.

'No,' Mona said. 'He doesn't train. Unless lifting beer-glasses counts.'

Jean laughed and shook her head as though Mona was a real wag, a card. 'Good for you,' she said. 'Haha. Good for you.'

They all smiled at each other again. Something had reached a natural conclusion. Mona looked into her orange juice and Stephanie and Carolyn began a slow drift in the direction of the buffet table.

Danny's voice, further off but still clean as a triangle, was asking where the toilets were.

'Well,' Jean said. 'It's been a pleasure meeting you.' She was turning away, not sure how to make the break without feeling she was doing the wrong thing. 'And that *charming* husband.'

Mona smiled, nodded.

'And tell him,' Jean stage-whispered, 'that lovely man of yours. He's *wonderful*.' Flashing aren't-I-awful eyes before she faded further off. Behind her back, Mona saw Danny heading off out the door. One hand in the pocket, raking for fags. Mona kept smiling till Jean turned away.

The buffet table was crowded now, mostly women: more empty glasses dotted round the place than full ones. Mona thought about going over and couldn't be bothered. Up too early again, bed too late, Danny haring about with an iron before breakfast. Getting here. You got out of practice for being out: rusty for dealing with people. All they knew was work, when you thought about it: Danny in his room all the time with the bloody piano, crashing away till midnight depending what else he'd had to do that day, her trying to write at the kitchen table till godknows. They hardly knew how to deal socially with each other never mind other people. And then there was the dizziness, the waves of nausea that washed up these days. What she wanted was a lie down. There was a chair over on the far side of the room with no one near it, just a man looking out the big bay window. The chair looked soft and Danny wouldn't be long. The man looked OK too: preoccupied. Safe. She was just about to go over when something touched her back.

A man was standing behind her with a wee book of some kind. It wasn't a concert programme, just a book.

'Sorry,' he said. 'Didn't mean to do that.'

He had very pale skin, freckles on his scalp. 'That's OK,' Mona said. 'Just don't do it again.'

It was meant to be funny, light or something but he just looked at her and didn't say anything. His eyes were watery, filmed over. He looked not well.

'Sorry,' she said.

'No,' he said. 'I am. My line.'

'Right,' she said. The watery eyes kept looking at her. Mona gesticulated towards the chair. 'Just . . . um . . . heading over here then.'

'What d'you think of this lot?' he said. He rustled the booklet between his hands. 'Lot of money to run an orchestra.'

Mona looked at him. Maybe he hadn't heard her. Maybe she hadn't heard him, the wheezy voice needing to be listened to harder to get more of a gist.

'People don't think about where it comes from,' he said. 'Money.'

The chair was still free. Mona could see it. The man was looking out at the night skyline.

'Dependent on things they know nothing about.' He wiped his mouth suddenly, the white end of a hanky disappearing back inside the jacket pocket. 'Parasitic. The whole thing. All parasites.'

The feeling in Mona's stomach was intensifying. It told her she wanted to get away but she couldn't think how. How to do it refused to occur.

'The people who come to concerts. Ignorant. Like everybody else.'

Mona waited.

'Am I not being interesting enough?' he said suddenly.

'No,' Mona said. She said it without thinking. 'No you're being. You're being what you're being.'

'People who come to concerts,' he said again. He looked at the floor.

'You're not the kind of people who come to concerts, then?'

'Oh yes,' he said. 'Wife likes them. Women do.' His eyes scanned the parquet. 'I'm also the director-general of this outfit. It's sort of expected.'

Something like a wince moved over his mouth, faded out. It was hard to tell whether he didn't know she hadn't a clue what he was talking about or simply didn't care. He kept looking down.

'Right,' she said.

They stood for a moment saying nothing.

'Not a musician yourself, are you?' He rolled the sore-looking eyes towards her briefly, lowered them again.

'No,' she said. 'You're safe there.'

He made the half-smile. 'No I'm not,' he said. 'You're a sympathizer. I can tell. I know you're thinking I'm a fool. A Philistine.'

'Oh?'

'You sense it,' he said. 'Like a smell.'

Mona had had enough. She didn't want any more of whatever this was. Not tonight.

'It's what's wrong,' he said. 'What's wrong with the whole country.'

Mona said nothing.

'No servant class.'

Mona looked suddenly at him. She couldn't help it. She stood very still, just looking.

'Given up our servant class. Self-evident that's no good. You look at the great civilizations and you'll see: give up your servant class and it all goes to hell. Too many people who don't know anything. They're not getting the proper guidance. Not getting a job where they're given reliable instruction. What are they supposed to do?'

Mona didn't know.

'Express themselves,' he said. 'They go about expressing themselves.'

He waved the paper limply, scanned the room. They had stopped looking at each other.

'Doesn't build pyramids, does it?'

'Pyramids,' Mona said. She kept watching him, the ironic smile or whatever it was, twitching at the corners of his mouth. 'Pyramids,' she said again. There was nothing else in the room to attach to. Not a thing. The man near the window had moved away and you couldn't even see the streetlights from here. She watched black sky for a while. Then spoke.

'My mother was a servant,' she said. 'She was in service for eight years.'

'So was mine.' The shape of him at the corner of her eye not budging. 'Interesting we should have that in common.'

Stephanie was there suddenly, fussing.

'Do you want anything Archie? He never eats properly.' She raised her eyebrows, the pencil lines moving into mock-furious arches. 'I need to do everything for him.'

She wiped his lapels and took the booklet out of his hand. He just stood there, letting her and Mona saw for the first time what it was. A score. He'd been in at the concert, if he'd been in at all, with a concerto score. Without it to hold onto, his hand started shaking. It trembled over the slit of his jacket pocket as though he was trying to pull out a stuck scarf. Like he had Parkinson's or something.

'Go away, Stephie,' he said. He was doing his smile, shifting the top lip. It occurred to Mona he might have had a stroke. She looked over at Stephanie and Stephanie smiled. Very gently.

'Go away,' he said again. She went.

'Well,' Mona said. She could see Danny at the door now, the travel bag over one arm, waving for her to come. Her coat was there too. 'Well. It's been . . . whatever.'

'Yes,' he said. 'It has.'

He reached to take the empty glass from her. He held onto it when she passed it to him, drew her nearer.

'You despise me, don't you?' he said.

It was just the same tone of voice he'd used all evening: even, disinterested.

'I can see that too.'

His eyes looked coated.

'I don't know you,' she said. She let the glass go. 'I know nothing about you. Of course I don't despise you.'

'You know the Koechel number of that concerto? The one they did tonight? The tempo for the second movement?'

'No,' Mona said.

'Thought not,' he said. 'Neither does that young man.'

'I have to go now.' She said it quite definitely, quite sure. She wanted away from him: this dying individual with his score tucked under his arm, thinking Mozart had written an instruction manual just for him, a set of tips on form. If she didn't go soon she'd say something and let Danny down. It was his do, not hers. This was Danny's work for godsake, not hers. 'Goodbye,' she said. She walked away without turning round, hoping she had sounded calm. Jean and Carolyn weren't anywhere. Heather was dancing. Only Stephanie waved.

'Christ I thought you were never coming,' he said when she got out. He was pacing from foot to foot like he was frozen. 'Come on then. I'm dying for a fish supper.'

Mona took Danny's tails on their hanger, her own coat.

'You got your flowers?' she said.

He hauled the tulips from under the sports bag, hers too. The roses. Mona had almost forgotten about them.

'Don't tell me,' he said. 'Simon said they weren't for me.'

Mona nodded.

'I told him you were pregnant. Did you tell him as well?'

Mona looked Danny hard in the eye, put one hand on his shoulder. The cloth of his jacket was warm, grainy.

'Danny,' she said. Her stomach was tight. 'What was the Koechel number of the concerto?'

'Eh?' he said. He stopped bouncing.

'The K number. D'you know it?'

'Four-six-six,' he said.

Mona looked at him.

'Look, you don't spend months with a piece, seeing it every day without knowing the Koechel number. I can give you the date of the first performance as well if you like. Eleventh of February, seventeen-eighty-five. And his dad was there. Not that they've got anything to do with anything but I'm throwing in extra free. What kind of question's that supposed to be? Koechel number?'

'Danny,' she said. She pulled him closer. He smelled of cigarette smoke, aftershave and sweat. A man after his work. 'Danny, tell me our child will not have to play the piano for a living, Danny. Tell me.'

He looked at her hard, his eyebrows tangled up. Mona kept her face dead straight.

'Mona,' he said quietly. 'I haven't a clue what you're talking about. Not a clue.'

'I know,' she said. 'Are you going to tell me anyway?'

'No,' he said. 'Of course I'm not.'

She knew that too.

'Can I assume the daft questions concluded?' He smiled when he said it but he was getting fed up with this, whatever it was. He wanted his chips and he wanted them now. Mona said nothing. Danny flexed his hands. 'Come on, Mona. It's perishing in here.'

He stopped for the plastic carrier, the straps of the overnight bag. The blond trumpet-player came out the reception room rubbing his temples.

'Thank God that's over,' he said. He nodded in their direction. 'See you in the pub OK?'

He walked off, shaking his head, down the corridor after his case. Mona watched him. When she turned back, Danny was standing, the weight of the big bag digging a groove into his shoulder. He was fit for the road.

'OK? The take-away on the corner. We'll catch the pubs as well if you're quick.' He smiled like the sun coming out, kissed her cheek and started walking.

Mona watched Danny moving towards the night air outside, his flowers under one arm. Her wrist was sore, the hanger with the tails biting into her fingers. It was so bloody heavy. She looked down at the thing, the stubborn crimson lining, hearing the sound of his footfalls recede. Monkey-jackets they called them. Livery. Faint laughter was drifting from behind the closed door. Danny walked on ahead, two bunches of flower-heads bobbing under his arm. She hadn't even told him how good he'd been, how proud she was of him. His work. And that, she realized suddenly, was what she very much wanted to say. Yellow tulips still fresh beneath the artificial light. 'I love you, Danny.' It was exactly what she wanted to say.

Polaris

FAY WELDON

The dog was called Thompson, a name without significance, except that Timmy's nephew, aged ten, had named him so. It was an innocent, respectable name. Thompson was a springer spaniel: a strong, handsome, long-haired creature, silky brown and white and full of powerful, unnamed emotions. 'Never seek to tell thy love,' misquoted Meg, from Blake, trying to stare Thompson out, 'love that never can be told –' And Thompson stared back at Meg, and seemed to be weeping. It was Meg who dropped her eyes.

The dog Thompson loved Timmy as a man loves another man, and the man Timmy loved Thompson as a man loves a dog. That, Meg decided, was the cause of Thompson's distress. 'He's perfectly happy,' protested Timmy, in the face of all evidence to the contrary. 'That is just the way dogs look at their masters. There is nothing unhealthy in it.'

They were plastering and painting their first house, their first marital home, on the hills above the naval base where Timmy was stationed, there where the cold North Sea meets the sandy Western Scottish shore, there where Polaris dwells. They were using white paint; no frills, just a bleak beauty, a background. That was what they both wanted. Security insisted they put in a telephone, otherwise they'd have gone without that too. They needed only each other. The telephone was in and working before anything else, before even the electricity cable arrived to link them to the mainstream of the world.

Now they mended and smoothed and renovated, making good what had gone before. The shaggy Scottish sheep came to stare at them through gaps in the old stone walls, where once windows had been, and soon would be again. The sheep made Thompson jump.

'Silly beast,' said Timmy fondly. 'He's afraid of them. He only understands southern sheep.' Yet he expected Meg, also transplanted from south to north, to be brave.

Meg and Timmy prayed that it would not rain until the roof was watertight, and God answered their prayers and sent a long hot dry summer, heather-scented. And Meg and Timmy sawed and hammered and twisted pipes and made love when the spirit moved them, which was often. Down at the Base the other wives trotted in and out of each other's nice new bungalows, with papered walls in pretty pinks and greens, and said that Meg was mad; but no doubt time would cure her, as it had cured each of them in turn. Time, and experience and winter. A cold lonely winter or two, with Timmy away, and she'd move down to the Base, for the company and the coffee and the moral support.

'I'll never be like them,' Meg told Timmy, of course she did. 'I'm different. I married you, I didn't marry the Navy.'

'You'll have Thompson for company,' was all he said, 'when I'm away.'

'Oh, Thompson!' scorned Meg. 'Scratching and bouncing and fussing! All feeling and no brain.'

'He's just alive,' said Timmy. 'He can't help it.'

'I'd rather look after a brain-damaged child than a dog,' said Meg. 'Any day! At least you'd know where you were.'

'You wouldn't rather,' Timmy said, his face not loving and laughing at all but serious and cold, just for an instant, before relaxing again into its pleasant ordinariness.

Her own, her lovely Timmy! How could she be afraid of him? He was handsome in the way heroes are handsome – broad-shouldered, big-framed, blond and blue-eyed – and had made her, who was accustomed to being always slightly delinquent, somehow not quite like other people, into the heroine of her own life. Timmy had given her a vision of perfectibility. He had married her. But she wished he didn't have a beard. If she couldn't see his mouth, how could she properly judge his feelings? Perhaps his flesh was warm but his bones were cold?

Timmy's beard and Thompson! Well, she could live with them.

She had had lovers more temperamental, more experimental, more — if it came to it — exciting than Timmy, but none who had made her happy. He moved her, she tried to explain to him, into some other state. He changed her in his love-making, she said one morning as they puttied glass into window-frames, into something that belonged to somewhere else, somewhere better.

'Perhaps it's the somewhere else you say Thompson comes from,' he said, joking, no doubt because her talking about intimate and emotional matters made him uneasy. But she chose to take it the wrong way, and didn't talk to him for a full six hours, banging and crashing through their still fragile, echoing house until he dropped a hammer on his toe, and made her laugh and she forgave him. Her anger was a luxury: both understood that and thought they could well afford it. Her little spats of bad behaviour were a status symbol of their love.

They made love outside in the yellow glow flung back from the old stone walls as the sun set.

'Never let the sun go down on thy wrath,' said Timmy. Sometimes he said such obvious things she was quite shaken; phrases that merely flitted through her head, and out again, Timmy would give actual voice to. She thought perhaps it was because she'd had more experience of the world than he. He'd spent a long time under the seas, some six months out of every twelve, since he joined the Navy as a cadet. Besides, he'd been to a public school and a naval college and only ever mixed with the same kind of people; she'd been to art school and had a hard time with herself in one way and another, brought up by a mother she never really got on with: without a father. Timmy took life simply and pleasantly and did as he wanted, without worrying, and was generous. She worried and was mean: she couldn't help it. She couldn't throw away a stale crust unless there was a bird waiting to eat it, whereas Timmy would pour milk down the sink, if the sink was nearer than the fridge and he was tidying up. She had to save, he to spend. But in a sense it didn't matter: between them the opposites balanced out. His prodigality and her frugality, caught steady on the fulcrum of their love.

Thompson slept under the bed, and when they made love at night would be both jealous and fascinated. He'd roam the room and shuffle and lick their toes.

'Dogs shouldn't be in bedrooms,' said Meg.

'Love me, love my dog,' said Timmy, and she found she'd been waiting for him to say it for a long time. Once he had, she settled down to put up with Thompson, third party to their marriage, the fixture under the marital bed. She even bought flea powder down at the PX on the Base, on one of their weekly trips in. And a special comb for Timmy's beard.

In the Autumn Timmy must expect to go on his tour of duty on Polaris. Three months on, three months off, more or less; sometimes longer, sometimes shorter. Security demanded uncertainty. But Meg could not believe it would ever happen. Timmy would say things like:

'You've got to take a driving test before the Autumn, Meg,' or, 'I have to have at least the kitchen finished before I go,' and she would somehow wonder what he was talking about. Her father had died when she was six. The death had been expected for a year, but how can a child expect a thing like that?

Timmy made her read a book about the care of dogs, and said, 'My brother used to take Thompson when I was away, but now I've got you he's your responsibility.'

But then September did come and the first cold wet day, and they lit the fires in smoky chimneys, and marvelled that the roof was rainproof and the walls windproof. The phone rang at six the following morning and Meg woke from sleep to hear Timmy saying, 'Aye-aye, sir', and she thought it must be a dream, but the space beside her in the bed became cold, and she saw Timmy, lean and naked, dragging out the suitcase from beneath the bed, and he put on a blue shirt and navy socks, and she saw, or thought she saw, Timmy put a pistol into a kind of shoulder harness which he slung over the shirt, and then a navy woollen jersey over that. Could one imagine such a nasty, arid, deathly black metal thing as that pistol? Surely not! And all of a sudden Timmy looked like one of his nephew's Action Men, the one with the beard. She thought his movements had become jerky. She closed her eyes. Timmy bent and kissed her.

'You can't go!' she cried, in panic. 'You can't!'

'Someone has to,' he said.

'What, blow up the world?' she demanded.

'Darling,' he said patiently, 'stop the world from blowing up. If you wanted to have this conversation you've had four months to do it. It isn't fair to start it now. I have to go.'

'But there has to be more notice than this!'

'There can't be,' he said. 'Security.'

His face had its carved look again, but elevated from the simple planes of the child's toy to the more complex and serious kind one might see on a monument to the dead, at the entrance to a War Graves Cemetery, where the rows of simple white crosses stand as such a dreadful rebuke to the frivolous. 'Look after Thompson for me,' he said, and left, closing the door between himself and the dog, and of course himself and her, but she felt that Thompson came first. She watched from the window as Timmy bounced down the stony path on his bicycle into the valley fog, and vanished into the white nothingness of the rest of the world.

Timmy left his bicycle with the security guard down at the docks. It was padlocked next to Rating Daly's new lightweight eight-speed racer, and the security guard undertook to oil it at weekly intervals.

'Hurry up, sir,' said the security man. 'They're waiting to do the fast cruise: said they needed their navigator.'

Polaris submarines, before setting off to sea, which they like to do at unprecedented times and unexpected states of tide, need to test their engines by running them at full speed. But so that the whole coast can't tell by the sudden rumble that a Polaris is on its way out, the engines are fast-cruised just for the sake of it, from time to time. A rumble in the water, the quivering of the sea and sand where children play, may mean something, but equally may not. No one wants to think about it too much.

There are five British Polaris submarines: these compose Britain's independent nuclear deterrent. They have a home base. They have to have that in the same way that people have to have beds. They are very large, like whales. They can't be hidden, so they try to be unexpected. In theory each Polaris slips in to home base every three months or so, under cover of dark, usually in the early morning. First Crew goes home silently, by bicycle or car. Second Crew, warned by a single phone call, eases itself from its bed and is on board with as little fuss as possible. Security would like to keep the crews secluded in barracks for maximum secrecy, if only they could. But you can't push submariners more than a certain way, or who's going to choose to be one? Polaris's crew have to stay sane; and it is common wisdom that the way to stay sane (at least for men) is to have lots of sex and lots of children. So they have to put up with married men, and though they prefer them to live on Base (as second best to barracks) if they insist on living with their wives in crumbling crofters' cottages on the bare hillside they put up with that too. It just makes a little more work.

Instead of hurrying on board Timmy asked if he could use the telephone in the security hut to call his wife.

'Just married, aren't you, sir,' said the security man enquiringly, and dialled the number himself. But he used a coded number from a list he held. He took no chances. Only then did he hand over the instrument.

'Meg,' said Timmy, 'how are you?'

'I'm in bed,' said Meg, 'and Thompson's on it, not even under it, and he's licking my face.'

'Look after yourself,' said Timmy, 'and think of me every morning at eleven-thirty.'

'I'll think of you all the time.'

'Make a special effort at eleven-thirty – it's a quiet time on board – and I'll try and pick up the signals.'

'Is it allowed?' asked Meg, not without bitterness. 'Isn't telepathy a breach of security?'

'It depends,' said Timmy, in all seriousness, 'on what you do with the information received.'

'Where are you calling from?' asked Meg.

'Somewhere,' said Timmy. 'But there's a grey wharf and a shiny wet bright sea. Has the mist cleared up there?'

'It has,' said Meg, and she looked out of the window on to a pristine day resting over autumn hills, and felt her sense of loss and anger subside. All the same, she said, crossly,

'I think all this security business is nonsense.'

'It's only for a few hours every now and then,' said Timmy. 'And we shouldn't be talking about it.'

'I don't care who's tapping this phone,' said Meg. 'The way to confound the tappers is to overwhelm them with detail! And what's to stop me ringing my cousin whose friend works in the Russian Embassy perhaps, and weeping on her shoulder and saying Timmy's just left me for his tour of duty?'

'My dearest,' said Timmy, cautiously. 'Two things. First, we'll lie about on the bottom of the loch for a while, before actually moving off, and secondly I expect you'll find you can't make outgoing calls on our phone, at least for a little while. It's for all our sakes. You want me home safely, don't you?' That silenced her.

'Of course,' she said, presently, in a small voice. 'Darling, I love you, and every morning at eleven-thirty I'll think of you and you'll think of me.'

'Two minutes to eleven-thirty, for two minutes. Every day a Remembrance Sunday,' he said. 'I must go now. I'm not supposed to be ringing you, really. It's just that I left – well, you know – all Navy and no man, and I want you to know the man always wins, and darling –'

'Yes?'

'If Thompson does actually ever catch a rabbit, make sure he gets worm pills. Tape as well as round: dogs pick them up if they hunt. Remember? It was in the book.'

'I'll look after Thompson,' she said, and meant it, and he said, 'I love you. I'll see you in three months. Well, roughly three months,' and put the phone down, leaving her to wonder if the reminder about the pills had been the real purpose of the call.

Timmy went on board, into the belly of leviathan, and joined the captain and the first officer on the bridge.

'Now we can get on with the fast cruise,' said the captain, reproachfully. That was as far as reprimand ever got. He was careful of his officers' feelings. They were to be a long time together beneath the sea. He had a beard so full you could hardly tell what his features were, and bright, bright blue eyes; a gentle manner and a reputation, even amongst submariners, for eccentricity.

'Sorry, Alec, sir,' said Timmy. 'I've never been last on board before,' he added in his defence.

'You've never been married before,' said the captain, but whether that compounded or excused Timmy's failing was not made clear. Those who captain Polaris submarines have to keep abreast of the private lives of their crew. They have, after all, to watch for signs of instability. There is a lot at stake.

The countdown for the fast cruise had begun, when Ratings Percival and Daly appeared to say there had been a mishap of which the captain should be at once informed.

'Some of the exotic veg, sir, aren't on board,' said Percival.

'We have no aubergines, no fresh chillies and no fresh ginger.'

The captain turned a concerned face towards his crewmen. 'Of course, sir,' said Rating Daly, 'we have powdered chilli and pow-dered ginger: that's stock issue. But I know how keen you are on the fresh, and it doesn't solve the aubergine question. The pimentos, courgettes, celeriac and so on came on board by crate okay, but the order clearly wasn't made up properly.'

'Chilli powder and fresh chilli have nothing in common at all,' said the captain, seriously discomposed. 'Only fools think they have.'

'Aye-aye, sir,' said Percival.

'Aye-aye, sir,' said Daly.

The root of the trouble is, sir,' said Jim, the first officer, pouring oil on troubled waters, as was his habit, 'that down in Stores they've only just about caught up with the mushroom as an exotic vegetable. Fresh ginger and so forth is way beyond them.'

But the captain just stared gloomily at Ratings Percival and Daly as if it were all their fault.

'And we hadn't even left port,' Percival complained later to Daly. 'I knew then what kind of tour this was going to be. Never allowed near the galley for the men's food, for hamburgers and beans, because the officers have commandeered it for sweet-and-sour pork with hot chilli sauce, or worse. It will all end in mutiny, not to mention ulcers.' But that conversation came later. Now another thought struck the captain.

'Olive oil?' he asked, over the murmur of warming engines.

'Some left by Crew No. 1, sir. Two litre bottles.'

'Not enough,' said the captain and closed down the engines.

An urgent approach was made to Security and in about an hour Zelda, Jim's wife, drove up to the dock gates with a couple of crates, which Security checked. They prodded ginger and peered into chillies, and nodded and let them through.

'This isn't alcohol?' they enquired, opening up one or two big plastic containers full of green liquid.

'It's olive oil,' said Zelda crossly, in her fluty officer's wife's voice.

She wore a headscarf decorated with ponies' heads and had rather large, brilliant teeth in a long thin face. She seemed to know what she was doing.

'Taste it,' she said, and made them; they put their fingers into the liquid and sucked and shuddered. Olive oil! Their wives still fried in lard, and used Heinz Salad Cream on the salad.

Polaris submarines are dry. No alcohol is allowed on board. To be drunk in charge of a submarine is an offence. Stores did let Captain Alec's crew take cooking wine with them, on condition that it was used in cooked dishes, never uncooked. Heating sends off alcohol in vapour, they explained. Thus sherry could be used in soup, so long as that soup was simmering when the sherry was added; but never in cold trifles. The regulations were strict.

Timmy left the boat to collect the crates.

'Where's Jim?' asked Zelda. 'Why did they send you?'

'You know what it's like,' said Timmy, embarrassed.

'I know what *he's* like,' she said. 'And more than one set of goodbyes in one day he just can't face.'

'That's about it,' said Timmy.

'Never mind,' said Zelda. 'I'll just have to say goodbye to you' – and she kissed him long and passionately on the mouth.

'Hey, hey,' said the security man, uneasily. 'That man's got to be celibate for the next three months. You should think of that.'

'It's just for old times' sake,' said Zelda, and Timmy looked flushed and self-conscious.

'Mind you look after Meg for me,' said Timmy. 'And not for old times' sake.'

'I'll look after her,' said Zelda.

'And do be discreet, Zelda,' said Timmy. 'And make sure she looks after Thompson.'

'Bloody Thompson,' said Zelda. 'Always licking one's toes in bed.'

Timmy went back inside, and the hatches were finally battened down, and the rumble of the fast cruise began. Presently Polaris slid away from its dock. Halfway down the estuary it submerged, and was gone.

A knock came on Meg's door as she sat on a clean, smooth patch of floor, doing yoga exercises. She had a small bony body, no-nonsense straight hair and a wide brow and a straight nose and rather thin lips. She had always wanted to live in the country. She'd been a fabric designer who thought she should have trained as a potter but might one day write novels, and had assumed she'd marry some country craftsman. Then she'd bring up her children (when she had them, which she would) without the aid of television or yellow additives in the food, and so forth. And now here she was, married to a man about whom she knew very little, except that she was addicted to him, body and soul, so that his profession and his politics and his social values meant nothing. And all she knew was that her chest ached from lack of him; and she had a pain where her heart was.

Yoga was part of her plan for self-improvement, put into action ten minutes after Timmy's phone-call, when she had stopped crying. Three months to achieve physical perfection, perhaps learn a language – certainly get the house in order. She would dedicate the time to Timmy.

She'd tried the telephone and found, as Timmy had predicted, that the line was now dead. Presumably it would come to life in its own good time. She didn't mind; the sense of being looked after for her own good was reassuring. It was like being a small child again, with parents at the ready to curb one's follies.

The postman rang the doorbell. Meg opened the door, holding Thompson back by his collar. 'It's all right,' she said. 'He's all bark and no bite. He might knock you down by accident but never on purpose.'

'That's always good to know,' said the postman, who was an elderly Scotsman. He rolled up his trouser leg to show a papery grey shin marked with livid patches, which he claimed were the results of dog bites. 'If he adds to these,' he said, 'you'll be getting no more letters up here, and that's certain. You'll have to come down to the Post Office, forbye. Recorded Delivery, sign here.'

He settled himself for a chat, balancing against the doorpost, but occasionally shifting, the better to balance against Thompson.

'You ought to keep the door properly latched,' he said. 'There're prowlers about.'

'Up here? Surely not!'

'Everywhere,' he said. 'It's the unemployment and Christmas coming, and worse. A young woman like yourself, your husband off –

'How do you know he's off?' Meg was startled.

'First Crew's back, that's why. He's Second Crew, so he's away. It's not difficult.'

'It's supposed to be secret,' complained Meg, but he was more interested in the letter for which she signed. It was in a brown envelope.

'That a bill?' he asked, following her into the kitchen.

'I don't know,' said Meg. 'It's for my husband, not me.'

'You'll have to open it,' he said. 'You're married to a sailor now. I've got to get on. There'll be a big collection down at the Base. The minute the husbands go the wives start writing. It calms down after a week or so. I'll come up here whenever I can. You're too isolated, you know. But you can always drive down, I suppose, for a cup of tea and a chat.'

'I don't drive and I don't much care for chats,' said Meg stiffly. She closed and latched the door after him, but then regretted her rudeness. She would need friends: the buses that passed on the hill road, below the cottage, came only once a week.

She put on another jersey because the wind was suddenly cold, and looked around the cottage. She realized that there was no real means of heating it through the winter, and wondered why it was that Timmy was so impractical, and why she had left all this kind of thing to him, knowing him to be so.

Thompson started barking. The milkman. She opened the door to him. She had always presumed that up here milkmen didn't just put the bottles on the step and leave, as they did in the city, and she was right.

'You'll be wanting less milk,' he said. He was even older than the postman, and wheezed. Perhaps Security vetted all visitors to the house, in the husband's absence, in the interests of domestic felicity?

'Will I?'

'With your husband off. Before we had the Base at least we knew where we were. Now it's chop and change all the time. Three pints one day, six the next. It's the goodnight cocoa. Navy men, get a taste for cocoa, don't they?'

'Do they?' she said, coldly.

'So you'll be all alone up here for three months! Only the sheep for company, forbye. Pity you don't have kiddies.'

'I've been married for less than a year.'

'I'd get on with it, all the same,' he advised. 'All the Navy wives do. The way I look at my work,' he went on, 'is as a Welfare job. Someone for the lonely wives to talk to. Does that dog bite?'

Thompson was sniffing round the old man's knees. 'Only barks,' said Meg.

'Pity. He'll need to do more than that. Prowlers about. Have you got stores in? What are you going to do when the snow starts? I don't come up here in the snow, you know. Couldn't even if I wanted to. No one's going to send a snow-plough just for you.'

Snow? It was almost impossible to imagine the landscape white. She had never seen it so.

'I'll dig myself out,' said Meg. She came from the city, where snow meant an awkward mush, not the implacable enemy country-dwellers know it to be.

She shut the door on the milkman and his aged crabbiness and went upstairs. She sat back on the bed and lost herself in an erotic haze and thought about Timmy, while Thompson grinned at her, as if he knew and sympathized with the tenor of her thoughts. She felt Timmy's presence near her. She looked at her watch. It was thirty-one minutes past eleven. Sea-lag, she thought. The telephone pinged slightly and when she lifted the receiver she could hear the dialling tone again.

'Hi,' she said, to whoever no doubt listened.

Again she had the feeling that she was known, noticed, that they were on her side, and the ping had been a whisper from the watchers to say, 'He's off, he's safe, all's clear! Now watch, and wait, and one morning in the New Year, or even earlier, you will hear him whistling up the frozen path, and we will have him home to you. We, the listeners!'

It was quite a sensuous feeling: a lying-back on strong, supporting arms. She replaced the receiver, smiling.

Polaris lay on the bottom of the loch and waited for the Routine from Base that would tell them where to go and how to go, and when. On the bridge, Timmy puzzled rather closely over the charts.

'Anything the matter, Mr Navigator?' enquired the captain. 'We don't want to end up in the Black Sea.'

It was a joke.

'Let alone up the Yangtze River, sir!' remarked Jim, who'd been reading about Red China in the papers. Security would have liked the crews not to read the papers, or only Rupert Murdoch's *Sun*, but the liberty of the individual in the West had to be respected, or what was everyone struggling for?

'That's for the politicians to decide,' said the captain, sternly. 'But I'm glad to hear you making a joke, Mr First Lieutenant, so early in the patrol. We're usually halfway round the world before you so much as smile. Is it the land that depresses you, or the sea?'

'The land, I think, sir,' said Jim.

Submariners are like artists, thought the captain, regretting his question. They'd really rather live alone, outside the married state, in order to pursue their vision in peace; yet they find the unmarried state lonely and sad. To have to feel guilty as they plunge seawards to what they really love, to see wifely tears flowing and hear their children's sobs is intolerable. But to have no one to care, to mark the difference between sea and land, is equally dreadful. Normal submarining, the captain knew, suits best the very young man: the man with parents who both love the child but look forward to his absence. Then all get the best of all possible worlds, with the added spice of a little danger, but not too much. Alas, on Polaris it was different. This was submarining-plus! How could you trust a young unmarried man with the future of Moscow, London, Sydney, Peking and so forth? You couldn't. They were too emotional. Down on Polaris every major city in the world was targeted: the co-ordinates ready and waiting. For the time might come (who knew what the future held?) when one of their own cities might have to be taken out, for good strategic or even peace-making reasons. It took a mature and steady man to recognize such necessities.

Timmy stared at the charts and wondered why they were so misty. He would have liked to have talked more to Jim about the land/sea divide but felt inhibited, as he so often was, with Jim, since having the affair with Zelda. A man, it seemed, could not sleep with his best friend's wife, however secretly and with however good intention, and still look him in the eye. Now that Timmy was himself married he could see more clearly just how great a folly and disloyalty the affair had been. He wished to apologize to Jim; but couldn't, of course. All the same, the fact remained: he was fond of Zelda, and could see that Jim was somewhat cavalier in his attitude towards her. For form's sake, and certainly in Zelda's presence, Jim should at least pretend to prefer life on shore to life at sea.

Under sea. Timmy wanted to be back in bed with Meg, with Thompson under it. Perhaps the mistiness was tears? He took off his glasses and wiped his eyes.

'Oh my God, sir,' he said. 'I've brought my wife's glasses.'

There was a short silence.

'Well,' said Jim, 'Yangtze, here we come!'

'It's all right, Alec, sir,' said Timmy. 'It's not too bad. I may get headaches, that's all.'

'Seeing with her eyes,' said the captain, 'while she sees with yours. Love's young dream. Don't let it happen again.' He softened the rebuke by returning to more rewarding subjects.

'How much peanut butter did we bring on board?'

'Two gallons,' said the first lieutenant.

'I hope it's enough,' said the captain. 'Many Indonesian dishes use quite large quantities of peanut butter. It is a country where food is eaten with the hands, and so a thicker consistency is needed.'

Presently the Routine from Base came through. The captain threw a switch or two, and the control board which linked with the nuclear reactor at Polaris's heart glowed warmly, as the mighty engines sucked its power and started up, and minutely vibrated the waves on the far-off shore where the children played, and bounced a grain of sand or so from here to there.

Polaris moved down the Irish Channel and out into the Atlantic. Down in the galley the captain pounded cummin seed and coriander and chilli to make a paste in which to coat a chicken. Jim peeled and diced and blanched baby white turnips preparatory to freezing. They brought fresh vegetables on board and prepared and froze them in the great freezer themselves, not trusting shore-men to do it properly. (There is no shortage of power on a nuclear submarine – lots of light, lots of hot water, lots of cool and elegantly recycled air. The crew swore the air smelt badly of garlic, like a French train on a school trip, but their officers denied it, hotly.)

The captain poured oil from Zelda's plastic can into a jug and thence into a pan. He meant to fry mustard seed in the oil, letting it sizzle for a few moments, then pour it over finely grated carrot, adding lemon juice, salt and pepper, for a simple but interesting salad to serve with the chicken. But the oil spattered in the pan.

'This isn't pure olive oil,' complained the captain.

He investigated and discovered that, beneath a thin top floating layer of olive oil, there was nothing more or less than white wine.

'That was very irresponsible of your wife,' he said sternly to Jim. 'You, me and Mr Navigator here are an Attack Team, not a musical comedy act.'

But he didn't pour the wine away; instead he put the canister up on a top cupboard, out of harm's reach.

While they were eating a Routine came through to say that Russian submarines were operating in their vicinity.

'When are they ever not?' yawned the captain.

But they took their plates through to the bridge and watched the lights on the radar screen, and listened to the bleeps as the leviathans from the other side neared and all but brushed them, and paused, and passed, in companionable fashion.

'I wonder if they've discovered food,' said the captain.

'I shouldn't think so, sir,' said Jim, who'd once been on a school trip to Leningrad, and been made sick by soused herring.

'Then what do they do all day?'

They couldn't remember themselves what they had done, in the days before they'd discovered the soothing art, and had dined on hamburgers like anyone else. But now the weeks were filled with a sense of purpose; and, indeed, accomplishment.

Two weeks passed. Thompson and Meg settled down to a state of truce. She tried to keep him out of the bedroom entirely, while he tried to get into the bed, and they compromised with under the bed. Now that Timmy was away Meg noticed the landscape. She watched the winter closing in, suddenly and crossly, like a shopkeeper closing up before a football match. Slam, slam! Down came the shutters, out went the sun, up sprang the wind, and life retreated, muttering, underground, leaving the hills lean and sinewy and blank. Even the slugs went from the kitchen cupboard. She missed them. How was it possible to miss such disgusting slimy things, which clung to damp walls in dark and unexpected places? She was obliged to conclude that it was because they were, simply, alive and of the animal not the plant kingdom, and had some kind of blind purpose and vague will which carried them into the rockiest and most inhospitable places, where even plants could not survive. They were life, carrying their message into the world of non-life.

Sometimes she was glad Timmy wasn't there. She would have muttered something about missing the slugs and he would have looked quizzical and she would have turned pink and felt silly. Some knowledge simply had to be borne alone: that was one of the penalties of being human. The suggestion was, inasmuch as one had the power of speech, that there was a sharing; but of course there wasn't. It was a pain that the slugs were spared. Thompson, on the other hand, was spared nothing. His suffering was the worse because, observing that humans talked to each other, he believed they would exchange notes on the wonders of the universe. He was wrong in this, but didn't know it. Meg and Timmy's real conversation, real agreement, was wordless and in bed. No wonder Thompson liked to be under it.

The bus was taken off for the winter months. Too few people used it. Meg cycled down to the Base – a half-hour journey going in, two hours back, uphill – to the library, and asked the librarian to find her a book on the life-cycle of slugs. The library had in stock many reference books on crocheting and knitting and jam-making and upholstery and Teach-Yourself-French and First Steps to Philosophy, but there was nothing on slugs.

'You can always try slug pellets,' said the librarian. 'The slugs eat them and simply deliquesce.'

'But that's horrible!' said Meg.

'I expect it is, when you think about it. The thing is, don't think about it. Simply do it.'

Meg met Zelda outside the library. Zelda swooped on her and

embraced her and said she must come in for coffee. Wasn't she going mad up there on her own? Meg was looking rather odd, said Zelda. Meg was wearing jeans and an old navy jersey of Timmy's. She felt protected in it. Zelda was wearing pink jeans and a pinker sweater, and a fashionable grey wool scarf tied as a shawl, and many gold bangles and rings.

'In what way odd?'

'You have a funny look in your eye,' said Zelda, 'as if you were pregnant.'

Meg thought.

'When I went to take my pill this morning,' she said, 'I found I had four left and yet I was at the end of the course.'

They went to Zelda's warm, pretty bungalow, with its picture windows and squared-off walls. Thompson had to stay outside. He wailed, but Zelda was ruthless.

'So you've missed four pills,' she said. 'That means you want a baby. It's your unconscious.'

'I don't want a baby,' said Meg. 'I want Timmy.'

'I don't want a baby either,' said Zelda, 'but I'm having one. I only found out this morning. Think of it, Jim won't know for another two months and two weeks. Give or take a day or two, for Security.'

'But you can tell him through the Family Telegram system,' said Meg.

'They only pass on good news, not bad,' said Zelda. 'Bad news waits until the men are back on shore.'

'I suppose your good news and Jim's good news aren't necessarily the same thing,' said Meg.

'Exactly,' said Zelda. 'But that's marriage, isn't it?'

Meg thought in her heart, *not mine and Timmy's, it isn't.*

It was eleven-forty-five and Meg had forgotten to think of Timmy. His thoughts had been flashing all around her but she hadn't noticed. She'd been thinking about the deliquescing of slugs.

At that moment Thompson discovered Zelda's lavatory window ajar and squeezed himself in, bending a hinge or so, and bounced into the living room. He threw himself on Zelda.

'Why does he go to you?' asked Meg, puzzled.

'Because I'm the owner of the house,' said Zelda crossly. 'And he's trying to get into my good books. Couldn't you have left him at home?'

She aimed a kick at Thompson with her little gold boot and he howled. Meg felt protective of him at once and said she must be getting back.

'I don't know much about dogs,' said Meg, as she got on her bicycle, 'but is Thompson extra-specially intelligent?'

'He's extra-specially *mad*,' said Zelda.

The next day Zelda rang Meg and asked her to dinner that very evening to meet Tony.

'You can't say no,' said Zelda, 'because your engagement book is empty.'

'I don't even have one,' said Meg.

'That figures.'

'Who's Tony?'

'He's the spare man, dear. There's always one about. He's a P R man: he deals with the press round here. His wife's away in New Zealand – she always is – and if she isn't she doesn't understand him. He mends fuses and walks dogs and all the husbands trust him. Some sensible woman put the word about that he's queer, which is why his wife's always away, but of course he isn't. He's very nice and funny and he might cheer you up.'

'It's very kind of you, Zelda, but I don't think I'll come.'

'Why not?'

'I don't think Timmy would like it.'

'I don't actually think submariners are very possessive men, or they wouldn't be away so much, would they?' It was an argument hard to refute. Meg tried to think her way round it, but failed. 'I suppose not,' she said. 'Thank you very much, Zelda, I'd love to come.'

Down on the bottom of the Indian Ocean Polaris kept the meal-times of the ships on the surface. Dinner that night was multinational – home-made ravioli done by Jim, who was so good at fiddly dishes;

Persian chicken – the kind stuffed with ground mixed nuts and simmered – produced by the captain; and a French *tarte aux poires*, prepared by Timmy, who could produce a more delicate confectioners' cream than anyone aboard. Timmy kept his watch on home time, in order to keep his eleven-thirty appointments with Meg.

When Meg got down to the Base that night she had to push her way through an angry Peace Movement crowd, milling about in the mud with banners and effigies of broken nuclear missiles, like broken phalluses, held aloft. They let Meg through easily enough. She was wearing jeans and an anorak and was riding a bicycle: she seemed near enough one of their own.

'Take the toys from the boys,' they chanted, and Meg thought of the two faces of Timmy, the bouncy, grinning little boy, and the cool, grave features she sometimes glimpsed, that of the man within, and wondered which of them it was she loved, and knew it was the man, who half-frightened her. She had fun with the little boy, and played sexy games with him, but love was reserved for the man, and the man, indeed, was dangerous.

She disliked the women for not understanding this: she thought they weren't adult women at all – just angry little girls in grown-up bodies, which they hated. She was glad that she'd brought a dress and some heeled sandals with her. She'd stuffed them crossly into a carrier bag before she'd left, cursing Zelda's social pretensions, but now she felt pleased with herself. The dress was of fine wool, navy, with white flowers embroidered around the neckline. She'd been married in it.

'What's making you so angry?' asked Zelda, once Meg was inside and changing.

'What do these women want?' demanded Meg.

'Peace,' observed Zelda. 'I always thought you were rather their sort.'

'Then you thought wrong,' said Meg shortly. 'I don't want anything to do with it. Timmy and I just want to be left alone. He's a navigator: all he does is steer ships about by the stars.'

'There are no stars under the sea,' said Zelda. 'It's more compli-cated than that. Timmy is cleverer than you think.'

'If the Navy chooses to put him on Polaris, that's their responsibil-ity. He's still just a navigator,' Meg persisted. 'A kind of timeless person.' And indeed, she saw Timmy as one of the heroes on Odysseus's boat, underneath a starry Grecian sky, steering between Scylla and Charybdis. She'd met him at a party. 'And what do *you* do?' she'd said. 'I'm a navigator,' he'd replied, and she had hardly heard. Her heart had gone; she had given it away, and that was that. She was like a child: she would not ask more, for fear of finding out more than she cared to know: of having to do what she ought, not what she wanted. A little girl who would not look down at her shoes before school, in case they needed cleaning.

'Darling!' said Zelda, pouring them both rather large gin-and-tonics. Dinner was ham salad and baked potatoes, and already on the table – except for the potatoes, which were keeping warm on the heated Hostess trolley. 'Darling, your husband is one of the Attack Team. There are three of them on Polaris. The captain, the first officer and the navigator. With a little help from the captain, your husband and mine could finish off the world. Didn't he ever tell you?'

'They wouldn't want to finish off the world,' said Meg, presently, taken aback. Timmy had never told her this.

'You know what men are,' said Zelda. 'They just love to obey orders. And if the Routine comes through from Base, "blow up Moscow, or Hanoi, or Peking", that's what they'll do. They'll sit down and push their buttons at the same time and whee! Off go the missiles as programmed. Men have no imagination, you see. One million, two million dead. It's only numbers. And women and children have to be sacrificed to the greater good. Well, we all know that. My father was a doctor; I know better than anyone. He looked after his patients, never us.'

'But the order won't come through,' said Meg.

'It hasn't so far,' said Zelda, glad to see Meg shaken out of what Zelda saw as a virtuous complacency, and pleased to shake a little more. 'But I suppose it must one day. If one owns a pair of nut-crackers one tends to crack nuts. But you knew all this when you married him; you can't complain now. When I meet those Peace Women I just push my way through them, shouting, "The Ruskies are coming, the Ruskies are coming." That makes them crosser still. Well, you have to laugh, don't you?'

'Not really,' said Meg.

'I do,' said Zelda. 'And at least when we're all nuked out of existence by the Ruskies – this whole country is just an unsinkable aircraft carrier for the USA: their forward line – our husbands will be safe enough. They can stay below for ever. We must take comfort from that.'

'Zelda,' said Meg, 'why don't you go and join them outside?'

'I don't have the right shoes,' said Zelda. The doorbell rang: it was Tony, the PR man.

'Tony will make you feel better,' said Zelda. 'He'll explain that we're all perfectly safe and our men are doing a grand job saving the world from itself, and protecting British women and children, and that those women out there are well-intentioned but misguided dupes of the Russians.'

Tony was as lean as Timmy was broad, and his nose hooked and aquiline and his charm very great. He looked into Meg's eyes as if he were looking into her soul, and valued it deeply. He looked past her body and into her mind, and liked it, and made her feel comfortable. She realized that she had never felt quite comfortable with Timmy, and wondered why.

'I can see Zelda's in a naughty mood,' said Tony. 'I hope she hasn't been upsetting you. One has every sympathy with the women outside: and yes, they are misguided, because nuclear weapons are a deterrent – they prevent wars, they don't cause them – but I wouldn't go so far as to say the women are dupes of the Russians. I am no "Reds under the Beds" man. Those women out there are brave and intelligent and have their point of view. We have a different point of view because we know more. We have more facts at our disposal.'

'You are employed by the Admiralty,' said Zelda, 'to say exactly that kind of thing. To pour any sort of oil on any sort of troubled water you happen to come across. Have some ham salad. Don't you think Meg is pretty?'

'Yes I do,' said Tony, 'and Zelda, couldn't I go into the kitchen and whip us up some spaghetti bolognese? You know I hate salads.'

'I was hoping you'd say that,' said Zelda. 'You know where everything is.'

Thompson growled when Tony rose: that was unusual, thought Meg. Thompson's sins were usually those of over-enthusiasm rather than ill-temper.

After supper Tony insisted on driving Meg home, with her bicycle on his roof-rack.

'I'll be perfectly safe,' she said.

'Good heavens, no,' he said. 'You might get raped by a Peace Woman. I'd never forgive myself. I'm perfectly respectable, aren't I, Zelda? Tell her I'm perfectly respectable.'

Zelda duly told her. Meg gave in, glad to be spared the long ride uphill, glad of the comfort of his smooth white car; uneasily conscious of the benefits money could buy.

They passed through the encampment of makeshift tents where the women had settled for the night.

'Everyone has to make a living,' said Meg sadly. 'And almost no one's occupation is guiltless, I suppose. Just think, Timmy might be an Arms Salesman. Now they're *really* wicked.'

'These women live off the State,' said Tony. 'The wretched tax-payer supports them.'

Tony had another face, too, thought Meg, just as Timmy did. When Tony was off-guard, the all-embracing, all-forgiving urbanity deserted him: she could see the impatient dislike shimmering beneath; a dislike of long-haired lefties, strident feminists, anti-blood-sport nuts, and so forth. She disliked them too, but somehow in a different way. She wanted to change their minds, not root them out. Were all men like this? Pretending to be civilized, but wanting in their hearts nice clean sudden final solutions? The drama of destruction?

She had a vision of After-Armageddon: the missiles flying through crevices in clouds over crowded seas; the hills black and poisoned;

the stuff of nightmares. She'd had such nightmares before she'd met Timmy. She'd assumed they were some kind of symbolic reflection of her own inner state, her own fear of sudden, awful events. Her father dying. Sudden, awful, the end of the world. But if everyone had a vision of the end of the world, wasn't that dangerous? Mightn't it then come true? Wasn't it better to keep the mind on what was kind and pure and hopeful? If one acknowledged the devil one gave birth to the devil. She believed that. She thought that was why she so resented the Peace Women. They were bringing Armageddon nearer, not keeping it away. Perhaps she was pregnant? How could she bring a baby into this world? But then again, how could she not? One had to affirm one's faith in the future, and affirm it, and affirm it, and affirm it.

Tony had his hand on her knee. How long had it been there? It was a pleasant hand, warm, sensible, and full of expectation.

She moved it gently away.

'No, thank you, Tony,' she said. 'I love Timmy.'

'Of course you do,' he said, cheerfully. 'And so you should, a nice girl like you.'

She wasn't sure she wanted to be a nice girl. He suggested she admire the landscape. It occurred to her that Timmy never suggested she admire anyone or anything other than himself, or his handiwork.

Tony asked to come in, but she said no, and he acquiesced, again pleasantly.

He offered his services in any way she liked.

'Anything un-innocent,' he said. 'Just say the word. But if I have to put up with the innocent for the pleasure of your company then I will. Mend fuses, fix shelves, lay lino: I'm the original Mr Fix-it. I'll even take the foul hound for walks.'

They lingered on the doorstep. He said he was a woman's man. He said he couldn't get on with Navy men, because they had no conversation. They could exchange information and tell jokes and swap prejudices, but they didn't deal in ideas. And now he had met Meg he wouldn't easily let her go. He had to talk to someone.

'There's Zelda,' said Meg.

She called Thompson and went in and shut the door, and looked at the bare rough decent walls and the plain deal table and was glad to be alone.

'I hope Zelda and Meg get together,' said Jim, the first officer. They ought to be friends. I'm afraid your Meg's going to be rather lonely up there on the hills.'

They themselves were under the polar ice-cap: it was a fairly edgy place to be. The radar man never liked it, and Rating Hoskins lay awake in his bunk at night (local night) worrying about what would happen if they set off a missile when they happened to be under some ice mountain. Would the initial thrust be enough to force it through, or would it turn, as in some children's cartoon, and destroy the destroyers? 'She has Thompson to keep her company,' said Timmy.

He felt the touch of Meg's thoughts. She was laughing. He looked at his watch. It was eleven-thirty, Greenwich Mean Time. That night he dreamt that Meg was taking Thompson for a walk in the woods of his childhood.

Meg, indeed, was taking Thompson for a walk, but out on the hills. Thompson had recovered from his fear of sheep since Timmy had gone, and now showed a desire to chase them – only strong words and a stern face prevented him. If she tried to put him on the lead he pulled her along over the rough ground, so she would stumble and fear for her ankles. She had to contain him by force of will alone. She thought that Tony was a good deal more controllable than Thompson.

Even as the notion occurred to her Thompson was off over the brow of the hill and though she yelled for a good five minutes he did not return. A cold wind had got up: the hills were hostile. She did not belong here. She thought she would leave Thompson to find his own way home. He was more part of the elements than she was: leaping and bounding into the chilly blast, exhilarated. The thought that he was Timmy's dog, and she was responsible for him, oppressed her. She could see down to the harbour below, and the docks and the grey sea, and the slow movement of the toy cranes, and on the next fold of hills the Base itself, with its squared-off roads and pretty bungalows and the thin tracery of the high wire fence, and outside it a kind of muddy unevenness, presumably where the Peace tents were pitched, or slung, or whatever they were. She was too far off to make out detail.

It's nothing to do with me, she thought, let them get on with their games, and leave me out of it. Leave me to love my husband, and walk my dog, and get on with my life.

And she ran bounding down the hill.

By five that evening Thompson had not returned and the postman, delivering an envelope marked with many red bands, said, 'A farmer will have got that dog with a gun, forbye. Out there worriting sheep again.'

'He doesn't worry sheep,' Meg said.

The red bands induced her to open the letter and she found inside notification that Timmy's Visa card had been withdrawn for non-payment of dues. She discovered that they owed the company £843.72 and at 12½ per cent accumulative interest, too. Timmy had told her to use the card to buy wallpaper, paint, carpets and so forth. She had used it the day before, down on the Base, to buy groceries, finding funds in the joint account she shared with Timmy running low. Timmy's monthly salary had not for some reason shown up on the balance.

Meg shivered. Cold had somehow got into her bones. She put on more jerseys and piled wood on the fire – though stocks were surprisingly low – but kept opening the door to see if she could see Thompson bounding home, which of course she didn't.

Night fell. No Thompson. Meg telephoned Tony and wept over the receiver.

'I'll come right up,' he said.

Thompson arrived home at the same time as Tony. He stood at the door laughing and panting and dropping and picking up a dead rat, for the death of which he expected to be congratulated.

'I hope he hasn't been worrying sheep,' said Tony. 'They shoot dogs for that round here.'

Tony removed the rat from Thompson's mouth, made Meg look for worm pills and thrust one down Thompson's throat. Then he told Meg what to write to Visa and gave her the number of the Families' Officer on the Base who looked after the financial affairs of the wives while their husbands were away. He claimed that submariners were notoriously impractical in money matters and, indeed, in most domestic matters.

'Their minds ebb and flow in tune with the mighty currents of the deep, I expect,' said Meg. 'Their wives have pathetic little sharp foamy wavelet minds. All detail, no grandeur.'

'Not so pathetic,' said Tony.

He put his hand into something he called a soot box in the Rayburn flue and told her the chimney needed sweeping, and he would send a man up to do it, and to fix a cowl to stop the smoke blowing back when the wind was from the north.

He told her he would bring up stores from the Base so she could sit out a snowstorm: otherwise they'd have to send a helicopter to fetch her down and she wouldn't like that, would she? And neither would he. He for one would like to see someone make a go of living independently, outside the Base. The Navy owned too much of people's souls: it had no business to.

He said he'd lend her a television set, and she said she didn't like TV, and he said oh she would, she would. By the time the New Year was here, and her husband back.

He said he expected nothing from her. He liked to be of use. He was a solitary kind of person, really. So was she. Let them both circle each other for a time.

And he went away, leaving Meg warm and comforted and stirring inside. She tried to remember what Timmy's face looked like, and was not able to. It was as if the presence of another man in the croft, his coat hanging on the back of the chair, seeing to things, doing things, had somehow driven out the lingering feel of Timmy.

'Did you know,' said the captain – they were back up in the Pacific now, and coral less of a problem than ice, though still tricky – 'that we nuclear submariners outnumber the blue whale? American, Russian, Chinese by the hundred! We're the rarity – the ones with the GB plates. Every city in the world with a missile pointed at it.

Our five just provide extra cover for the major capitals: a drop of wine in the child's glass, to stop him making a fuss, to make him feel grown up.'

'Ours not to reason why,' said Jim. 'Ours just to do and die –'

'Only we won't be doing the dying,' said Timmy. 'That's for those at the end of our doing.'

Men get meditative at the bottom of the sea. On some days even *haute cuisine* fails. Rating Hoskins played good guitar, but only knew peace-songs from the sixties; which made everyone maudlin.

Meg said to Tony, 'The trouble with Thompson is, he acts as if I were his sister, not his mistress. He doesn't respect me.'

'I don't act as if you were my sister,' said Tony. He was in bed with Meg. He had just got in; for warmth, he said. The man who came to sweep the chimney said the whole thing was about to fall down and the fire mustn't be lit until he'd come back, which he would do the following day, with materials to rebuild it.

Cold had struck afresh into Meg's bones. The Families' Officer had explained to her that nearly all Timmy's monthly salary cheque was bespoken on credit purchase arrangements, mortgage payments and so forth. There was next-to-nothing left over for daily living; and she, Meg, had been living like a spendthrift, buying cream when top-of-the-milk would do, sending letters first-class, buying wallpaper when whitewash would serve. He would advance her money, of course, against Timmy's next salary. The Navy, he said, believed in looking after wives – and frequently had to. Naval pay was designed to keep single men in beer, not married men in homes. But where was it all to end? If only Meg would agree to sell the croft and come and live on Base, she'd find the living more economical. Meg told the Families' Officer she'd think about it. Tony said he'd pay off the Visa, and they wouldn't tell Timmy. Meg agreed. Meg crept into bed not caring whether Tony followed.

Tony did follow, with a bottle of champagne and two glasses.

'I suppose,' he said, 'you spent most of the last three months in bed with Timmy.'

'Not necessarily in bed,' said Meg. 'It was warmer then – outdoors was always very nice and we grew fond of under the kitchen table, except for Thompson.'

'When it suddenly stops,' he said, 'it must be very hard.'

'Of course it's hard,' said Meg, crossly.

He had all his clothes off. Meg had taken off her jeans, for comfort's sake, but had her other clothes on, the usual vests and body warmers. (And winter not even truly started.) She was in bed for warmth and comfort, nothing else.

'I wish you wouldn't act like some kind of servicing agency,' she said, shaking off his enquiring hand. 'For all I know you're put in by Security to keep me happy.'

'Security don't want people to be happy,' he said. 'Merely silent.'

'It's much the same thing,' she said, 'when it comes to wives.' And she sat up and accepted the proffered champagne.

'You aren't *really* Security?' she asked, fascinated and a little alarmed.

'Of course not,' he said. 'How paranoid you are. Would they really go to such lengths for the simple wife of a simple navigator?'

'They have to occupy themselves somehow,' said Meg. 'And he *is* one third of an Attack Team: that is, one fifteenth of Britain's Independent Nuclear Deterrent.'

'Is he really Attack Team?' asked Tony. 'How do you know?'

'Zelda told me,' said Meg.

'Ah, Zelda,' said Tony. 'Zelda would never go to bed with a man wearing a body warmer and a thermal vest.'

'Well, you'd know,' said Meg. He did not deny it.

He removed her body warmer and thermal vest.

'I haven't said I will,' she warned him. 'You got into this bed on your own account. I didn't ask you in.'

'You didn't get out of it either,' he said. 'A man takes these little hints to heart. You have lovely nipples. Pinkish. Much nicer than Zelda's.'

'I wish you'd be serious,' she complained. 'How am I going to survive this life? How can Timmy afford to leave the Navy, if he doesn't try and save?'

'Dear heart,' said Tony, 'I am serious, and Timmy doesn't want to leave the Navy.'

'Oh yes he does.' She covered her breasts with the sheet.

'Consciously perhaps, but not deep down in his subconscious, where it really counts.'

Meg believed him and her hand lost its will. The sheet dropped. There was a noise at the door, a scraping sound, and the fragile catch gave way. Thompson lumbered in and lay beneath the bed.

'That's it,' said Meg. 'Please get out of this bed, Tony.'

'Why? He can't talk,' said Tony.

'I wouldn't be too sure of that,' said Meg.

So Tony got out of bed and dressed, forgetting his tie. Thompson dragged that under the bed and chewed it a little, having been deprived of his rat, and needing some small revenge.

Meg felt quite fond of Thompson, for having rescued her. At the same time the rain had started to fall, and the ground around the croft, disturbed by months of building work, had turned to mud. Whenever Thompson went out, which seemed to be every fifteen minutes, he took shafts of expensive hot air with him; and when he came in, clouts of mud. He would run upstairs to the bedroom and shake himself there. If she tried to keep him in, or out, he would holler and bang like a naughty child until she let him out, or in. She was plastering and papering the kitchen and it was, because of Thompson, taking twice as long as she had estimated.

Meg's mother- and father-in-law came to visit and admire and sympathize – they were the nicest and remotest of nice remote people – and she suggested they take Thompson away with them. They seemed surprised, even – had they been a little less nice – a fraction shocked.

'But he's company for you. And protection!'

He is disorder, Meg longed to reply: he is distraction and débâcle. He is expensive – 75p a day to feed – he is dirty, and what's more, he is Timmy's. And Timmy, she longed to say, having the uncomfortable feeling that somehow they had shifted the whole responsibility of their son on to her, is yours more than mine. It was you two, after all – and she knew she was being childish – who *thought Timmy up*.

She smiled sweetly and made drop-scones on the stove which, thanks to Tony, roared warmingly and cooked beautifully and was no trouble at all except when Thompson lay too close to it, filling the air with the smell of singeing dog hair. They went away, patting Thompson.

Four more weeks and Timmy would return. Perhaps even in time for Christmas!

'I bet you know when Second Crew's coming back,' she said to Tony, when she met him down at the Base, outside the library. But he only shimmered a smile and said to ask Zelda. She didn't see much of Zelda. She thought Zelda to blame for practically pushing her into Tony's bed (or rather Tony into hers). She was sorry for Zelda's husband, Jim, that nice, simple, beaming man. Wives ought to be virtuous: it was a kind of magic which kept disaster away.

The Peace Women struck camp and moved off, and she felt the magic had worked. When Tony came to help her tile behind the kitchen sink and ran his hand up the back of her jumper she slapped him down very hard, so that tears came to his eyes.

'I didn't expect quite that,' he complained. 'You're so unpredictable.'

'I don't sleep very well.'

'You know the cure for that.'

'It's not that. I think I have cystitis or something. I keep having to get up in the night to spend a penny.'

'You're pregnant,' he said, and took her down to the doctor, who confirmed the diagnosis.

'I wish it was my baby,' said Tony. 'I love babies. But now I'm going south, for a month or so.'

Meg phoned Zelda to tell her the news.

'Should I tell the Families' Officer?' she asked. 'Then he could send a telegram.'

'No point,' said Zelda. 'They'll be back in a few days. And he'll be in a bad temper. They always come back cross. Be warned.'

★

Timmy stepped out on to firm land, which rocked beneath his feet, and breathed rich cold air which stunned him. It seemed to him that no time at all had passed since he had gone on board. He had two quite different lives. One up here, one down there. It was safer down there, longing for ever for journey's end. He took his bicycle from the security shed. It had been kept well-oiled, he was glad to see. Zelda was waiting for Jim and as Timmy cycled past she said, 'Meg's pregnant,' and he whooped with – what? Pleasure, surprise, shock? – Or just the strength of life in this clean cold unfetid place? He stopped at the Base wine shop to buy champagne. When he got home Meg was in bed and asleep and he got in beside her – as did Thompson, half-mad with ecstasy. Thompson, Timmy observed, had put on weight. Meg couldn't be giving him enough exercise.

'Champagne in bed,' said Meg. 'We're supposed to be saving. It's unbearably extravagant.'

That hurt him.

'Of course I'm glad to see you home.' She shouldn't have said it: it made it sound forced. They had made love furiously and fast and were left uncompanionable and dissatisfied.

'You've put on weight,' she said next, and shouldn't have. 'And you're pale.'

'It's just that the rest of the world is over-coloured,' he said, retreating, wanting peace, and the gentle lilt of expected life. Just the captain, Jim and himself.

'What do they give you to eat under the sea? Baked beans and corned beef?'

'More or less,' said Timmy.

'I made us a nice cottage pie,' she said. And then: 'Put your head on my tummy. All that life going on down there!'

'It doesn't feel any different,' he said, and shouldn't have. 'I'm glad you forgot your pills,' he added, to make things better.

'How much did the champagne cost?' She returned to the theme of his extravagance. She wished he'd go away again.

'I think you should have trained Thompson to stay out of the bedroom,' said Timmy. 'He's not a poodle or a lapdog; he's a gun dog.'

'I love him being in here,' said Meg. 'I even like the sound of him scratching his fleas.'

'*Fleas*?' said Timmy in alarm.

'All dogs have fleas.'

'Not if they're properly looked after.'

It was intolerable. Meg shrieked and Timmy shouted. She said she was going home to her mother: he said he was going back to sea. She said she'd have a termination and he said good. When both had voiced exhaustion and outrage, and Thompson had stopped pattering and whuffling and fallen asleep with a dribble of saliva drying on his jowls, Timmy laughed.

'Sorry about all that,' he said. They went to bed and to sleep, twined, then woke up and made love again, in a calmer way, and seemed able to resume their life where they had left off. Except not quite. Timmy was alarmed at the consumption of fuel for the Rayburn and said the new chimney was responsible: she shouldn't have had it done. He said she'd have to keep the damper in and she said 'then it smokes' and he said 'nonsense' and she said 'allow me to know my own stove' and he said 'but I installed it' and she said 'badly' and then he laughed and they both stopped, and kissed.

'I'm not supposed to upset you,' confided Meg. 'The Families' Officer said so. Save him from worry: for the sake of the Navy, for the sake of the country, for the sake of the world. He didn't mention for your sake, or mine. But that's what I'm thinking of. See my smile? Set fair for you?' And so it was, until the last day of the leave.

Then, when Timmy had been home for nearly three months, Thompson, cross no doubt because he'd been put on a diet and run off his feet, dragged Tony's tie from under the bed and laid it by Timmy's face as Timmy did his press-ups.

The telephone rang as Timmy stared at the tie. He answered it, listened, said 'yes' and put the receiver down.

She said, 'is that them?' and he said 'yes' again and went on staring at the tie. It was late March. It had been a mild winter, with very little snow. Tony had not been seen, nor mentioned by anyone, except as the person who'd recommended the builder who'd done the damage to the chimney. Timmy had had to rebuild it. They'd spent Christmas with Timmy's nice remote parents, and the New Year with Meg's vaguely reproachful mother. Meg was six months' pregnant.

'How did that tie get there?' asked Timmy.

'I don't know,' she said. 'It's very dusty.'

'How long has it been there? About six months? You were on the pill. How do women get pregnant when they're on the pill? You got pregnant after I left, by a man who wears a green tie with red stars on it. Christ!'

Meg laughed, from shock. She shouldn't have.

'And now you're laughing. No wonder. You have my income, is that it? But you don't have to have me!'

He had on his hard cold face. Meg felt her own grow hard and cold.

'Is your objection to the quality of the tie?' she asked. She did deign to defend herself.

He did not reply. He was packing his few things. The gun was under his arm. Perhaps he'll shoot me, she thought, and part of her hoped he would.

'Nothing's been right since I've been home,' he said. '*Nothing*. I understand why.'

'You must ask the doctor,' she said. 'He'll tell you.'

'How can I ask the doctor? I'm going away for three months, now, with this to think about!'

Meg wept. Thompson howled. Timmy stamped and banged and departed.

'But I'm pregnant!' she called after him, weeping.

'Complain to its father, not to me,' he called back, and was gone. She waited for him to telephone from the dock, but he didn't. She went up to the hills and sat there and watched and presently saw Polaris glide away out of its dock and sink beneath the water halfway down the loch. Thompson laid his bony chin upon her knee and pressed, and the next day she found a bruise there. She bruised easily, now that she was pregnant.

★

' "Truly the light was sweet," ' misquoted the captain, at the peri-
scope, ' "and a pleasant thing it was for the eyes to behold the sun."
You see these lumps on my eyelids, Mr Navigator? Cholesterol spots,
they say. According to the MD I have to cut down on animal fats.
You were first on board this time, Mr Navigator. Have a good leave?'

'No, sir,' said Timmy.

Meg went down to Zelda's, piteously. Zelda was bright and very
pregnant. She had new doorbell chimes, 'Pling-plong,' they went,
when you rang. 'Pling, pling, plong.'

'Woodland bells!' cried Zelda, in triumph. 'Jim thought I'd like
them. Well, that's the way it goes! Work together, live together,
think together. What's the matter with you, red eyes? No, don't
tell me. You had a row with Timmy and he walked off with a harsh
word on his lips.'

'Yes. Several. Whore. Adulteress. That kind.'

'And you won't see him for another three months! Never mind.
It always happens. You get used to it. What was it Jim said this
time? I can't remember. It doesn't matter. Something perfectly
horrid. Ah yes, they want me to help out at the library but Jim said
if I took a job I'd grow a worse moustache than I have already.
Statistics show career-women grow moustaches. What do they do
down on that boat of theirs – study statistics?'

'But Zelda,' Meg wept, 'supposing, supposing – supposing something happens to Timmy and those are the last words he ever said
to me.'

'You're very egocentric,' said Zelda. 'You should be thinking of
him, not you. Mind you, he'll forget he ever said them. Men do.
They have no memory for insults given, only those received. Did
you say anything terrible to him?'

'No.'

'Then that will be next leave. Jim and I take it in turns. It's the
strain, you know. Bad-tempered when they go, bad-tempered when
they get back, and a little bit of peace in the middle. Is it worth it?'

The pling-plong of the woodland chimes sounded and Tony
came into the hall.

'Hi,' he said. 'Long time no see.'
'Hi,' said the women, cheering up.

It was late spring. The cold wet weather continued unseasonably into April. A few daffodils came up on the hills, but were paled and shredded by the winds, and if the birds sang no one stood about to hear. Meg stayed in the croft and continued to regard herself as a married woman, and to believe what Zelda had said. She was tempted to storm around Tony, shower him with gusts of blame and torrents of reproaches, but somehow it was all too grave and grown-up for that. She had to be still, for the baby's. It was an easy pregnancy: she was fortunate.

Thompson grew more excitable, less controllable. He actually caught rabbits now, and came back bloodied, as if he too had reached man's estate.

It's all the men's fault, thought Meg. All the bombs and the missiles and the schemes and the theories and the rival forms of government, and they make believe that the way to solve things is to see who can blow each other up best: all male, male and angry and mad.

If the Peace Women had still been there, she thought, she would have joined them. You couldn't in the full flush of early sexual love, but you could later on: you could chant with the rest of them, 'Take the toys from the boys.' Oh yes, easily.

In the middle of April a strange thing happened. It was on a morning that had dawned so clear and still and fine that there was no mistaking winter had ended: and Meg could see that for weeks now, hidden by the windy, unseasonable veil, the spring had been preparing for its surprises. The trees, which only the day before had seemed lean and black, could today be seen to be plump and hazy with fresh green leaves. Peonies had sprung up where she'd thought there was nothing but brown earth: and there were pansies and polyanthus underfoot. Meg stood on the doorstep, her face raised to the warmth of the sun, and knew that summer and good times were coming. Thompson sat on the path and did the same. She saw now that every branch seemed to have a bird upon it; and a row of starlings sat on the drystone wall and that they too had their heads turned towards the warmth. And where the wall had crumbled to the ground sat a rabbit, perfectly still, and behind that a sheep, quietly staring in at her. The cat – borrowed from Amanda down at the library to keep the mice population down – jumped from the path to the windowsill, and sat there, and one or two of the assembled company twitched a little, but quickly settled again. It was as if all living creatures united in their pleasure in the day, in their relief that the hard times were over and the knowledge that good times were coming; and that all, in this, were equal and understood one another.

Thompson was the first to break the unnatural peace. He yelped and barked and shot after the rabbit. The sheep trotted off, the birds rose squawking, the cat disappeared into the bushes after them. The normal rules of kill or be killed reasserted themselves. It seemed, at least in the animal kingdom, a kind of game, to which everyone consented.

Meg blamed Thompson. When he came back from his chase, leaping and prancing and slavering, she hit him and shouted at him and chased him through the house, shrieking. Then she was ashamed of herself. Thompson crawled under the sofa and growled when she came near, and when she put her hand beneath it to make friends he snapped at her.

A little later the telephone rang. It was one of the local farmers, asking her to keep her dog under control. He was running the profit off his sheep. If it went on, he'd have to shoot him.

'It's not my dog,' said Meg, feebly. 'It's my husband's, and he's away. He's in the Navy.' She thought that might soften his heart.

'Aye, I know all about that,' said the farmer. 'And I know you're pregnant, and I'm sorry for you, lass. But what are you Navy folk doing up here on our land? You've got your own world, you stick to it. Your dog's your luxury. My sheep are my necessity. That dog's an untrained working dog, and there's nothing worse. He'd be better off dead.'

After that Meg kept Thompson in the house, or took him for

walks on a lead, and in her heart Thompson and Timmy became the same thing, the same burden.

Down below the China Seas Jim said to Timmy, 'What's the matter, old man?'

'Nothing's the matter,' said Timmy. He was surprised Jim had noticed anything: he saw himself as a bright clear day, sunny and smiling. The black clouds rolled and swirled about the edges of his unconscious, but with an effort of will he kept them back. Blue skies, smiling at me!

'If it's Zelda,' said Jim, 'don't worry. I know all about that. These things happen. It's all over now. Zelda doesn't like me being in the Navy. It's a half-life for a woman. They have a right to something more. So she has her revenge: then tells me. I don't blame you, old man, and I don't blame her.'

Timmy counted the sentences as Jim spoke them. Nine. He'd never known Jim say more than four in a row before. He was moved by a sense of the importance of the occasion, and presently felt a burden had gone from him he didn't even know he had been carrying.

'I wonder what the time is at home?' he said. The captain consulted a dial or so.

'Eleven-thirty in the morning,' he said. 'Why?' 'Because that's my time for contacting Meg,' he said.

'Telepathy?' asked the captain. 'The Ruskies do it all the time. I suppose we shouldn't lag behind.'

Timmy listened in, but felt no answering call from Meg, and felt at once lost and vulnerable and said, 'I suppose there are many innocent ways a man's tie could get to be under one's wife's bed,' and the captain said, 'Quite so.'

'I blame myself, sir,' said Timmy.

'That's the secret to it all,' said the captain. 'Let's drink to that!'

'Drink, sir?'

'Life is sweet,' said the captain, 'and a little white wine won't do us any harm.'

He took down from the back of the shelf one of Zelda's two canisters of white wine.

'But, sir,' said Jim, 'it's *bœuf au poivre* for dinner, with green peppers, not black, the way it ought to be. Shouldn't we be drinking red?'

'Desperate times, desperate measures!' said the captain, opening one of the canisters of white wine. Then he pricked his finger with a needle and let a drop or two of blood fall inside. 'Here's to universal brotherhood!' he said. 'And to all our faults!' The blood barely discoloured the wine so he added some drops of cochineal as well. 'We'll leave it a rosé,' he said. 'Compromise, that's the thing.'

The midwife knocked upon Meg's door and found her sitting grimly on a chair, Thompson's lead wound round her wrist, and Thompson sitting at her feet, unwilling, and chafing and wild-eyed. He barked at the midwife, and strained to get to her, not to attack, but to welcome her in.

'I should let the dog go,' said the midwife. Meg did, and Thompson leapt forward and the midwife went towards him instead of cringing back, as most people did when faced with the noisy, welcoming Thompson, and thus managed to keep her balance. Presently Thompson calmed.

'How long had you been sitting like that?' she asked.

'About an hour,' said Meg. 'But I know his moods. If I let him out when his eyes look like that, he goes straight after the sheep, and then he'll get shot.'

'It might be the best thing,' observed the midwife.

'Timmy would never forgive me,' said Meg, who had begun to weep. She was seven months' pregnant. She lay on the bed while the midwife felt round her belly.

'You didn't come down to the clinic,' said the midwife, 'so I thought I'd just pop up here to see if all was well, which it is.'

She took a casual look round the kitchen shelves to see if there was any food, which there was. But she still wasn't easy.

'Hubby away, I suppose,' she said, 'being Crew No. 2. And we mustn't ask when he's due back, must we?'

'No, we mustn't,' said Meg. 'And he couldn't be fetched back, even if I were dying. Not that he'd want to be fetched. He might miss the end of the world, and he wouldn't like that.'

'Can your mother come and stay?' asked the midwife.

'She doesn't like dogs,' said Meg shortly. 'And she doesn't like Timmy, and she doesn't like the Navy, and she told me this would happen and I said let me run my own life, Mother. And I don't think she likes me either, come to think of it.'

'What about your husband's parents? You don't seem to be in a state to be left alone.'

'I hardly know them. What I do know, I don't like. It's mutual, I think.'

'Isn't there somebody who could take the dog?'

'The dog is my responsibility. I'll see it through if it kills me.'

'Your legs are very scratched. Why is that?'

'Because I was taking Thompson for a walk. He pulled me through some bushes.'

'Put him in kennels.'

'Timmy would never forgive me. Perhaps I should go into kennels and Thompson could have the bed all to himself. Until Timmy comes back. Then they'd share it and be perfectly happy. He only married me because he needed a kennel-maid.'

'I think I'd better ring the doctor up,' said the midwife. 'I can't leave you in this state.'

'I'm not in a state,' said Meg, weeping copiously. 'I was only trying to entertain you. Pow! Three schoolboys with their fingers on the trigger. It's all so funny!'

The midwife made Meg take a tranquillizing pill, and Meg asked for a few extra for Thompson, but the midwife wouldn't oblige. She said she'd return later with the doctor and Meg was to stay where she was.

But after the midwife had gone for half an hour or so, Meg gave in to Thompson's whinings and snappings and put him on the lead and took him for a walk. Thompson walked sedately for a little but then started pulling and tugging, and finally wrenched the lead right out of her hand – or perhaps she just gave up holding it – and was off after a rabbit. She stood on the brow of the brackeny hill and looked down to a slight valley and a wooded culvert and then the hill rose again and on the opposite slope were sheep. She saw Thompson's small shape pelting downhill: she watched him lose the rabbit in the undergrowth of the valley, and then saw him emerge the other side and stand for a while, watching the sheep.

'But I knew this would happen,' she said aloud. 'It was bound to happen.'

And the sheep scattered as Thompson leapt amongst them, biting and yelping, and she saw a man with a gun coming over the top of the hill. She waved her arms and yelled and started running, but watched the gun being raised and pointed and saw a little puff and then heard a crack, and Thompson had jumped in the air and fallen, in slow motion, and the sheep spread out, away from the centre of the scene, as if interpreting some formal dance routine. And because she was looking at the farmer she didn't watch where she was going, and tripped, with her foot in a rabbit hole, and fell; lost consciousness and, regaining it seconds later, felt a dreadful pain in her side and an even worse one in her head, for which she was totally responsible. She was manufacturing hate, and rage, and pain; all by herself, with enormous energy.

The farmer was putting his coat beneath her head. She felt her eyes cross and wary and her mouth pulled up in a sneer. He said something which ended, as so much did in these parts, 'forbye'; and then his face had gone and so was he, and if she turned her head – her body being pinned by so much pain – she could see where Thompson lay. His skull was partly gone; bits of shredded flesh stuck to something which was white and presumably bone, and also bits of a kind of grey badly wrapped parcel, which was presumably brain; the seat of all Thompson's troubles.

She was glad Thompson was dead. She hoped the baby was dying too, and then herself. She wanted the world to end: if she could have ended it then and there she would have. Pressed the button, finished it all. Ashes and dust and silence. The thought was so strong it seemed like an explosion in her head: not a sharp decent crack, like the one which had shattered Thompson, but a kind of reddish rumble, which presently carried consciousness away with it.

Zelda bent over her; she was in an ambulance. The midwife was there, too. She was knitting a white scarf with red stripes as best she could, for the road was bumpy. An ambulance attendant studied his nails.

'What *is* Timmy going to say?' reproached Zelda. 'Poor Thompson!'

'Oh, shut up, Zelda,' said Meg, automatically.

'Is she coming round?' asked the midwife.

'She's being very rude,' said Zelda. 'Is that the same thing?'

'What happened?' asked Meg.

'Acute abdominal pain for no apparent reason,' said the midwife. 'It happens sometimes. Don't worry, the foetal heart's strong and steady: so's yours.'

'Did I dream it?' asked Meg. 'Is Thompson dead?'

'Thompson's dead,' said Zelda. 'What *is* Timmy going to say? You should have put him in kennels, Meg.'

'Don't persecute the wee lassie,' said the midwife.

'It's the best thing for her,' said Zelda. 'I know her backwards. Look! It's brought the colour back to her cheeks.'

Meg wept for Thompson.

'I thought I'd blown up the world,' she said, presently. 'I'm glad it's still here.'

'Takes more than you, dear,' said the midwife.

'Three of us like me, and we might,' said Meg, 'all too easily,' but the midwife didn't take the reference. Zelda did. Zelda said, 'Well, I'll have no talk of the end of the world in front of the children. So far as I'm concerned their fathers are guarding our shores and protecting our future, not to mention paying the rent, and to say anything else is negativism. Women for the Bomb, that's me!'

'You've been seeing too much of Tony,' said Meg.

'I just hope,' said Zelda, 'that when my baby's born it manages to look like Jim. So now you know.'

Meg spent the rest of the day in the Base hospital and in the evening they sent her home by ambulance. She kept thinking she saw Thompson, out of the corner of her eye; but when she looked fairly and squarely he wasn't there. But his spirit lingered around the house, on the stairs and under the bed; and every door and window-frame had been scored by his strong claws.

The next morning Meg spoke to him seriously.

'Thompson,' she said, 'you're here and yet you're not here. You'll be off soon, I expect. Did you die for a purpose, to teach me a lesson? I feel there is something to be learned. I wish I knew more clearly what it was. I know I wasn't grateful for what I had, and I should have been. I expected a humble, grateful, easy animal, who would consent to be loved, who could be controlled; and instead I had you. I wanted for a husband the projection of my own fantasies, and instead I had Timmy. No wonder he fought back. I thought it was other people who were angry and violent, not me; but it wasn't so. It was me as well. It's never *them*, is it? It's *us*.'

And she was silent, and seemed to hear Thompson's patient, heavy breathing.

'Thompson,' she said, 'take your spirit out of here, and go to the bottom of the sea, where the big silent ships glide in and out, and tell your master I'm sorry.'

Down on Polaris two Routines came through. One was from the Family News Service. The captain put it in a folder and said nothing.

'I know it's for me, sir. Is it Meg? Is she all right?'

'Perfectly all right.'

'Then what is it, sir? Is it Thompson?'

'Custom is, my boy, to keep bad news to the last day of the tour. Since there's nothing one can do about it –'

But Jim told him.

'Thompson was shot by a farmer. He'd been worrying the sheep.'

Timmy was silent for a while. The smell of chicken *à l'ail* – chicken stuffed with twenty heads of garlic, and simmered in stock – filled the galley and indeed the rest of the boat. It was a comforting smell.

'Poor Meg,' was what Timmy said. 'Poor Meg! All alone up there without even a dog to keep her company. At least I'll be home for the birth.'

'I think I'll just about miss Zelda's,' said Jim, thankfully.

'I'm not much good at childbirth.'

The second Routine was from Operations Base and told them to make for home at all speed. The captain passed the news on to the Engine Room and opened the second canister of Zelda's wine and again he added a little blood, in the interests of universal brotherhood, and a little cochineal: they drank, and Jim carved. The cooked garlic cut and tasted somewhere between fresh young turnip and good potato. They savoured that, and the good red wine. It was half past eleven. (Dinner had drifted earlier and earlier, through the tour. Hunger seemed to gnaw more anxiously as the weeks passed.)

' "Go thy way, saith the preacher," ' quoted the captain. ' "Eat thy bread with joy, and drink thy wine with a merry heart, for God now accepteth thy works." '

Timmy, it being time, thought of Meg and heard a dog barking. It was so firm and real and loud a noise he looked round for its source.

'Sir,' said Timmy, 'do you hear a dog barking?'

'I hear no barking,' said the captain. 'How could I? We are under the sea.'

But whether it was the agreeable sound of the banana and rum fritters frying; or the richness of the red forbidden wine – or perhaps indeed the spirit of poor murdered Thompson touched him – at any rate, presently the captain said –

'You know, if a Routine came through to push those buttons, I wouldn't! What, and lose all this?'

The First Wife

PENELOPE LIVELY

At his niece's wedding Clive Harper fell in love with his first wife. At least that was what it felt like. There she was, not seen for many a long year, and he found himself in a turmoil. He stood staring at her through the chattering groups. Mary. Older, greyer, but unaccountably alluring. He was startled by his own response. Women of his own age did not appeal to him, generally speaking. His present wife was ten years younger.

It had not occurred to him that Mary might be at the wedding. He now remembered that she had always kept up with his brother and sister-in-law, with whom he himself was not on particularly close terms. He was looked upon with slight disapproval, which amused him. Well — they would, wouldn't they? He contrasted with satisfaction his own vigorous and varied life and their staid and complacent routine. Moreover, his brother was always taken for the elder, though he was in fact four years younger than Clive. Gratifying, that.

Clive surveyed the room. A dull gathering, on the whole. Neighbours, old friends, the statutory sprinkling of relatives. Gaggles of young — the niece's cronies. There was only one person here he wanted to talk to.

He watched her being patiently nice to an ancient aunt of his. Mary had always been good about that sort of thing. He edged nearer, to inspect more closely. She hadn't seen him yet. She of course would be expecting him to be here, so there was not for her the element of surprise. She presumably anticipated a meeting. And the very fact that she was here must mean that she . . . wanted to see him? He felt a further thrill of interest.

She was looking handsome – distinctly handsome. She seemed somehow more positive than the Mary he remembered. There she stood, a tall woman in a light green suit, with greying hair becomingly arranged, a creamy silk scarf knotted at her neck. Good legs, elegant shoes. Clive noticed this sort of thing about a woman. Mary had not used to dress thus, in the old days. He observed the pretty Victorian brooch on the lapel of her jacket and her unusual silver earrings. No rings on her hands. A warm, responsive smile on her face as she talked to this importunate aunt.

He was overcome with a quite desperate sense of loss. There she stood, who once had been entirely his, and who no longer was. She seemed a reinstatement of his own past, of his own unattainable youth. A miraculous reincarnation – tangible and present. All he knew was that he had to be near her, had to talk to her, had to have her turn that smile upon him.

He quite forgot that he had left her, all those years ago, because he was suddenly aware that she had begun to look old. Someone had said jokingly that she looked like his mother. A young mother, mind, the person had added hastily – but the damage was done. Clive had gone home in a state of jitters, and a month later he had left Mary and moved in with Michele, who was twenty-four and half French, an irresistible combination.

He was terrified of age. The terror had begun – oh, back in his twenties when he had looked around and realized with surprise and dismay that there were others younger than himself. His thirtieth birthday had risen up and smashed into him like a rock in a tranquil sea. He was incredulous. Thirty? Me? And then he had rallied and told himself that thirty was nothing, thirty was fine. Well – no great disaster, anyway. But he found himself looking in the mirror more often, and watching the faces of his contemporaries to see how he was doing by comparison. And every now and then there would come one of those moments of chilling realization. Thirty-six. Thirty-nine – Christ! Forty.

He was forty-one when he left Mary. She had never understood his fits of terror. She had made light of his panic, when she perceived what he felt. Look, she had said, so what? You're getting older. So am I, so's everyone. She simply didn't understand. She had no conception of those awful seizures – the cold fear in the stomach. No, no – this can't be happening. Not to me. To other people, maybe. Not to me.

And now he was fifty-nine. Sometimes, in dark moments, the awful fact reared up and sent him reeling. But he had learned, over the years, how to keep it all at bay. Activity was the thing. Fill the days, the evenings. Travel. Go out. Be with others. Talk, laugh. He made sure to surround himself with younger people. When his old friends showed signs of becoming a touch decrepit he slid away from them. And of course Susan, his present wife, was not yet fifty.

The arrangement with Michele had not lasted long. Indeed, he could barely remember Michele now. She had had many successors, over the years. Little affairs – never intense enough to rock his marriage (one must have a base, a calm centre), just something to keep the adrenalin flowing. He had to have that constant frisson of interest – the anticipation of a discreet meeting, the flattery of a new face turned attentively to his.

And now – astonishingly, bewilderingly – here was Mary's face with all the allure of some stranger sighted and marked down. She was still talking to the aunt, still had not seen him. He thought with a pleasurable tingle of how she might respond when she did. How would he look to her? He was glad he had put on his rather dashing new shirt. Susan had pulled a face, for some inexplicable reason – had got out a plain white one and proposed that instead. Thank God, though, that Susan had woken with what looked like incipient flu and had decided to cry off the wedding. What luck.

He would have expected that by now Mary would be wondering if he was here, would be casting furtive glances round the room. She did not. She continued with her patient attention to the aunt until some acquaintance joined them, when she took the opportunity to slide gracefully away. But still she did not search for him. She walked over to his brother and sister-in-law and stood talking and laughing with them in a casual intimacy that had Clive in a sudden fret of jealousy.

He tried to remember what news of her had reached him over the last few years. She had never remarried. There had been a relationship that had lasted for some while but he knew that it was over now. She was alone, he was sure of that – if she were not he would have heard. She lived alone and worked in hospital administration, a career on which she had embarked after their marriage broke up.

Long ago now, all of that. He could no longer remember very precisely the sequence of events. Just that catastrophic remark by some acquaintance, and his jitters. Michele hoving upon the scene with her beguiling youth. The way in which he himself had flailed between guilt and the panic-stricken knowledge that he was going to do what he subsequently did. He had to – it had been inevitable. And there had been outrage. His brother and sister-in-law had not spoken to him for a year. One or two friends had dropped him. And of course Mary had been badly hurt. He could see that now, could feel compunction. He had behaved badly – he would be the first to accept that.

And now was his chance – not to make amends but to initiate a new, rewarding relationship. That was so very much what he needed, he suddenly realized. Not some transitory flirtation with an agreeable newcomer, but a dependable, mutually supportive liaison with the person he had once known best in the world. It need not affect his marriage in any way. The thing would be tactfully concealed, and provide a marvellous private uplift for them both. He was amazed still at the excitement the sight of her had induced in him.

His brother and sister-in-law had been distracted by other guests. Mary was alone. It was time to act. She was already moving away.

He arrived at her side. 'Well . . . It's wonderful to see you, Mary.'

At the sound of his voice she turned her head. There was no surprise on her face – indeed no identifiable expression at all. 'Hello, Clive.'

'Well!' he said again. He put everything into the look he gave her. He was good at that kind of tacit eloquence, he knew. His look

conveyed admiration and regret and pleading anticipation. It told
her that he admired her appearance, that he thought she seemed
years younger than he knew her to be, that he had a thousand things
to say to her, that he needed time in which to say them. It told her,
in effect, that he had fallen in love with her. Clive had himself been
on the receiving end of such looks in his day and knew them to be
instantly unsettling. He waited for Mary to display unsettlement.

She did indeed seem taken aback. She was silent for a moment,
apparently studying him. Then she said, 'I gather poor Susan's got
flu.'

This was not the direction in which he meant them to go. He
dealt quickly with Susan's flu and tried to bring things back to a
more personal focus. He asked where she was living, and was told.
Good – now he could get her address and phone number from the
directory. He inquired about her work, and was given a dispassionate
account of what she did. She was quite high-powered, he recognized.
This also was disorienting, like her dress and manner. The earlier
Mary – his Mary – had been a more self-effacing person. But this
authority was undoubtedly part of her new appeal. A woman of her
time, he thought approvingly. Good for you. He finished what he
was saying – something about his own present doings – and gazed
at her again with unashamed admiration. Let her know what he was
feeling, what he was thinking.

She seemed a touch restive. She glanced over his shoulder, sipped
at her drink. She was affected, by him, no doubt about that. He had
disconcerted her. Now, perhaps, was the moment to make a direct
approach.

'Could we perhaps . . . meet?' he said.

She hesitated. And now that wretched aunt was heading for them.

'Mary,' she was crying. 'Mary – I quite forgot to give you my
new address.'

Clive gave his first wife his most beseeching smile. 'Soon? I'll call
you. All right?'

She seemed about to speak, hesitated again. And then the aunt
was there, chuntering on. Clive touched Mary's arm for a second
and left them.

He could understand her hesitation – he could sympathize entirely. She didn't know how to respond. She mistrusted her own feelings, perhaps – was confused by the whole encounter. He would wait a couple of days, and then phone her. No – he would write a brief note first, maybe send some flowers, phone the day after that.

For the rest of the afternoon he made perfunctory conversation with others while trying to keep Mary within his sights. He did not manage to speak to her alone again, and when he searched for her to say goodbye she had already gone. Never mind, the groundwork had been done.

He decided against the flowers – a banal touch, that would be. He wrote her a letter – short but intense. He told her how deeply moved he had been at seeing her. He hinted delicately at years of regret. He implied a sense of void in his own life. He included one or two veiled references and muted jokes which referred back to their life together. He concluded by saying that he wanted very much to see her. Perhaps they could meet for lunch or dinner? He would phone her next week.

She did not reply. He had anticipated this – naturally, she would not wish to seem precipitate. He called, and was confronted with an answerphone. He rang off without leaving a message, and tried again the next evening. Still the answerphone. This time he spoke. He proposed lunch in three days' time. He named a restaurant. If he did not hear from her he would take it that this was acceptable and would look forward with immense pleasure to seeing her.

He arrived slightly late at the restaurant, stymied by traffic. Handing his coat to the waiter, he looked round anxiously – no sight of her. Good – it would not do to have kept her waiting. And then the waiter said, 'A lady came earlier, sir. She left you this note.'

Clive stared at the man. He took the envelope. He felt a trickle of fear. He sat down, pulled out a single sheet of paper, and began to read.

Dear Clive: No, thank you. Not lunch nor anything else. I wonder what makes you think I should wish to? Well – empathy was never your strong point.

Your letter implied a certain desolation – nicely understated but poignant none the less, which was no doubt the intention. A state of mind with which I have been deeply familiar. However, I am not I feel the right person to offer solace. I'm sure you will find someone more receptive, unless you have entirely lost your touch, which everything suggests that you have not.

Thank you for your compliments – most acceptable to a woman of my age. You haven't changed all that much yourself, though more I fear than you would like. The signs of a desperate rearguard action are plainly visible. You seem anxious to remind me of the old days, so I'm sure you won't mind if I presume on former intimacy and make a point or two. The hair *en brosse* is not a good idea, and I wouldn't tint the grey bits if I were you – it shows in a strong light. Also, the puce shirt is unwise on a man of your age and figure. I do hope Susan's flu is better. Poor thing. Yours, Mary.

'Would you care for an aperitif, sir?' the waiter was saying.

Through a Glass Brightly

BERYL BAINBRIDGE

Norman Pearson went to the meeting because his neighbour's wife, Alison Freely, told him he ought to mix more. He was afraid that Alison's reference to the meeting was a roundabout way of telling him that he was taking up too much of her time, and instantly said that he had every intention of going, that indeed he had already made inquiries about it long before she had brought up the subject.

Two years before, his wife had left him for a career woman with a villa in Spain. He had never met the woman, but his wife had cruelly left a photograph of her in the suitcase on top of the wardrobe. He often took down the photograph and studied that unknown face, those eyes that had winked at his wife across a crowded room and spirited her out of his life. In spite of every effort, he had not yet adjusted to being on his own. He had read that single men were in demand at dinner parties and things, but though he had casually let drop, in conversations with colleagues at the office, that he was on the loose, in a manner of speaking, no one had ever taken him up on it, not even to the extent of asking him round for a cup of tea. Last February he had become quite pally with a divorcee in Mount Street – patting her dog, passing the time of day – until she sent him a note complaining about the dilapidation of the party wall at the back of his house. It wasn't that he objected to sharing the cost of doing something about it, rather that he dreaded some cowboy builder mutilating the rambler rose that he had planted against the wall in happier times. Actually, his wife had planted it; lately, he couldn't rid himself of the superstitious thought that if the rose didn't thrive, neither would he. The divorcee was still sending him solicitors' letters, because of course they were no longer on speaking terms and even the dog ignored him. He had come to the conclusion that if there was a demand for deserted men, men on the loose, then it existed somewhere else, in exotic Islington perhaps, or Hampstead, and had not yet reached East Croydon.

The meeting was called to discuss arrangements for the Mary Street Carnival, and was held upstairs in the Hare and Hounds. The accountant from No. 111, who owned a typist and a photocopying machine, had sent out the notices. It went without saying that his close friend J.J. Roberts, who was something controversial in the television world, took the chair. Not that people were fighting for the privilege of being that involved; not any more. Mary Street had organized a carnival, in summer, for the past eight years, and those serving on the Committee usually ended up out of pocket. It was a headache trying to recuperate expenses once the Steel Bands and the Inter-Action Groups had muscled in on the occasion. Nor had anyone forgotten the year the Committee, accused of being too middle-class in its attitude, had been persuaded to join forces with the Youth Centre at the end of the street. The youth leader, who was called Sunday and was an ethnic minority, had talked the landlord of the Hare and Hounds into applying for an extended licence. Afterwards, a majority of the residents, particularly those who had suffered broken windows, had protested that it was meant to be a day for the children. There was no denying that the Carnival itself had been a great success, at least until eight o'clock when the Committee were counting the day's takings in the Church Hall. Then someone shouted out the word 'Fire!', and naturally they had all run to see what was up. They only went as far as the door. Even so, when they turned round the cash boxes had simply vanished into thin air. There were the usual reasoned arguments along the lines of shooting being too good for 'them', and, send 'them' back on the next banana boat, but nothing came of it. The accountant had gone so far as to have notices printed, which were wired to the lamp posts, promising forgiveness all round and pleading for the money to be returned anonymously. Needless to say, he never heard a dicky bird. Since then, the accountant and J.J. Roberts, accompanied by a minder from the Leisure Centre, had gone round the stalls every half hour collecting whatever had accumulated in the cash boxes.

Carnival Day had evolved out of a desire to beautify the street. The proceeds of that first event had gone towards buying, and subsequently planting, trees along the edges of the pavement. This idea of environmental improvement was abandoned shortly after it was discovered that no one had taken into account the camber of the road. In no time at all the roots of the trees had begun to interfere with the drains, and the Council had to come round and uproot them − it came out of the rates, of course − and stick them back into huge concrete tubs that were an eyesore. Alison Freely had a tub right outside her house, which meant she couldn't park her car properly. She put poison in the soil and killed off her tree, but the Council said they hadn't the manpower to remove the tub. Now nobody really knew what the Carnival was in aid of, or indeed what happened to the proceeds. For many it was just an excuse to get rid of worn-out clothing and broken furniture.

At the meeting, when suggestions were called for, Mrs Riley the architect said what about a competition for a model of the street as it might be in fifty years' time.

'Marvellous,' said J.J. Roberts. 'Bloody marvellous.'

Nobody else came up with anything quite as complicated, though the graphic designer from No. 89 attempted to persuade people that it would be a fun thing to paint their balconies in different colours. He said it wouldn't cost much and urged them to think of those sticks of rock one used to buy at seaside resorts: such colours − such luminous pinks and greens.

Betty Taylor, whom J.J. Roberts always referred to as Elizabeth Taylor, and who lived in compulsorily purchased property, said that it wasn't fair on people who didn't have balconies. A senior citizen, she had recently attended a talk given in the Church Hall by a member of the Women's Workshop and was becoming increasingly aware of the divisions caused by privilege. She said that if sticks of rock were only going to be distributed to balcony owners, then she would vote against it. The accountant told her that in his opinion balconies gave easy access to thieves, and she should thank her lucky stars she was without one.

It was then that Norman Pearson remarked that his mother had once been burgled in Streatham. The swine had taken her television set and the transistor radio but ignored her crystal ball on the mantelpiece. He was astonished at the reaction resulting from this routine, though undoubtedly sad, little tale.

'Fortune telling,' hissed Mrs Riley. 'Fortune telling.' The accountant beat at his thigh with his fist and laughed uncontrollably. 'Christ,' exploded J. J. Roberts. 'How bloody marvellous.'

The next morning, when they were both emptying rubbish into their respective bins, Alison asked Norman how he had got on at the meeting. He said he had found it stimulating. 'That show-off Roberts was in charge.'

'Of course,' Alison said. 'Many others turn up?'

'One or two,' he said, and as she was going back into the house, called out, 'I'm going to tell fortunes.' But his words were lost in the slamming of her door and he was glad that she hadn't heard, because he had promised not to tell anybody, so as to be more mysterious on the day.

He collected the crystal ball from his mother's a week before the Carnival. She didn't want to part with it; she said it was valuable. In the end he almost snatched it from her, and was surprised at its weight. Though he looked into it for hours, even after he had drunk three-quarters of a bottle of retsina, he could see nothing within its depths but a milk-white cloud. Irritated, he shook it, as though it was one of those children's snow-flake scenes encased in glass, but still he saw nothing beyond that impenetrable mist. His own life, he thought, staring gloomily out at the bunting already strung across the street, was becoming equally opaque. Deep down, he blamed his wife, for if she had not been so flighty he would never have been in such a predicament.

Preparations for the Carnival began at eight o'clock in the morning. They were lucky with the weather, in that it wasn't actually raining. J.J. Roberts strode up and down in a pair of shorts, chalking lines and circles on the surface of the road, and pointing at the sky. 'Lots of blue,' he shouted optimistically, whenever anybody appeared on the balconies. When he saw Norman, he cried out, 'Looking forward to it, Pearson?'

'Rather,' said Norman, wishing he had the courage to go to a main-line station and take a train in any direction.

At one o'clock the merry-go-round, the slide, the racks of second-hand clothing were in their allotted spaces. The home-made cakes, the bags of fudge and toffee, the rag dolls and the tea-cosies lay spread along the trestle tables. From behind each privet hedge wafted a smell of frying sausages and hamburgers, of kebabs roasting above charcoal. A man on stilts, thin arms held wide, stood like a pylon in the middle of the road. Hordes or little children, pursued by parents, ran between his legs, screaming.

The Lady Mayoress opened the proceedings, standing on J.J. Roberts's balcony and shouting through a loudspeaker. Norman was crouched at a rickety table inside a wigwam anchored precariously in the gutter. He wore a flouncy dress loaned to him by the accountant's wife, dark glasses and a Davy Crockett hat. No one had recognized him when he appeared in the street. He was straining to hear the Mayoress's words when some children pushed against the wigwam. The table collapsed, sending the crystal ball flying into the gutter. When he picked it up there were tiny hair-line cracks upon its surface. It made all the difference.

His first customers were a man and a woman, neither of whom had he ever seen before, and he was able to tell them that they were going on a long journey, somewhere hot, without vegetation.

'Good heavens,' breathed the woman.

Encouraged, Norman studied the scratches carefully and, screwing up his eyes, fancied he saw the marks of tyre tracks.

'It's not going to be all plain sailing,' he said. 'I foresee trouble.' He charged the couple ten pence and realized, too late, that he could have asked for fifty. He heard them outside the tent, informing someone that the crystal gazer was incredible, absolutely incredible.

She had told them all about that documentary they had made for 'War on Want', when the crank shaft went and David, but for the champagne, would almost certainly have died of dehydration.

A queue began to form outside the wigwam. The noise, the jostling, was tremendous.

'Stop it,' Norman protested, as a youth with a plug of cotton-wool in his ear insisted on entering with two of his friends.

'There's no room,' he warned, hanging on to his Davy Crockett hat as the tent lurched sideways.

'Get on with it,' ordered the youth belligerently.

'Well,' said Norman. 'You've been ill recently, with headaches.'

'Rubbish,' sneered the youth.

'Earache, then,' said Norman. 'I see a tall man with very long legs. He's waving his arms.'

'Bugger me,' said the youth, all the cockiness gone from him.

'You were mugged,' said Norman confidently, staring at a wavy line that looked not unlike the handle of a teacup. 'Attacked in some way.'

'Gerroff,' cried the youth, recovering. 'I weren't attacked, you stupid bag. Me Dad hit me with a poker.'

When Betty Taylor came into the wigwam, Norman found himself telling her that she had not had much of a life.

'You're right,' she said. 'You're right.'

'You've never had it easy, right from a child.'

'No,' she sniffed. 'I haven't.'

'And I can't see anything better in the future,' Norman said. 'You're not one of Nature's darlings. I wish I could pretend otherwise, but the crystal ball never lies.'

Betty Taylor left the wigwam in tears. Norman felt dreadful the moment she had gone, and wondered what had made him so peculiarly truthful. After all, she had done nothing to him.

Nevertheless he enjoyed himself; it was simple once he'd got the hang of it. Nicotine stains on the fingers pointed to a death-wish, blood-shot eyes denoted too much dependence on the bottle, nervous laughter was a sure sign of inferiority. It was all a matter of observation.

Half way through the afternoon a woman in a white dress squeezed into the wigwam. She was coughing. 'You're supposed to be frightfully good,' she said huskily. 'Do tell what's in store for me.'

Norman looked at her face, at her eyes, and then peered into the crystal ball. 'Sometimes,' he told her, 'I find it's not altogether wise to pass on the information. It might upset people – some people – if the exact picture were given.'

'Oh, come now,' she said. 'You can tell me. I've paid my ten pence.'

'I see a house,' he said. 'It's painted white. It's not here . . . it's somewhere abroad.' He glanced at her sunburnt arms and went on, 'You've only recently returned. You weren't alone.'

'Go on,' said the woman. 'You're awfully good so far.'

'This other person,' he said, 'is unhappy. It's a woman. Her surname begins with P, I think. Yes, it's definitely P.'

'What does this P person do?' asked the woman She was holding a little fold of skin at the base of her neck, twisting it between thumb and forefinger.

'Nothing at the moment,' said Norman, 'that's the trouble. She used to look after someone, but then she walked out.'

The woman stared at Norman.

'I think it was her mother,' he said. 'Someone close, anyway. At any rate they took it badly. I see a station platform and a figure standing very near the rails. There's a train coming.'

'Oh, God!' said the woman.

'There's something else,' Norman said, 'something else coming through. I've got it. I've a picture of a woman lying down and someone bending over her, someone in a white coat. Is she at the dentist's, I wonder?' He took his time; he was sweating and his dark glasses kept sliding on the bridge of his nose. At last he said, 'The woman has a sore . . . no, not a sore, more like a small lump just beneath her adam's apple. It's serious.'

After a moment the woman asked, 'Which one is it? The woman at the station or the one with the name beginning with P?'

'Ah, well,' said Norman, 'I'm only the projector, not the identifier.

I leave it to those who consult me to work out whose life is in danger.'

The woman put a pound note on the table and ducked out into the street. Norman could hear her coughing above the noise of the Steel Band on the corner.

When it was all over and he'd been congratulated on his success – more than one member of the Committee asked if he was free next week for drinks, for supper – Norman went home, and removing the suitcase from the wardrobe took out the photograph and tore it in half across the throat.

Then he sat at the table and wrote a note to the divorcee, telling her that she could pull down his wall whenever she felt like it. If necessary he would pay for the whole caboodle.

Life wasn't all roses.

On the Antler

E. ANNIE PROULX

Hawkheel's face was as finely wrinkled as grass-dried linen, his thin back bent like a branch weighted with snow. He still spent most of his time in the field and on the streams, sweeter days than when he was that half-wild boy who ran panting up the muddy logging road, smashing branches to mute the receding roar of the school bus. Then he had hated books, had despised everything except the woods.

But in the insomnia of old age he read half the night, the patinated words gliding under his eyes like a river coursing over polished stones: books on wild geese, nymph patterns for brook trout, wolves fanning across the snow. He went through his catalogues, putting red stars against the few books he could buy and black crosses like tiny grave markers against the rarities he would never be able to afford – Halford's *Floating Flies and How to Dress Them*, Lanman's *Haw-Ho-Noo*, Phillips' *A Natural History of the Ducks* with color plates as fine as if the wild waterfowl had been pressed like flowers between the pages.

His trailer was on the north bank of the Feather River in the shadow of Antler Mountain. These few narrow acres were all that was left of the home place. He'd sold it off little by little since Josepha had left him, until he was down to the trailer, ten spongy acres of river bottom and his social security checks.

Yet he thought this was the best part of his life. It was as if he'd come into flat water after half a century and more of running the rapids. He was glad to put the paddle down and float the rest of the way.

He had his secret places hidden all through Chopping County and he visited them like stations of the cross; in order, in reverence and in expectation of results. In late May he followed the trout up the narrow, sun-warmed streams, his rod thrusting skillfully through the alders, crushing underfoot ferns whose broken stems released an elusive bitter scent. In October, mists came down on him as he waded through drenched goldenrod meadows, alert for grouse. And in the numb silence of November Hawkheel was a deer hunter up on the shoulder of Antler Mountain, his back against a beech while frozen threads of ice formed on the rifle's blue metal.

The deer hunt was the end and summit of his year: the irrevocable shot, the thin, ringing silence that followed, the buck down and still, the sky like clouded marble from which sifted snow finer than dust, and the sense of a completed cycle as the cooling blood ran into the dead leaves.

Bill Stong couldn't leave things alone. All through their lives there had been sparks and brushfires of hatred between Hawkheel and him, never quite quenched, but smoldering low until some wind fanned up the little flames.

In school Hawkheel had been The Lone Woodsman, a moody, insubordinate figure prowling the backcountry. Stong was a wiseacre with a streak of meanness. He hunted with his father and brothers and shot his first buck when he was eleven. How could he miss, thought woman-raised Hawkheel bitterly, how, when he sat in a big pine right over a deer trail and his old man whispered 'Now! Shoot now!' at the moment?

Stong's father farmed a little, ran a feed store and got a small salary to play town constable. He broke up Saturday-night dance fights, shot dogs that ran sheep and sometimes acted as the truant officer. His big, pebbled face was waiting for Hawkheel one school morning when he slid down the rocks to a trout pool.

'Plannin' to cut school again? Well, since your old man's not in a position to do it for you, I'm going to give you a lesson you'll remember.' He flailed Hawkheel with a trimmed ash sapling and then drove him to school.

'You don't skip no more school, buddy, or I'll come get you again.'

In the classroom Bill Stong's sliding eyes told Hawkheel he had been set up. 'I'll fix him,' Hawkheel told his sister, Urna, at noon. 'I'll think up something. He won't know what hit him when I'm done.' The game began, and the thread of rage endured like a footnote to their lives.

In late October, on the Sunday before Stong's fifteenth birthday, an event that exposed his mother's slovenly housekeeping ways took his family away.

Chopping County farmers soaked their seed corn in strychnine to kill the swaggering crows that gorged on the germinating kernels. One of the Stongs, no one knew which one, had mixed the deadly solution in a big roasting pan. The seed was sown and the unwashed pan shoved beneath the blackened iron griddles on the pantry floor where it stayed until autumn hog butchering.

The day was cold and windy, the last of summer thrown up into the sky by turbulent air. Stong's mother pulled out the pan and loaded it with a pork roast big enough to feed the Sunday gathering of family. The pork killed them all except Bill Stong, who was rolling around in Willard Iron's hayloft on a first shameful adventure. The equation of sex and death tainted his adolescent years.

As Stong grew older, he let the farm go down. He sat in the feed store year after year listening in on the party line. His sharp-tongued gossip rasped at the shells of others' lives until the quick was exposed. At the weekend dances Stong showed up alone, never dancing himself, but watching the women gallop past, their print blouses damp with sweat under the arms, their skirts sticking to their hot legs. At night he walked through town seeing which ones left the window shades up. He went uninvited to church suppers and card parties, winked out juicy tales and stained the absent with mean innuendo. Often his razor tongue stropped itself on the faults and flaws of his dead parents as though he had come fresh from a rancorous argument with them, and at other times he called them saints in a tearful voice.

Stong caught Hawkheel with petty tricks again and again. After Hawkheel started farming, once or twice a year he found the mailbox knocked over, water in the tractor's gas tank or the gate opened so the cows got onto the highway. He knew who'd done it.

Still, he kept on buying grain at the feed store until Stong told him about Josepha. Stong's eyes shone like those of a greedy barn cat who has learned to fry mice in butter.

'Hell, everybody in town knows she's doin' it but you,' he whispered. He ate Hawkheel up with his eyes, sucked all the juice out of his sad condition.

It was cold in the store and the windows were coated with grain dust. Hawkheel felt the fine powder between his fingers and in his dry mouth. They stared at each other, then Stong scurried out through the chilly passageway that led to the house.

'He's got something coming now,' said Hawkheel to Urna. 'I could wire him up out in the woods and leave him for the dogs. I could do something real bad to him any time, but I want to see how far he goes.'

Stong had sour tricks for everybody. Trade dropped away at the feed store, and there were some, like Hawkheel, who spat when they saw the black pickup heading out of town, Stong's big head turning from side to side to get his fill of the sights before the woods closed in.

For a long time Urna made excuses for Stong, saying that his parents' death had 'turned' him, as though he were a bowl of milk gone sour in thundery weather. But when Stong told the game warden there was a summer doe in her cellar she got on the phone and burned Hawkheel's ear.

'Leverd, what kind of a man turns in his neighbor over some deer meat he likes to eat just as good as anybody?'

Hawkheel had an answer, but he didn't give it.

A few years after Josepha left, Hawkheel began to slide deep into the books. He was at Mosely's auction hoping the shotguns would come up early so he could get out of the crowd and take off. But it dragged on, hundreds of the old lady's doilies and quilts going one by one to the summer people. Hawkheel poked through the boxes on the back porch, away from the noise. A book called *Further Adventures of the One-Eyed Poacher* sounded good and he dipped into it like a swallow picking mosquitoes off the water, keeping one ear on the auctioneer's patter. He sat on the broken porch glider and read until the auctioneer, pulling the crowd behind him like a train, came around to the back and shouted 'Who'll give me five dollars for them boxes a books!'

Surrounded in his trailer by those books and the hundreds he'd added to them over the decades, Hawkheel enjoyed his solitude.

Stong, too, was more and more alone up at the store as he got older, his trade dwindled to a few hard-pressed farmers who still bought feed from him because they always had and because Stong carried them until their milk checks came in. Listening in on the phone wasn't enough now; he interrupted conversations, shouting 'Get off the line! I got a emergency.'

'You ask me,' said Urna to Hawkheel, 'he's funny in the head. The only emergency he's got is himself. You watch, they'll find him laying on the kitchen floor some day as stiff as a January barn nail.'

'When I get through with him,' said Hawkheel, 'he'll be stiff, all right.'

Stong might have fallen to the cold kitchen linoleum with an iron ringing sound, but in his sixties his hair turned a fine platinum white and his face thinned to show good bones. It was a time when people were coming into the country, buying up the old farmhouses and fields and making the sugarhouses into guest cottages.

'Bill, you look like a character out of a Rupert Frost poem,' said the woman who'd bought Potter's farm and planted a thousand weedy birches on prime pasture. The new people said Stong was a character. They liked his stories, they read morals into his rambling lies and encouraged him by standing around the feed store playing farmer – buying salt blocks for the deer, sunflower seeds for the bluejays and laying mash for the pet chickens they had to give away each fall.

Stong set his tattered sails to catch this changing wind. In late life he found himself admired and popular for the first time, and he was grateful. He saw what the summer people liked, and to please them he carried armloads of canning jars, books, tools and other family goods down from the house to the store. He arranged generations of his family's possessions on the shelves beside the work gloves and udder balm. He filled the dusty window with pieces of old harness, wooden canes and chipped china.

In autumn he laid in ammunition for the summer men who came back for their week of deer hunting. The sign in his window read GUNS BLUE SEAL FEED WINE ANTIQUES, a small part of what he offered, for all his family's interests and enterprises were tangled together on the shelves as if he had drawn a rake through their lives and piled the debris in the store.

'They say,' said Urna, 'that he's cleaned out everything from kettles to cobwebs and put a price tag on it. You know, don't you, that he's selling all them old books his grandfather used to have. He's got them out there in the barn, higgledy-piggledy where the mice can gnaw on them.'

'Has he,' said Hawkheel.

'I suppose you're going up there to look at them.'

'Well,' said Hawkheel, 'I might.'

The Stong place was high on a bluff, a mile upstream from Hawkheel's trailer as the crow flew. To Hawkheel, every turn of the road was like the bite of an auger into the past. He did not remember his adult journeys up Stong's driveway, but recalled with vivid clarity sitting in the dust-colored passenger seat of their old Ford while his father drove over a sodden mat of leaves. The car window had been cranked down, and far below, the hissing river, heavy with rain, cracked boulders along its bottom. His father drove jerkily, lips moving in whispered conversation with invisible imps. Hawkheel had kept his hand on the door handle in case the old man steered for the edge and he had to jump. It was one of the last memories he had of his father.

The Stong place, he saw now, had run down. The real-estate agents would get it pretty soon. The sagging clapboard house tapered away into a long ell and the barn. The store was still in the ell, but Hawkheel took the old shortcut around back, driving through the stinging nettles and just catching a glimpse through the store window of Stong's white head bobbing over a handful of papers.

The barn was filled with dim, brown light shot through like Indian silk with brilliant threads of sunlight. There was a faint smell of apples. On the other side of the wall a rooster beat his wings. Hawkheel looked around and saw, behind the grain sacks, hundreds of books, some in boxes, some stacked on shelves and windowsills. The first one he took up was a perfect copy of Thad Norris's 1865 *The American Angler's Book*. He'd seen it listed in his catalogue at home at $85. Stong wanted one dollar.

Hawkheel went at the boxes. He turned out Judge Nutting's nice little book on grouse, *The History of One Day Out of Seventeen Thousand*. A box of stained magazines was hiding a rare 1886 copy of Halford's *Floating Flies*, the slipcase deeply marked with Stong's penciled price of $1.50.

'Oh God,' said Hawkheel, 'I got him now.'

He disguised the valuable books by mixing them with dull-jacketed works on potatoes and surveying, and carried the stack into the feed store. Stong sat at the counter, working his adding machine. Hawkheel noticed he had taken to wearing overalls, and a bandana knotted around his big neck. He looked to see if there was a straw hat on a nail.

'Good to see you, Leverd,' said Stong in a creamy voice. He gossiped and joked as if Hawkheel were one of the summer people, winked and said, 'Don't spend your whole social security check on books, Leverd. Save a little out for a good time. You seen the new Ruger shotguns?' Mellowed and ripened Stong, improved by admiration, thought Hawkheel.

The books had belonged to Stong's grandfather, a hero of the waters whose name had once been in the Boston papers for his record trout. The stuffed and mounted trout still hung on the store

On the Antler 163

wall beside the old man's enlarged photograph showing his tilted face and milky eyes behind the oval curve of glass.

'Bill, what will you take for your grandpa today?' cried the summer people who jammed the store on Saturdays, and Stong always answered, 'Take what I can get,' making a country virtue out of avarice.

Stong was ready to jump into his grandfather stories with a turn of the listener's eye. 'The old fool was so slack-brained he got himself killed with crow bait.'

Hawkheel, coming in from the barn with book dust on him, saw that Stong still lied as easily as he breathed. The summer people stood around him like grinning dogs waiting for the warm hearts and livers of slain hares.

Stong's best customers were the autumn hunters. They reopened their summer camps, free now from wives and children, burned the wood they had bought in August from Bucky Pincoke and let the bottle of bourbon stand out on the kitchen table with the deck of cards.

'Roughin' it, are you?' Stong would cry jovially to Mr Rose, splendid in his new red L.L. Bean suspenders. The hunters bought Stong's knives and ammunition and went away with rusted traps, worn horseshoes and bent pokers pulled from the bins labeled 'Collector's Items'. In their game pockets were bottles of Stong's cheap Spanish wine, faded orange from standing in the sun. Stong filled their ears to overflowing with his inventions.

'Yes,' he would say, 'that's what Antler Mountain is named for, not because there's any big bucks up there, which there is *not*' – with a half wink for Hawkheel who stood in the doorway holding rare books like hot bricks – 'but because this couple named Antler, Jane and Anton Antler, lived up there years ago. Kind of simple, like some old families hereabouts get.'

A sly look. Did he mean Hawkheel's father who was carted away with wet chin and shaking hands to the state asylum believing pitchfork handles were adders?

'Yes, they had a little cabin up there. Lived off raccoons and weeds. Then old Jane had this baby, only one they ever had. Thought

a lot of it, couldn't do enough for it, but it didn't survive their care
and when it was only a few months old it died.'

Stong, like a petulant tenor, turned away then and arranged the
dimes in the cash register. The hunters rubbed their soft hands along
the counter and begged for the rest of the story. Hawkheel himself
wondered how it would come out.

'Well, sir, they couldn't bear to lay that baby away in the ground,
so they put it in a five-gallon jar of pure alcohol. My own grandfather
– used to stand right here behind the counter where I'm standing
now – sold 'em the jar. We used to carry them big jars. Can't get
'em any more. They set that jar with the baby on a stump in front
of their cabin the way we might set out a plaster duck on the lawn.'
He would pause a moment for good effect, then say, '*The stump's
still there.*'

They asked him to draw maps on the back of paper bags and
went up onto the Antler to stare at the stump as if the impression
of the jar had been burned into it by holy fire. Stong, with a laugh
like a broken cream separator, told Hawkheel that every stick from
that cut maple was in his woodshed. For each lie he heard, Hawkheel
took three extra books.

All winter long Hawkheel kept digging away at the book mine in
the barn, putting good ones at the bottom of the deepest pile so no
one else would find them, cautiously buying only a few each week.

'Why, you're getting to be my best customer, Leverd,' said
Stong, looking through the narrow, handmade Dutch pages of John
Beever's *Practical Fly-fishing*, which Hawkheel guessed was worth
$200 on the collector's market, but for which Stong wanted only
fifty cents. Hawkheel was afraid Stong would feel the quality of
paper, notice that it was a numbered copy, somehow sense its rarity
and value. He tried a diversion.

'Bill! You'll be interested that last week I seen the heaviest buck
I seen in many years. He was pawing through the leaves about thirty
yards from My Place.'

In Chopping County 'My Place' meant the speaker's private deer
stand. It was a county of still hunting, and good stands were passed

from father to son. Hawkheel's Place on the Antler regularly gave him big deer, usually the biggest deer in Feather River. Stong's old Place in the comfortable pine was useless, discovered by weekend hunters from out of state who shot his bucks and left beer cans under the tree while he tended the store. They brought the deer to be weighed on Stong's reporting scales, bragging, not knowing they'd usurped his stand, while he smiled and nodded. Stong had not even had a small doe in five years.

'Your Place up on the Antler, Leverd?' said Stong, letting the cover of the Beever fall closed. 'Wasn't that over on the south slope?'

'No, it's in that beech stand on the shoulder. Too steep for flatlanders to climb so I do pretty good there. A big buck. I'd say he'd run close to one-eighty, dressed.'

Stong raked the two quarters toward him and commenced a long lie about a herd of white deer that used to live in the swamp in the old days, but his eyes went back to the book in Hawkheel's hands.

The long fine fishing days began a few weeks later, and Hawkheel decided to walk the high northeast corner of the county looking for new water. In late summer he found it.

At the head of a rough mountain pass a waterfall poured into a large trout pool like champagne into a wine glass. Images of clouds and leaves lay on the slowly revolving surface. Dew, like crystal insect eggs, shone in the untrodden moss along the stream. The kingfisher screamed and clattered his wings as Hawkheel played a heavy rainbow into the shallows. In a few weeks he came to think that since the time of the St Francis Indians, only he had ever found the way there.

As August waned Hawkheel grew possessive of the pool and arranged stones and twigs when he could not come for several days, searching later for signs of their disarray from trespassing feet. Nothing was ever changed, except when a cloudburst washed his twigs into a huddle.

One afternoon the wind came up too strong to cast from below the pool, and Hawkheel took off his shoes and stockings and crept cautiously onto the steep rock slab above the waterfall. He gripped his bare white toes into the granite fissures, climbing the rough face. The wind blew his hair up the wrong way and he felt he must look like the kingfisher.

From above the pool he could see the trout swimming smoothly in the direction of the current. The whole perspective of the place was new; it was as if he were seeing it for the first time. There was the back of the dead spruce and the kingfisher's hidden entrance revealed. There, too, swinging from an invisible length of line wound around a branch stub, was a faded red and white plastic bobber that the Indians had not left.

'Isn't anything safe any more?' shouted Hawkheel, coming across the rock too fast. He went down hard and heard his knee crack. He cursed the trout, the spruce, the rock, the invader of his private peace, and made a bad trip home leaning on a forked stick.

Urna brought over hot suppers until he could get around and do for himself again. The inside of the trailer was packed with books and furniture and the cramped space made him listless. He got in the habit of cooking only every three or four days, making up big pots of venison stew or pea soup and picking at it until it was used up or went bad.

He saw in the mirror that he looked old. He glared at his reflection and asked, 'Where's your medicine bottle and sweater?' He thought of his mother who sat for years in the rocker, her thick, ginger-shellacked cane hooked over the arm, and fled into his books, reading until his eyes stung and his favorites were too familiar to open. The heavy autumnal rain hammered on the trailer and stripped the leaves from the trees. Not until the day before deer season was he well enough to drive up to Stong's feed store for more books.

He went through the familiar stacks gloomily, keeping his weight off the bad leg and hoping to find something he'd overlooked among the stacks of fine-printed agricultural reports and ink-stained geographies.

He picked up a big dark album that he'd passed over a dozen times. The old-fashioned leather cover was stamped with a design of flowing feathers in gold, and tortured gothic letters spelled 'Family Album.' Inside he saw photographs, snapshots, ocher newspaper clippings whose paste had disintegrated, postcards, prize ribbons. The snapshots showed scores of curd-faced Stongs squinting into the sun, Stong children with fat knees holding wooden pull-along ducks, and a black and white dog Hawkheel dimly remembered.

He looked closer at one snapshot, drawn by something familiar. A heavy boy stood on a slab of rock, grinning up into the sky. In his hand a fishing rod pointed at the upper branches of a spruce where a bobber was hopelessly entangled in the dark needles. A blur of moving water rushed past the boy into a black pool.

'You bastard,' said Hawkheel, closing the album on the picture of Stong, Bill Stong of years ago, trespassing at Hawkheel's secret pool.

He pushed the album up under the back of his shirt so it lay against his skin. It felt the size of a Sears' catalogue and made him throw out his shoulders stiffly. He took a musty book at random – *The Boy's Companion* – and went out to the treacherous Stong.

'Haven't seen you for quite a while, Leverd. Hear you been laid up,' said Stong.

'Bruised my knee.' Hawkheel put the book on the counter.

'Got to expect to be laid up now and then at our age,' said Stong. 'I had trouble with my hip off and on since April. I got something here that'll fix you up.' He took a squat, foreign bottle out from under the counter.

'Mr Rose give me this for checking his place last winter. Apple brandy, and about as strong as anything you ever tasted. Too strong for me, Leverd. I get dizzy just smelling the cork.' He poured a little into a paper cup and pushed it at Hawkheel.

The fragrance of apple wood and autumn spread out as Hawkheel tasted the Calvados. A column of fire rose in the chimney of his throat with a bitter aftertaste like old cigar smoke.

'I suppose you're all ready for opening day, Leverd. Where you going for deer this year?'

'Same place I always go – My Place up on the Antler.'

'You been up there lately?'

'No, not since spring.' Hawkheel felt the album's feathered design transferring to his back.

'Well, Leverd,' said Stong in a mournful voice, 'there's no deer up there now. Got some people bought land up there this summer, think the end of the world is coming so they built a cement cabin, got in a ton of dried apricots and pinto beans. They got some terrible weapons to keep the crowds away. Shot up half the trees on the Antler testing their machine guns. Surprised you didn't hear it. No deer within ten miles of the Antler now. You might want to try someplace else. They say it's good over to Slab City.'

Hawkheel knew one of Stong's lies when he heard it and wondered what it meant. He wanted to get home with the album and examine the proof of Stong's trespass at the secret pool, but Stong poured from the bottle again and Hawkheel knocked it back.

'Where does you fancy friend get this stuff?' he asked, feeling electrical impulses sweep through his fingers as though they itched to play the piano.

'Frawnce,' said Stong in an elegant tone. 'He goes there every year to talk about books at some college.' His hard eyes glittered with malice. 'He's a liberian.' Stong's thick forefinger opened the cover of *The Boy's Companion*, exposing a red-bordered label Hawkheel had missed; it was marked $55.

'He says I been getting skinned over my books, Leverd.'

'Must of been quite a shock to you,' said Hawkheel, thinking he didn't like the taste of apple brandy, didn't like librarian Rose. He left the inflated *Boy's Companion* on the counter and hobbled out to the truck, the photograph album between his shoulder blades giving him a ramrod dignity. In the rearview mirror he saw Stong at the door staring after him.

Clouds like grey waterweed under the ice choked the sky and a gusting wind banged the door against the trailer. Inside, Hawkheel worked the album out from under his shirt and laid it on the table while he built up the fire and put on some leftover pea soup to heat. ' "Liberian!" ' he said once and snorted. After supper he felt queasy and went to bed early thinking the pea soup might have stood too long.

In the morning Hawkheel's bowels beat with urgent tides of distress and there was a foul taste in his mouth. When he came back from the bathroom he gripped the edge of the table which bent and surged in his hands, then gave up and took to his bed. He could hear sounds like distant popcorn and thought it was knotty wood in the stove until he remembered it was the first day of deer season. 'Goddammit,' he cried, 'I already been stuck here six weeks and now I'm doing it again.'

A sound woke him in late afternoon. He was thirsty enough to drink tepid water from the spout of the teakettle. There was another shot on the Antler and he peered out the window at the shoulder of the mountain. He thought he could see specks of brightness in the dull grey smear of hardwood and brush, and he shuffled over to the gun rack to get his .30–.30, clinging to the backs of the chairs for balance. He rested the barrel on the breadbox and looked through the scope, scanning the slope for his deer stand, and at once caught the flash of orange.

He could see two of them kneeling beside the bark-colored curve of a dead deer at his Place. He could make out the bandana at the big one's neck, see a knife gleam briefly like falling water. He watched them drag the buck down toward the logging road until the light faded and their orange vests turned black under the trees.

'Made sure I couldn't go out with your goddamned poison brandy, didn't you?' said Hawkheel.

He sat by the stove with the old red Indian blanket pulled around him, feeling like he's stared at a light bulb too long. Urna called after supper. Her metallic voice range in his ear.

'I suppose you heard all about it.'

'Only thing I heard was the shots, but I seen him through the scope from the window. What'd it weight out at?'

'I heard two-thirty, dressed out, so live weight must of been towards three hundred. Warden said it's probably the biggest buck ever took in the county, a sixteen-pointer, too, and probably a state record. I didn't know you could see onto the Antler from your window.'

'Oh, I can see good, but not good enough to see who was with him.'

'He's the one bought Willard Iron's place and put a tennis court onto the garden,' said Urna scornfully. 'Rose. They say he was worse than Bill, jumping around and screaming for them to take pictures.'

'Did they?'

'Course they did. Then they all went up to Mr Tennis Court's to have a party. Stick your head out the door and you'll hear them on the wind.'

Hawkheel did not stick his head out the door, but opened the album to look at the Stongs, their big, rocklike faces bent over wedding cakes and infants. Many of the photographs were captioned in a spiky, antique hand: 'Cousin Mattie with her new skates', 'Pa on the porch swing', simple statements of what was already clear as though the writer feared the images would some-day dissolve into blankness, leaving the happiness of the Stongs unknown.

He glared, seeing Stong at the secret pool, the familiar sly eyes, the fatuous gaping mouth unchanged. He turned the pages to a stiff portrait of Stong's parents, the grandfather standing behind them holding what Hawkheel thought was a cat until he recognized the stuffed trout. On the funeral page the same portraits were reduced in size and joined by a flowing black ribbon that bent and curled in ornate flourishes. The obituary from the *Rutland Herald* was head-lined 'A Farm Tragedy'.

'Too bad Bill missed that dinner,' said Hawkheel.

He saw that on many pages there were empty places where photographs had been wrenched away. He found them, mutilated and torn, at the end of the album. Stong was in every photograph. In the high-school graduation picture, surrounded by clouds of organdy and stiff new suits, Stong's face was inked out and black blood ran from the bottoms of his trousers. Here was another, Stong on a fat-tired white bicycle with a dozen arrows drawn piercing his body. A self-composed obituary, written in a hand like infernal corrosive lace that scorched the page, told how this miserable boy, 'too bad to live' and 'hated by everybody' had met his various ends. Over and over Stong had killed his photographic images. He listed every member of his family as a survivor.

Hawkheel was up and about the next morning, a little unsteady but with a clear head. At first light the shots had begun on the Antler, hunters trying for a buck to match the giant that Stong had brought down. The Antler, thought Hawkheel, was as good as bulldozed.

By afternoon he felt well enough for a few chores, stacking hay bales around the trailer foundation and covering the windows over with plastic. He took two trout out of the freezer and fried them for supper. He was washing the frying pan when Urna called.

'They was on TV with the deer,' she said. 'They showed the game commissioner looking up the record in some book and saying this one beat it. I been half expecting to hear from you all day, wondering what you're going to do.'

'Don't you worry,' said Hawkheel. 'Bill's got it comin' from me. There's a hundred things I could do.'

'Well,' said Urna. 'He's got it coming.'

It took Hawkheel forty minutes to pack the boxes and load them into the pickup. The truck started hard after sitting in the cold blowing rain for two days, but by the time he got it onto the main road it ran smooth and steady, the headlights opening a sharp yellow path through the night.

At the top of Stong's drive he switched the lights off and coasted along in neutral. A half-full moon, ragged with rushing clouds, floated in the sky. Another storm breeder, thought Hawkheel.

The buck hung from a gambrel in the big maple, swaying slowly in the gusting wind. The body cavity gaped black in the moonlight. 'Big,' said Hawkheel, seeing the glint of light on the hooves scraping an arc in the leaves, 'damn big.' He got out of the truck and leaned his forehead against the cold metal for a minute.

From a box in the back of the truck he took one of his books and opened it. It was *Haw-Ho-Noo*. He leaned over a page as if he could read the faint print in the moonlight, then gripped it and tore it out. One after another he seized the books, ripped the pages and cracked their spines. He hurled them at the black, swaying deer and they fell to the bloodied ground beneath it.

'Fool with me, will you?' shouted Hawkheel, tearing soft paper with both hands, tossing books up at the moon, and his blaring sob rose over the sound of the boulders cracking in the river below.

The Unthinkable Happens to People Every Day

ALI SMITH

'I'm sorry son but there's no one of that name lives here.'

The man hung up, stood in the phone box and breathed out slowly. Without warning London surrounded him, widening round him like rings in water with its scruffy paint-peeled shops, its streets leading into other insignificant streets, its anonymous houses for all the grey seeable distance. Someone rapped on the glass, a woman scowling from under her umbrella, and as he came out he saw people waiting in a line behind her. He crossed the road and stood outside a television shop with the sets in the windows showing one of the daytime programmes where two presenters and an expert discuss an issue and viewers phone in and talk about it. That was when he went inside the shop and within a few minutes had smashed several of the sets.

Now the man was driving too fast for his car, he could hear it rattling and straining under the tape of The Corries, the one tape that had been in the glove compartment when he looked. Above the noise there was a hum in his ears like when you wet your finger and run it round the rim of a glass. He thought that's what it had been like, like going into a room full of wine glasses. Nothing but wine glasses from one end of the floor to the other, imagine. As soon as you got into a room like that, he thought, the temptation to kick would be too strong. The same as when he was a boy and they visited the McGuinness's, when he was handed that china saucer and the cup with the fragile handle, with the lip of it so thin against his own that it would be really easy to bite through. As soon as a thought like that came into your head you wanted to try it. That ache in his arm to twitch suddenly and send the tea into the air. That would have made his folks laugh. They might have been cross to start with, but after that it'd have been something to remember.

He had stepped inside the TV shop to get out of the way of passers-by. Sleek new televisions were ranged in front of him, small ones on the top shelf, larger ones in the middle, massive wide-screen sets on the floor on metal stands. All except two were showing the same picture and the sound was turned up on one; he heard the presenter hurrying a caller off the air so as to bring the next person on. The woman he was hurrying had apparently just told them about a wasting disease her daughter aged nineteen had been diagnosed as having and the bespectacled expert, presumably a doctor giving advice, was shaking his head dolefully at the camera. The presenter said, 'Well thank you for that call Yvonne, we hope we've brought a little bit of comfort to you on that, and your daughter too, but now let's go over to Tom who's calling from Coventry, I believe he's just heard he's been found HIV positive, am I right, Tom?' The maps on the screens flashed where Coventry was.

The man leaned forward and tipped the television in front of him off its shelf; it crashed on to the top of the television below it. Its screen fragmented and there was a small explosion as all the sets in the shop went blank. In the time it took the young woman serving another man in the video section to get to the door of the shop, he had launched a portable cassette radio through the screen of another set and sent a line of small televisions chained together hurtling one after the other simply by nudging the first.

'I'm sorry, it couldn't be helped,' was what the man said. The woman told her boss Mr Brewer this, and that before she had a chance to call for help or anything he was off and because she was so shocked she didn't see which way. What the woman didn't tell

Mr Brewer was that actually the man had stood in the debris before he left and had slowly and carefully written down an address and a telephone number on one of the price display cards as he apologized. She had the piece of card folded in her back pocket and could feel it pressing against her as she spoke to Mr Brewer. Maybe the man hadn't given her his real address. That was something she didn't want to know. Maybe he had, though. That was what she didn't want Mr Brewer to know.

Side Two of The Corries ended again and the machine switched automatically back over to Side One. The last sign had flashed past before he'd had a chance to see where he was. In the middle years of his life, in the middle of a dark wood. He couldn't remember what that was from. In the middle lane of the motorway in the middle of the night. In a service station in the middle of nowhere in the middle of a cigarette. He held his coffee and stared out into the dark. He ought to phone his wife, they'd maybe be frantic. Or perhaps he could try the number again. There were three payphones by the exit. Think about just picking up the receiver, putting the coin in, pressing the number he knew the shape of like he knew the shape of his own hands, the telephone ringing there in the dark. But look at the time, he didn't want to wake anybody, that wouldn't do, and so he drained his coffee and headed back to the car.

At first light the road was so full of steep drops and sudden lifts that it was like being at sea; he had to travel most of it in second gear. It was light enough to read the word Scotland on the big rock as he passed. The Corries snapped near Pitlochry in the middle of the Skye Boat Song. Since Scotland is only a few hours long, it was about ten when he tried the number again, this time from a call box in sight of the house.

He lifted the receiver and pressed the numbers, he closed his eyes tightly and opened them again to try to get rid of the dizzy feeling. The garden, the walls, the door. The tree, much bigger. The lawn, the hedge. The next door. The whole block. The sky above it. The bus-shelter, the grass where the bus-shelter met the concrete, the little cracks in the edges of the kerb, different, the same. The same, but new houses had been built at the back where the field had been.

The windows of the new houses, with their different kinds and colours of curtains. Even before the phone was answered, he knew.

'No, I'm sorry. Look, is it not you that's phoned a few times already? I'm sorry, I can't help you there son. There's nobody of that name here.'

'I know,' he said. 'I won't call again. I'm really sorry to have bothered you. I'm just being stupid.'

After that it was random. Soon he was coasting the wet green carsick roads of the north; a little later he saw that the petrol he had bought in Edinburgh was almost gone. His car eventually ground to a halt on a gravelly back-road next to a small loch. The man wound down the window and as the sound of his car in his ears died away he heard water and birds. He opened the door and stood up. Further down the beach a child was crouched like a frog on the stones, her hair hanging; behind her was a big white-painted house converted into a roadside restaurant, closed for the season. A pock-marked sign on the roof of the house said HIELAN HAME, underneath in smaller letters BURGERS BAR-B-Q TRADITIONAL SCOTTISH FARE LICENSED. Behind this a mass of trees, behind them in the distance two mountains still with snow on the peaks, then the sky, empty.

The man walked across the stones and stood in the litter at the edge of the water. The car door hung open behind him, and the engine clicked as it cooled down. A bird sang in the grey air. Water seeped cold over the sides of his shoes.

It was the Easter holidays and the girl was out on the stones looking for insects or good skimmers. Sometimes if you turned a big stone over you could find slaters underneath, it depended how close to the water it was. The real name for slaters was woodlice. The girl had decided to collect insects for various experiments. She wanted to try racing them, she also wanted to try putting different kinds in a tupperware box together and to see which kinds survived when you left them in water. Last summer she had discovered tiny tunnels in the back garden and she had followed one to an ant colony in the manure heap. To see what would happen she had poured

Domestos from the kitchen cupboard on to it. First a white scum had come and some ants had writhed in it, taking a long time to die. The others had gone mad, running in all directions, some carrying white egg-looking things bigger than themselves. They had set up another colony on the other side of the heap and for days she had watched them cleaning out their old place, lines of ants carrying the dead bodies away and leaving them in neat piles under one of the rose-bushes. She was very sorry she had done that thing. This year she was going to be more scientific but kind as well, except to wasps. If they were stupid enough to go in the jam-jars and drown it was their own fault.

Here was a good flat stone. As she stood up to see how many skims it would have she saw the man who had left his car in the middle of the road walking into the loch. He sat down in the water about ten feet out. Then his top half fell backwards and he disappeared.

She ran along the bay to look for him; she heard a splash some-where behind her and turned round. The man was sitting up in the water again. He looked about the same age as her uncle, and she watched him take some things out of his pocket and fiddle about with them. As she got closer she saw he was trying to light a wet cigarette.

'Mister, excuse me,' she said, 'but your car's in the middle of the road, people can't get by.'

The man shook his hand away from himself so he wouldn't drip water down on to a match.

'Excuse me Mister, but is it not a bit cold, the water? Anyway your matches are soaking – my mother's got a lighter. I know where it's kept.'

The man looked embarrassed. He pulled himself to his feet unsteadily and wiped his hair back off his face, then stumbled back through the shallows. The girl watched the water running off him. She didn't know whether to call him Mister or Sir.

'Are you drunk, Sir?'

'No, I'm not drunk,' the man said smiling. Water from his clothes darkened the stones. 'How old are you then?' he asked.

The girl kept her distance. 'I'm nine,' she said. 'My mother says I'm not to talk to strangers.'

'Your mother's quite right. I've got a daughter your age. Her name's Fiona,' the man said, looking at his feet and shivering.

'I told you it was cold,' said the girl. She twisted round to skim her stone.

'I could show you how to skim stones,' said the man.

'I know how to skim stones,' the girl said, giving him her most scornful look. She expertly pitched the stone against the surface of the loch. The man scrabbled about at his feet to find himself a good stone and she stepped out of the range of the drips that flew off him when he threw.

'Not as good as you,' said the man. 'You're an expert right enough.'

'That's because I do it every day,' said the girl so the man wouldn't feel too bad. 'I live here, so I can. Are you on holiday here? Where do you live?' she asked.

The man went a funny colour. Then he said, 'Well when I was your age I used to live not far from here.'

'You don't sound very Scottish,' said the girl.

'That's because I've lived in London for a long time,' said the man.

The girl said she'd like to live in London, she'd been there once and seen all the places they show you on TV. When she grew up, she wanted to work for TV, maybe on programmes about animals. Then she asked the man did he know that Terry Wogan owned all those trees over there.

'Does he?' said the man.

Yes, and a Japanese man whose name she couldn't remember owned the land over there behind the loch.

'Who owns the loch?' the man asked.

'Me, I do,' said the girl. 'And my father owns the house and my mother runs the restaurant. Are you redundant? My uncle was made redundant.'

The man told the girl that no, he wasn't redundant and that, believe it or not, he worked for television. Had she ever heard of the programme called The Unthinkable Happens to People Every Day? The girl said she thought her mother watched it. Then she said suspiciously, 'I don't recognize you from off the TV.'

'No,' said the man, 'I'm not *on* the TV. I work in the background. I do things like phone up the people who write to us and ask them to come on the show to talk about the unthinkable thing that's happened to them. Then I add up how much it'll cost for them to come, and decide how long they'll get to talk about it.'

The girl had grown respectful and faintly excited about talking to someone who might work for TV. She couldn't tell whether the water running down the man's face was from his eyes or his hair. He looked very sad and she suddenly felt sorry for him even though he wasn't actually redundant. She decided to do something about it.

'Would you like to come up on to the roof?' she asked the man.

'Would I what?' he said.

'Would you like to come up on to the roof and throw some stones? I know this really easy way to get up there,' said the girl.

The man filled his wet jacket pockets with stones the girl selected. She showed him, springing up lightly, how to climb from the coalshed roof on to the extension. From there the man could heave himself after her up the drainpipe.

'You have to be very quiet or my mother'll hear,' said the girl. 'It's a wonderful view even on a day like today, isn't it?'

'Yes,' the man whispered.

The girl pointed at the HIELAN HAME sign twenty feet away. She was obviously a good shot; the paint had been chipped in hundreds of small dents.

'It's two points for big letters and five points for small ones. There's a special bonus if you can hit the c of Scottish,' she said. 'But *your* arms are probably long enough so that you could even reach the loch from here if you wanted,' she added hopefully.

'Right,' said the man. Taking a stone as big as his palm, he hurled it. They watched it soar in silence, then there was a distant splash as it hit the water.

'Yes!' cried the girl. 'Yes! You did it! Nobody's ever done that before. Nobody ever reached the loch before.' She jumped up and down. The man looked surprised and then very pleased.

'Anne-Marie!' called her mother at the thumping. 'Anne-Marie, I've *told* you about that roof. Now get down here. If you're at that sign again you'll feel the back of my hand.'

The girl led the man down off the roof, watching that he put his feet in all the right places. Her mother, angry at first at a stranger being up on her roof, was soon amazed and delighted to meet someone who worked on The Unthinkable Happens to People Every Day. She made him tea and a salad, apologizing for the fact that the restaurant was closed and there wasn't anything grander, and she dried his suit off for him. He told her that he was sort of a local boy really, but that he'd lived in England for a while. She said she could spot it in his accent. Had he been up visiting his parents, then? No, they were both dead, both some years ago now. He'd been up for a drive and to look at the place again. She asked him how he'd got wet. He said he'd fallen into the loch. He filled his car from a tank of petrol in the garage and before he left he promised the girl that he'd get the autographs of some famous children's TV presenters for her when he got back to work.

Some weeks later a packet arrived addressed to the Hielan Hame. Inside was a thank you letter for the girl's mother and several photographs of celebrities all signed 'To Ann Marie with best wishes.' The girl took them to school and showed them to all her friends. She didn't even mind that they'd spelled her name wrong.

'These are from the man who hit the loch,' she told her friends. 'He works for the TV and he's been up on our roof.'

Tuataras

BARBARA ANDERSON

They fascinated him, the hatching tuataras. Inch-long dragons pecking their way to a wider world. Shells are expected to enclose endearing and vulnerable balls of yellow, grey, or black fluff, but these were different. Leathery, wrinkled like dirty white gloves, the discarded ones resembled something unattractive and crumpled in the bottom of a laundry basket. Each shell had a number written on it with a felt pen. Charles Renshawe opened the inner glass door of the incubator and picked up 18 with care. The occupant had made little progress since his last inspection. The minuscule eyes stared, their sudden blink as startling as a wink from a blank face. They peered at him above a jagged rim, the body still completely enclosed.

Charles despised anthropomorphism in any form. Dogs with parasols teetering on their hind legs, advertisements in which chimpanzees jabbered their delight at cups of tea, made him very angry. 'What happened to the Mesozoic reptiles?' he asked the head.

He replaced the egg quickly, closed the double doors of the incubator, then turned to watch the juveniles which had hatched during the last week.

They were housed in a display case the base of which was covered with a deep layer of dry compost. The tuatara-hatching project was the work of one of his brighter honours students and had been almost too successful. 'We'll have them coming out our ears soon,

Doctor,' said Mrs Blume, crooning and pecking at the department's computer in the back room.

Charles relit his pipe yet again and counted them. Still eleven. The juveniles were exact miniatures of the adult forms except that they had no upstanding spines along the midline of their backs. Three of them had red dots between their eyes, the identification system of another student's research. This too pleased Charles. Class distinction among the archaic reptiles.

You hardly ever saw them moving. Their immobility was one of the things which fascinated him. He stared at one which was standing on three legs, willing it to ground the fragment of claw. He thought of the toads he had seen on an overnight stop in Guam on his way to present a paper at a Royal Society conference in Tokyo. They had appeared from this tropical dark, dozens of them, to squat motionless on the floodlit concrete path beneath his host's window. Suddenly one would move. Hop. Hop hop hop. Hop. Hop hop. Then resume its rock-like squat, immobile as a pro-grammed chess piece between moves.

Charles glanced at his watch. He had had his five minutes. He gave a faint sigh, turned off the light and returned through Mrs Blume's office to his own shambles. He sat at the desk which was submerged beneath piles of examination papers and resumed his marking. He worked steadily for an hour, ballpoint in hand, ticking, marking, deciding.

His laugh crashed through the silence of the still building, an explosion of pleasure as he rocked back in his chair. He had used the metaphor 'a dishcover of membrane bones' in an unfortunate attempt at clarification in a second-year lecture. He remembered standing in front of a hundred faces, the Asians and their tape recorders intent in the front rows, the rest a haze, a sea of uninterest. Every one of the papers already marked had chanted back the inane phrase. This candidate wrote with authority about a dishcloth of membrane bones. Charles read on, his heart sinking. You would think they would pick up something. At least have a glimmer. Hopeless. Hopeless.

At two a.m. he gave up. He stretched his arms above his head in capitulation, yawned wide as the goodnight kiwi, marched out of the mess and locked the door.

He lay very still when he woke next morning, then shut his eyes again quickly. Marking, he thought. That's all. Marking. Then he remembered. Last night had been bad. Very bad. So bad that he had picked up the pile of papers and retreated to his office at the University leaving Rhona red-faced and outraged at the table, abandoned among the chop bones and wilting salad. Charles heaved himself up in the bed. His thin hair stood up from his head in a caricature of fright, his myopic eyes searched with his groping fingers for the spectacles on the bedside table. No sound. Rhona must have finished in the bathroom. Her knuckles tapped against his door. 'Out,' said his sister, stumping back along the passage to her room.

She was still a good-looking woman. Her fine papery skin lay virtually unlined across the 'good bones' of her face. Her grey hair was puffed and gentle about her face except when Ashley did it too tight. 'Don't worry,' Charles said. 'It'll grow out.' 'All very well for you,' replied Rhona, her eyes snapping. And of course it was all very well for him, it had no effect whatsoever, even if she had had it dyed purple as she'd once threatened to do.

Rhona had been the toast of the town when towns still had toasts. She had appeared frequently among the photographs on the Social Page of slim girls 'escorted' by haunted-looking young men with jug ears. Her face, even in the smudged print, was flawless, her eyes large, the corners of her mouth curving upwards with pleasure. And she was friendly too, and generous. Often she would hiss at one of the young men hovering around her, Go on, go and dance with Leonie. She's been there all night. And the youth would retreat and return to be rewarded by a smile, that smile.

As the years passed the lesser toasts married, their nuptial photographs splashing through the pages of *The Free Lance*. 'Broad acres united,' sang the caption beneath the bucolic groom and the hysterical-looking girl clinging to his arm. 'Titian bride' followed 'Twins unite in double ceremony,' and still Rhona was unmarried. Nobody could understand it.

Charles was not interested. He was grateful to his sister for being a success and thus freeing him from responsibilities often hissed upon other young men. 'And look after your sister. Especially the Supper Waltz.' He flatly refused to go to dances. Mrs Renshawe, a strong-minded woman, threatened, cajoled, pleaded. Charles wore her down. 'I am not going to the Combined Dance.' 'I am not going to the Leavers' Dance.' 'I am not going.' Endless scraps of paper bearing such messages haunted Mrs Renshawe in the ball season. They greeted her from every box, container, drawer. They confronted her as she reached for an ivory tip, fluttered from the inside of her rolled napkin, lay beneath the knives in the knife drawer, even, she found once with a slight shock, fell from inside the toilet roll. Defeated, Mrs Renshawe decided that Charles would be better copy as an embryo intellectual. And he was a boy.

Charles fulfilled his mother's predictions. A good student, his interest in Zoology was quickened in the sixth form by one of the few effective teachers left behind during the war. Mr Beson was 4F, unfit for active service. He taught science, taught it well, and Charles was hooked. He enrolled at Otago as soon as he left school and majored in Chemistry and Zoology before going Overseas for postgraduate study.

It never occurred to Charles not to go home from Dunedin each holiday. He was quite happy in Hobson Street. He was quite happy anywhere. And besides, he knew he was not staying. He drove his mother about the town, opened the door of the Buick for her as he had been instructed since childhood, stowed her parcels with care, smiled at her when she had finished her shopping and asked with a professional backwards chuck of his head, 'Home, Mum?' He accompanied his father to the Club occasionally, but not often. He stood around politely as his father played snooker in the Billiard Room with Neville Frensham, and the light glinted on the bottles in the bar and the tension heightened and Charles thought what a balls-aching waste of time it all was.

Neville Frensham was a stockbroker in the same firm as his father. Younger, but not a great deal. He and Mr Renshawe walked home together after work and his father often asked Frensham in for a drink. Charles remembered the man, relaxed, at his ease in a large chair, the evening sunlight falling on the hand which held a full glass, a 'mixed trough' of dahlias and Michaelmas daisies on the mantelpiece above him. Mrs Renshawe sat smiling at him from a smaller chair. She liked large, decisive men with firm handshakes. Charles and his father sat on the padded window seat with cushions at their backs. Rhona, calm, still, beautiful, was perched on the edge of a spindly unpadded thing. She proffered nuts while Charles poured the drinks, the women's gin and tonics in small cut glasses, the men's whiskies in things twice the size; strong, hefty containers you could get a grip on. He saw Mr Frensham shake his head in rejection at the nuts. He patted his stomach, smiling up at Rhona.

'And do you know what he said?' he asked. Welcomed after toil, Mr Frensham was enjoying himself. Four pairs of eyes watched him, four faces were attentive. The saga concerned a friend of his son's, a lad about seventeen, to whom Mr Frensham had offered a whisky. He had then enquired about diluents. 'And do you know what he said? He asked for ginger ale!' exploded Mr Frensham. He rocked back in his flowery chair, a wary eye on his glass. 'I ask you!' Shock was registered. Excessive from Mr Renshawe, milder from his wife. None from Charles, who was refusing to play. His usual chameleon-like attribute of melding into any social décor seemed to have deserted him. He stared moodily into his beer. Rhona's smile blessed them all.

'Well you can imagine!' Mr Frensham gave a little kick with both feet in his excitement. 'I'll give you a whisky if you want one,' I said, 'but I'm damned if I'm going to let any callow youth ruin my hard-found whisky with lolly water. I told him! He got short shift from me.'

'Shrift,' said Charles.

The bristling bad-tempered eyebrows leapt at him.

'Pardon?'

'The word's shrift,' said Charles.

He always enjoyed seeing Rhona, who was now more beautiful than ever. Her pale skin seemed to be illuminated from within. He supposed her capillaries must lie close to the surface, but had the wit not to say so. They had the ease together of those who expect and require nothing from each other. She was still rather notably unmarried.

The next day they trailed upstairs after Sunday Lunch, Rhona in front, Charles two steps behind. She stopped and gripped the newel post on the landing.

'Charles,' she said.

'Yes,' he said, his eyes on her hand.

'Come along to my room for a minute.'

'OK.'

It was a pleasant room, low-ceilinged, a small window framed with flowered curtains. He watched the leaves blowing about on the striped lawn below them. His father appeared with the hand mower and began shaving the stripes. Charles pulled the curtain slightly to screen himself, and smiled at Rhona. She took no notice.

'Sit down,' she said, patting the bed beside her. The bedcover was the same flowered pattern of poppies, daisies and cornflowers. A pastoralist's nightmare, he thought, and opened his mouth to say so.

'Charles,' said Rhona.

'Yes?' He sat down beside her and crossed his legs. The bed tipped them towards each other. Charles moved slightly.

'Charles, I want to tell you something.'

'Yes,' said Charles.

She seemed remarkably agitated. She scrambled up onto the pillow and hugged her knees, wrapping the Liberty's skirt tight around them.

'Aren't you going to ask me what it is?' she demanded.

'You'll tell me,' he said.

'Oh!' The gasp was a rasping intake of air.

'I'm having an affair with Neville Frensham,' she said.

'Oh,' said Charles.

'Is that all you've got to say!' Her blues eyes seared him. His skin prickled.

'He's married isn't he?' said Charles miserably.

'Of course he's married, you clot. That's why it's an affair.'

An affair, thought Charles. Good heavens. And with that sod. He thought of that hand, that stomach.

'Why are you telling me?' he asked.

'God knows,' said Rhona, and burst into tears all over him.

She went Overseas soon afterwards. Charles was home when they farewelled her on the *Rangitoto*. They inspected the cabin she was to share with her friend Penelope, large, fair, a good sort. Rhona's side of the cabin was deep in flowers, hot spikes of gladioli were piled upon her bunk, the tiny inadequate shelves spilled over with pyramid-shaped 'arrangements' in posy bowls. Charles watched his sister's face as she read the card attached to a large bouquet of fleshy white orchids.

'Whoever sent those, dear?' said Mrs Renshawe.

'The girls from the office,' replied Rhona. Charles removed his spectacles, blew on them and wiped them with care. When they left the ship Rhona clung to him, sobbing, hiccoughing with the abandoned despair of a lost child. Mrs Renshawe was puzzled.

Rhona did various jobs in London. She was sacked from Harrods for suggesting to a customer who complained of the high price of the handkerchiefs that perhaps she should shop elsewhere. She trained at an exclusive interior design shop and developed the languid hauteur required. She was hardworking, used her initiative, and they enjoyed her slightly flattened vowels. She lived with English girls which pleased her mother. 'What is the point,' Mrs Renshawe asked her friend Rita, 'of going twelve thousand miles across the world to flat with Penelope Parsons?'

Rhona wrote cheerful letters home which told nothing. Charles read them and was glad she was happy. They exchanged postcards. He collected all the interesting ones, the bottle at Paeroa, the floral clock at Napier, diners with their mouths open stuffing food at the Hermitage. Rhona replied with reproductions of naked male sculptures from the Louvre, the Uffizi, wherever. 'Wish you were here.' Charles liked her.

She came home occasionally. She was now elegant as well as beautiful. She was invited to meals with all her married friends and played on floors with her many godchildren to whom she gave expensive English-type presents. Corals, for example, for the little girls to wear with their party frocks. Large Dinky Toy milk floats and rubbish collection vans which the little boys did not recognize, and which had to be explained and demonstrated by Rhona from England.

She came home when their father died, and two years later when they moved Mrs Renshawe into a home. 'I'm not coming home to look after her,' she said, glaring at Charles. 'Good God, no,' he answered. 'And you can't can you?' 'No,' said Charles. He had done his best but fortunately it was not enough.

Charles stayed on, rattling around in the Hobson Street house where he had lived since he returned to take up his appointment in Wellington. He gardened, he visited his mother, he invited people for meals. 'Anyone who can read can cook,' he said, though the hard part was having it all ready at the same countdown. He enjoyed his work and was good at it. He was glad his mother had given up on grandchildren.

He and Rhona never discussed Neville Frensham. He wondered whether to tell her when he died, but did nothing. Someone else would and anyway it was forty years ago. Good God.

He was astounded when Rhona's letter arrived. 'I am returning to New Zealand. Presumably it's all right by you if I come to Hobson Street. Mother can't last much longer and I should be there. Anyway, I want to come home. Very odd. Obviously I'll take over the cooking etc. It might be rather fun. Two of us bumbling towards extinction together. Much love, Rhona.'

Charles thought hard, his mind scurrying for solutions. He thought of cabling 'Don't come. Have made alternative arrangements.' Or just plain 'No. Don't.' But how could he? Under the terms of their father's will she had an equal share in the house. And anyway, how could he?

★

She came. She stayed. She moved into their mother's bedroom, a large room with a fireplace in one corner, a dressing table on which Mrs Renshawe's silver brushes still sat, a high bed covered with a crocheted bedspread and a long box thing covered in flowered cretonne. When he carried Rhona's suitcases up she had touched the box with the tip of her small pointed shoe. 'Good God,' she said 'the ottoman. What on earth would *Zaharis Interior Design* say?' She flung her squashy leather bag on the bed and flopped down beside it. She stared up at Charles with something like panic. He was puffing slightly. 'Mr Parkin begged me,' she said. 'They didn't want me to leave, you know.' Then why the hell did you, thought Charles, disliking himself. He put an arm around the padded shoulder of her Italian knit and pressed slightly. She buried her fluffy grey head against his jacket for a moment and sniffed.

'Oh well,' she said standing up, silver bangles jangling. 'Is there any sherry?'

But things got worse. He could have told her. He should have told her.

Charles stumped down the stairs, his right hand touching the wall lightly at intervals in a gesture imitated by his students. He turned left through the hall and padded into the kitchen. Rhona was sitting at the table with her back to the sun in the chair in which he had always sat, reading the paper.

'Good morning,' said Charles.

'Hullo.' She didn't look up.

He lifted the small blue and white striped teapot from the bench. 'Old or new?' he said. She glanced up briefly. 'Old,' she said. Charles opened the window and emptied the teapot onto the rose beneath. He pressed down the red flag of the Russell Hobbs kettle. A plastic bag, its contents weeping and bloody, lay beside it. Charles poked it.

'What's this?'

She glanced up, frowning. 'What?'

He poked again. 'This.'

'Plums,' said Rhona.

'Ah.'

Charles made tea, poured himself a cup and pulled out a chair which raked loudly on the faded green vinyl. A blackbird sang, defining its territory. He glanced out across the sunlit lawn. There it was as usual, singing its proprietorial heart out from the spindly kauri in the next-door garden. Charles sat down and helped himself to cornflakes, refolding Rhona's open packet of muesli and placing it on the bench. 'Which is the whole milk?' he asked. Head down, still reading, Rhona handed him a jug embellished with the crowned image of George VI. She had finished her breakfast and was smoking the first of her day's cigarettes. She was a tidy smoker, meticulous in the removal of butts, the emptying of ashtrays. Unlike Charles whose pipe dottle and matchstick-filled messes overflowed through-out the house. He poured milk onto the cereal and attacked the mush with quick scooping movements of his spoon, herding it into his mouth. He bonged a striped cotton napkin at his face and reached for the toast.

'Any chance of a piece of the paper?' he asked.

Rhona swung into action, slapping and tugging at the paper as though it was putting up enormous resistance. Still clutching the overseas news page she handed a crumpled heap to Charles.

'Thank you,' said Charles, smoothing and refolding the thing. They read in bristling silence for a while.

'I heard on the radio that Lange's not going to Paris,' he said, raising a tentative flag of truce.

It was shot to ribbons. 'Would you,' snapped Rhona, 'in the circumstances?'

'Perhaps not,' said Charles.

Rhona snorted, flicking her ash into the small brass ashtray with a quick decisive tap. She finished the cigarette and ground the glowing butt into extinction, then heaved herself up against the unstable plastic table. It rocked, slopping milky tea into Charles' saucer. She emptied the ashtray into the Pelican bag beneath the sink and reclosed the door. She remained planted in front of the sink, a strong white arm clasping the stained blue formica either side of her. Charles, from the corner of his eye, saw her put her head in her hands. Oh God, he thought dully. A miasma of dread enclosed him, paralysing action, thought, threatening his very existence as a civilized thinking being.

He made an enormous effort. 'What's the matter, Rhona?' he said.

Rhona swung around, her pearls about her plump neck, her hands clasped in agony. 'It's so bloody *awful* here,' she said.

Charles glared at her. Who was she to stand in his familiar old-fashioned kitchen, to breathe its slightly gas-scented air and mouth such antediluvian, anti-colonial crap?

'Are you pining for dear dirty old London?' he asked.

Rhona's eyes blinked with surprise. Charles was surprised himself.

'Yes,' snapped Rhona. 'Yes, I am.'

Charles felt rage thickening in his throat. Stronger even than his interest in the Comparative Anatomy of Vertebrates was his feeling for the land forms, the fauna and flora of the country where he grew up. When he had been a postgraduate student in England many of his New Zealand contemporaries had worked and schemed for the glittering prizes of Overseas Appointments. Charles, more able than most, had regarded these men (there were no women) as unusual genetic aberrations who could not be blamed for their imperfections. He knew he was going home and did so.

'And you're so *boring!*' continued Rhona, angrily banging her wrists in search of her handkerchief.

Charles breathed out, a liberating puff of relief. 'I've always been boring,' he said.

Rhona slammed back to the table and crashed her behind onto the unstable silly little chair opposite him.

'Don't you care?' she demanded.

'Not in the slightest,' said Charles.

She thumped the table with her closed fist.

'And I suppose you're proud of that! Proud of your Intellectual Honesty!' she cried. Her face, usually a pleasant sight, was mottled, despairing, damp.

'I don't bore me,' said Charles mildly.

To his horror, just when Charles thought he had cushioned the trauma, siphoned off the excess, set things on an even keel again, Rhona, for only the third time in his experience, burst into tears.

'You're only half a . . .' She gasped. 'Only half *there*!'

She disintegrated before him. She laid her rounded arms on the plastic table and howled like a – like a what? Charles had never seen anything like it in his life. He stared at her. What should he do? Slap her? God forbid. Ice? Wet towels? He slipped sideways from his skittery little chair and tiptoed from the kitchen.

He felt bad about it. Very bad. Twice in twenty-four hours he had abandoned a suffering human being. Charles was not an uncaring man. He gave to things. Not only to any conservation scheme however bizarre or impractical, but also to humanity. His donations to the City Mission had been regular and substantial. They had asked him to join the Board but he had declined owing to pressure of work. They quite understood.

He felt miserable all day. He chaired a Scholarship Board meeting with firm detachment. He continued with his marking, refusing as always to count how many papers remained unmarked. He lunched in the Staff Cafeteria, sitting with his salami and tomato roll, staring across the tossing windblown harbour a thousand miles away. He exchanged pleasantries with Mrs Blume who was suffering from a completely unjustified excess of work, but there you were.

He had not visited the tuataras all day. He finished his last second-year paper and leaned back, reaching out a spatulate-fingered hand for the striped tobacco pouch on his desk. He tamped the tobacco into his Lovat Saddle pipe with a nicotine-stained forefinger, wiped the finger on the carpet, and lit up, puffing his pipe with the catharsis of release. After a few minutes he pushed his chair back and ambled out of his office, through Mrs Blume's room into the small laboratory which housed the tuataras.

His fingers quivered as he opened the inner glass door of the incubator. He had timed it well. Before him the tuatara which last night had been a shell, a half head with eyes, climbed out from the remnants of its shell. With a backwards flick of its fragmentary left rear leg it tossed the shell aside. The movement reminded Charles of a stripper in a Soho dive thirty years ago as she kicked aside the irrelevant sloughed-off garments beneath her feet. Charles clutched the sides of the incubator. He felt weak with pleasure. Infinitely tender he picked the newly hatched tuatara up from the incubator and enrolled it among its associates in the compost. It did nothing. It just squatted there, planted on its four angled legs, occasionally moving its head very slowly to one side or the other. Charles picked up a piece of waste paper from the bench on which the incubator stood, pulled out his ballpoint and wrote, 'Have removed No. 18 (contents of) from incubator. In display case. C.R.' He slipped the note into the incubator door as he closed it.

He stood back. A transfusion of happiness flowed through him. He had thought of something. He hurried back to his office, giving Mrs Blume no more than a perfunctory nod. He would do something. Show his concern, his love almost. He reached for the telephone and dialled his home number. 'Rhona,' he said into the quacking receiver. 'Would you like to see the juvenile tuataras? The babies?'

Silver Water

AMY BLOOM

My sister's voice was like mountain water in a silver pitcher; the clear blue beauty of it cools you and lifts you up beyond your heat, beyond your body. After we went to see *La Traviata*, when she was fourteen and I was twelve, she elbowed me in the parking lot and said, 'Check this out.' And she opened her mouth unnaturally wide and her voice came out, so crystalline and bright that all the departing operagoers stood frozen by their cars, unable to take out their keys or open their doors until she had finished, and then they cheered like hell.

That's what I like to remember, and that's the story I told to all of her therapists. I wanted them to know her, to know that who they saw was not all there was to see. That before her constant tinkling of commercials and fast-food jingles there had been Puccini and Mozart and hymns so sweet and mighty you expected Jesus to come down off his cross and clap. That before there was a mountain of Thorazined fat, swaying down the halls in nylon maternity tops and sweatpants, there had been the prettiest girl in Arrandale Elementary School, the belle of Landmark Junior High. Maybe there were other pretty girls, but I didn't see them. To me, Rose, my beautiful blonde defender, my guide to Tampax and my mother's moods, was perfect.

She had her first psychotic break when she was fifteen. She had been coming home moody and tearful, then quietly beaming, then she stopped coming home. She would go out into the woods behind our house and not come in until my mother went after her at dusk, and stepped gently into the briars and saplings and pulled her out, blank-faced, her pale blue sweater covered with crumbled leaves, her white jeans smeared with dirt. After three weeks of this, my mother, who is a musician and widely regarded as eccentric, said to my father, who is a psychiatrist and a kind, sad man, 'She's going off.'

'What is that, your professional opinion?' He picked up the newspaper and put it down again, sighing. 'I'm sorry, I didn't mean to snap at you. I know something's bothering her. Have you talked to her?'

'What's there to say? David, she's going crazy. She doesn't need a heart-to-heart talk with Mom, she needs a hospital.'

They went back and forth, and my father sat down with Rose for a few hours, and she sat there licking the hairs on her forearm, first one way, then the other. My mother stood in the hallway, dry-eyed and pale, watching the two of them. She had already packed, and when three of my father's friends dropped by to offer free consultations and recommendations, my mother and Rose's suitcase were already in the car. My mother hugged me and told me that they would be back that night, but not with Rose. She also said, divining my worst fear, 'It won't happen to you, honey. Some people go crazy and some people never do. You never will.' She smiled and stroked my hair. 'Not even when you want to.'

Rose was in hospitals, great and small, for the next ten years. She had lots of terrible therapists and a few good ones. One place had no pictures on the walls, no windows, and the patients all wore slippers with the hospital crest on them. My mother didn't even bother to go to Admissions. She turned Rose around and the two of them marched out, my father walking behind them, apologizing to his colleagues. My mother ignored the psychiatrists, the social workers, and the nurses, and played Handel and Bessie Smith for the patients on whatever was available. At some places, she had a Steinway donated by a grateful, or optimistic, family; at others, she banged out 'Gimme a Pigfoot and a Bottle of Beer' on an old, scarred box that hadn't been tuned since there'd been English-speaking physicians on the grounds. My father talked in serious, appreciative tones to the administrators and unit chiefs and tried to be friendly with whoever was managing Rose's case. We all hated the family therapists.

The worst family therapist we ever had sat in a pale green room with us, visibly taking stock of my mother's ethereal beauty and her faded blue T-shirt and girl-sized jeans, my father's rumpled suit and stained tie, and my own unreadable seventeen-year-old fashion statement. Rose was beyond fashion that year, in one of her dancing teddybear smocks and extra-extra-large Celtics sweatpants. Mr Walker read Rose's file in front of us and then watched in alarm as Rose began crooning, beautifully, and slowly massaging her breasts. My mother and I laughed, and even my father started to smile. This was Rose's usual opening salvo for new therapists.

Mr Walker said, 'I wonder why it is that everyone is so entertained by Rose behaving inappropriately.'

Rose burped, and then we all laughed. This was the seventh family therapist we had seen, and none of them had lasted very long. Mr Walker, unfortunately, was determined to do right by us.

'What do you think of Rose's behavior, Violet?' They did this sometimes. In their manual it must say, If you think the parents are too weird, try talking to the sister.

'I don't know. Maybe she's trying to get you to stop talking about her in the third person.'

'Nicely put,' my mother said.

'Indeed,' my father said.

'Fuckin' A,' Rose said.

'Well, this is something that the whole family agrees upon,' Mr Walker said, trying to act as if he understood or even liked us.

'That was not a successful intervention, Ferret Face.' Rose tended to function better when she was angry. He did look like a blond ferret, and we all laughed again. Even my father, who tried to give these people a chance, out of some sense of collegiality, had given it up.

After fourteen minutes, Mr Walker decided that our time was

up and walked out, leaving us grinning at each other. Rose was still nuts, but at least we'd all had a little fun.

The day we met our best family therapist started out almost as badly. We scared off a resident and then scared off her supervisor, who sent us Dr Thorne. Three hundred pounds of Texas chili, combread, and Lone Star beer, finished off with big black cowboy boots and a small string tie around the area of his neck.

'O frabjous day, it's Big Nut.' Rose was in heaven and stopped massaging her breasts immediately.

'Hey, Little Nut.' You have to understand how big a man would have to be to call my sister 'little'. He christened us all, right away. 'And it's the good Doctor Nut, and Madame Hickory Nut, 'cause they are the hardest damn' nuts to crack, and over here in the overalls and not much else is No One's Nut' – a name that summed up both my sanity and my loneliness. We all relaxed.

Dr Thorne was good for us. Rose moved into a halfway house whose director loved Big Nut so much that she kept Rose even when Rose went through a period of having sex with everyone who passed her door. She was in a fever for a while, trying to still the voices by fucking her brains out.

Big Nut said, 'Darlin', I can't. I cannot make love to every beautiful woman I meet, and furthermore, I can't do that and be your therapist too. It's a great shame, but I think you might be able to find a really nice guy, someone who treats you just as sweet and kind as I would if I were lucky enough to be your beau. I don't want you to settle for less.' And she stopped propositioning the crack addicts and the alcoholics and the guys at the shelter. We loved Dr Thorne.

My father went back to seeing rich neurotics and helped out one day a week at Dr Thorne's Walk-In Clinic. My mother finished a recording of Mozart concerti and played at fund-raisers for Rose's halfway house. I went back to college and found a wonderful linebacker from Texas to sleep with. In the dark, I would make him call me 'darlin''. Rose took her meds, lost about fifty pounds, and began singing at the A.M.E. Zion Church, down the street from the halfway house.

At first they didn't know what to do with this big blonde lady, dressed funny and hovering wistfully in the doorway during their rehearsals, but she gave them a few bars of 'Precious Lord' and the choir director felt God's hand and saw that with the help of His sweet child Rose, the Prospect Street Choir was going all the way to the Gospel Olympics.

Amidst a sea of beige, umber, cinnamon, and espresso faces, there was Rose, bigger, blonder, and pinker than any two white women could be. And Rose and the choir's contralto, Addie Robicheaux, laid out their gold and silver voices and wove them together in strands as fine as silk, as strong as steel. And we wept as Rose and Addie, in their billowing garnet robes, swayed together, clasping hands until the last perfect note floated up to God, and then they smiled down at us.

Rose would still go off from time to time and the voices would tell her to do bad things, but Dr Thorne or Addie or my mother could usually bring her back. After five good years, Big Nut died. Stuffing his face with a chili dog, sitting in his unair-conditioned office in the middle of July, he had one big, Texas-sized aneurysm and died.

Rose held on tight for seven days; she took her meds, went to choir practice, and rearranged her room about a hundred times. His funeral was like a Lourdes for the mentally ill. If you were psychotic, borderline, bad-off neurotic, or just very hard to get along with, you were there. People shaking so bad from years of heavy meds that they fell out of the pews. People holding hands, crying, moaning, talking to themselves. The crazy people and the not-so-crazy people were all huddled together, like puppies at the pound.

Rose stopped taking her meds, and the halfway house wouldn't keep her after she pitched another patient down the stairs. My father called the insurance company and found out that Rose's new, improved psychiatric coverage wouldn't begin for forty-five days. I put all of her stuff in a garbage bag, and we walked out of the halfway house, Rose winking at the poor drooling boy on the couch.

'This is going to be difficult – not all bad, but difficult – for the whole family, and I thought we should discuss everybody's expectations. I know I have some concerns.' My father had convened a family meeting as soon as Rose finished putting each one of her thirty stuffed bears in its own special place.

'No meds,' Rose said, her eyes lowered, her stubby fingers, those fingers that had braided my hair and painted tulips on my cheeks, pulling hard on the hem of her dirty smock.

My father looked in despair at my mother.

'Rosie, do you want to drive the new car?' my mother asked.

Rose's face lit up. 'I'd love to drive that car. I'd drive to California, I'd go see the bears at the San Diego Zoo. I would take you, Violet, but you always hated the zoo. Remember how she cried at the Bronx Zoo when she found out that the animals didn't get to go home at closing?' Rose put her damp hand on mine and squeezed it sympathetically. 'Poor Vi.'

'If you take your medication, after a while you'll be able to drive the car. That's the deal. Meds, car.' My mother sounded accommodating but unenthusiastic, careful not to heat up Rose's paranoia.

'You got yourself a deal, darlin'.'

I was living about an hour away then, teaching English during the day, writing poetry at night. I went home every few days for dinner. I called every night.

My father said, quietly, 'It's very hard. We're doing all right, I think. Rose has been walking in the mornings with your mother, and she watches a lot of TV. She won't go to the day hospital, and she won't go back to the choir. Her friend Mrs Robicheaux came by a couple of times. What a sweet woman. Rose wouldn't even talk to her. She just sat there, staring at the wall and humming. We're not doing all that well, actually, but I guess we're getting by. I'm sorry, sweetheart, I don't mean to depress you.'

My mother said, emphatically, 'We're doing fine. We've got our routine and we stick to it and we're fine. You don't need to come home so often, you know. Wait 'til Sunday, just come for the day. Lead your life, Vi. She's leading hers.'

I stayed away all week, afraid to pick up my phone, grateful to my mother for her harsh calm and her reticence, the qualities that had enraged me throughout my childhood.

I came on Sunday, in the early afternoon, to help my father garden, something we had always enjoyed together. We weeded and staked tomatoes and killed aphids while my mother and Rose were down at the lake. I didn't even go into the house until four, when I needed a glass of water.

Someone had broken the piano bench into five neatly stacked pieces and placed them where the piano bench usually was.

'We were having such a nice time, I couldn't bear to bring it up,' my father said, standing in the doorway, carefully keeping his gardening boots out of the kitchen.

'What did Mommy say?'

'She said, "Better the bench than the piano." And your sister lay down on the floor and just wept. Then your mother took her down to the lake. This can't go on, Vi. We have twenty-seven days left, your mother gets no sleep because Rose doesn't sleep, and if I could just pay twenty-seven thousand dollars to keep her in the hospital until the insurance takes over, I'd do it.'

'All right. Do it. Pay the money and take her back to Hartley-Rees. It was the prettiest place, and she liked the art therapy there.'

'I would if I could. The policy states that she must be symptom-free for at least forty-five days before her coverage begins. Symptom-free means no hospitalization.'

'Jesus, Daddy, how could you get that kind of policy? She hasn't been symptom-free for forty-five minutes.'

'It's the only one I could get for long-term psychiatric.' He put his hand over his mouth, to block whatever he was about to say, and went back out to the garden. I couldn't see if he was crying.

He stayed outside and I stayed inside until Rose and my mother came home from the lake. Rose's soggy sweatpants were rolled up to her knees, and she had a bucketful of shells and seaweed, which my mother persuaded her to leave on the back porch. My mother kissed me lightly and told Rose to go up to her room and change out of her wet pants.

Rose's eyes grew very wide. 'Never. I will never . . .' She knelt down and began banging her head on the kitchen floor with rhythmic intensity, throwing all her weight behind each attack. My mother put her arms around Rose's waist and tried to hold her back. Rose shook her off, not even looking around to see what was slowing her down. My mother lay up against the refrigerator.

'Violet, please . . .'

I threw myself onto the kitchen floor, becoming the spot that Rose was smacking her head against. She stopped a fraction of an inch short of my stomach.

'Oh, Vi, Mommy, I'm sorry. I'm sorry, don't hate me.' She staggered to her feet and ran wailing to her room.

My mother got up and washed her face brusquely, rubbing it dry with a dishcloth. My father heard the wailing and came running in, slipping his long bare feet out of his rubber boots.

'Galen, Galen, let me see.' He held her head and looked closely for bruises on her pale, small face. 'What happened?' My mother looked at me. 'Violet, what happened? Where's Rose?'

'Rose got upset, and when she went running upstairs she pushed Mommy out of the way.' I've only told three lies in my life, and that was my second.

'She must feel terrible, pushing you, of all people. It would have to be you, but I know she didn't want it to be.' He made my mother a cup of tea, and all the love he had for her, despite her silent rages and her vague stares, came pouring through the teapot, warming her cup, filling her small, long-fingered hands. She rested her head against his hip, and I looked away.

'Let's make dinner, then I'll call her. Or you call her, David, maybe she'd rather see your face first.'

Dinner was filled with all of our starts and stops and Rose's desperate efforts to control herself. She could barely eat and hummed the McDonald's theme song over and over again, pausing only to spill her juice down the front of her smock and begin weeping. My father looked at my mother and handed Rose his napkin. She dabbed at herself listlessly, but the tears stopped.

'I want to go to bed. I want to go to bed and be in my head. I want to go to bed and be in my bed and in my head and just wear red. For red is the color that my baby wore and once more, it's true, yes, it is, it's true. Please don't wear red tonight, oh, oh, please don't wear red tonight, for red is the color –'

'Okay, okay, Rose. It's okay. I'll go upstairs with you and you can get ready for bed. Then Mommy will come up and say good night too. It's okay, Rose.' My father reached out his hand and Rose grasped it, and they walked out of the dining-room together, his long arm around her middle.

My mother sat at the table for a moment, her face in her hands, and then she began clearing the plates. We cleared without talking, my mother humming Schubert's 'Schlummerlied', a lullaby about the woods and the river calling to the child to go to sleep. She sang it to us every night when we were small.

My father came into the kitchen and signaled to my mother. They went upstairs and came back down together a few minutes later.

'She's asleep,' they said, and we went to sit on the porch and listen to the crickets. I don't remember the rest of the evening, but I remember it as quietly sad, and I remember the rare sight of my parents holding hands, sitting on the picnic table, watching the sunset.

I woke up at three o'clock in the morning, feeling the cool night air through my sheet. I went down the hall for a blanket and looked into Rose's room, for no reason. She wasn't there. I put on my jeans and a sweater and went downstairs. I could feel her absence. I went outside and saw her wide, draggy footprints darkening the wet grass into the woods.

'Rosie,' I called, too softly, not wanting to wake my parents, not wanting to startle Rose. 'Rosie, it's me. Are you here? Are you all right?'

I almost fell over her. Huge and white in the moonlight, her flowered smock bleached in the light and shadow, her sweatpants now completely wet. Her head was flung back, her white, white neck exposed like a lost Greek column.

'Rosie, Rosie –' Her breathing was very slow, and her lips were not as pink as they usually were. Her eyelids fluttered.

'Closing time,' she whispered. I believe that's what she said.

I sat with her, uncovering the bottle of Seconal by her hand, and watched the stars fade.

When the stars were invisible and the sun was warming the air, I went back to the house. My mother was standing on the porch, wrapped in a blanket, watching me. Every step I took overwhelmed me; I could picture my mother slapping me, shooting me for letting her favorite die.

'Warrior queens,' she said, wrapping her thin strong arms around me. 'I raised warrior queens.' She kissed me fiercely and went into the woods by herself.

Later in the morning she woke my father, who could not go into the woods, and still later she called the police and the funeral parlor. She hung up the phone, lay down, and didn't get back out of bed until the day of the funeral. My father fed us both and called the people who needed to be called and picked out Rose's coffin by himself.

My mother played the piano and Addie sang her pure gold notes and I closed my eyes and saw my sister, fourteen years old, lion's mane thrown back and eyes tightly closed against the glare of the parking-lot lights. That sweet sound held us tight, flowing around us, eddying through our hearts, rising, still rising.

Walker Brothers Cowboy

ALICE MUNRO

After supper my father says, 'Want to go down and see if the Lake's still there?' We leave my mother sewing under the dining-room light, making clothes for me against the opening of school. She has ripped up for this purpose an old suit and an old plaid wool dress of hers, and she has to cut and match very cleverly and also make me stand and turn for endless fittings, sweaty, itching from the hot wool, ungrateful. We leave my brother in bed in the little screened porch at the end of the front veranda, and sometimes he kneels on his bed and presses his face against the screen and calls mournfully, 'Bring me an ice-cream cone!' but I call back, 'You will be asleep,' and do not even turn my head.

Then my father and I walk gradually down a long, shabby sort of street, with Silverwoods Ice Cream signs standing on the sidewalk, outside tiny, lighted stores. This is in Tuppertown, an old town on Lake Huron, an old grain port. The street is shaded, in some places, by maple trees whose roots have cracked and heaved the sidewalk and spread out like crocodiles into the bare yards. People are sitting out, men in shirtsleeves and undershirts and women in aprons – not people we know but if anybody looks ready to nod and say, 'Warm night,' my father will nod too and say something the same. Children are still playing. I don't know them either because my mother keeps my brother and me in our own yard, saying he is too young to leave it and I have to mind him. I am not so sad to watch their evening games because the games themselves are ragged, dissolving. Children, of their own will, draw apart, separate into islands of two or one under the heavy trees, occupying themselves in such solitary ways as I do all day, planting pebbles in the dirt or writing in it with a stick.

Presently we leave these yards and houses behind; we pass a factory with boarded-up windows, a lumberyard whose high wooden gates are locked for the night. Then the town falls away in a defeated jumble of sheds and small junkyards, the sidewalk gives up and we are walking on a sandy path with burdocks, plantains, humble nameless weeds all around. We enter a vacant lot, a kind of park really, for it is kept clear of junk and there is one bench with a slat missing on the back, a place to sit and look at the water. Which is generally gray in the evening, under a lightly overcast sky, no sunsets, the horizon dim. A very quiet, washing noise on the stones of the beach. Further along, towards the main part of town, there is a stretch of sand, a water slide, floats bobbing around the safe swimming area, a lifeguard's rickety throne. Also a long dark-green building, like a roofed veranda, called the Pavilion, full of farmers and their wives, in stiff good clothes, on Sundays. That is the part of the town we used to know when we lived at Dungannon and came here three or four times a summer, to the Lake. That, and the docks where we would go and look at the grain boats, ancient, rusty, wallowing, making us wonder how they got past the breakwater let alone to Fort William.

Tramps hang around the docks and occasionally on these evenings wander up the dwindling beach and climb the shifting, precarious path boys have made, hanging on to dry bushes, and say something to my father which, being frightened of tramps, I am too alarmed to catch. My father says he is a bit hard up himself. 'I'll roll you a cigarette if it's any use to you,' he says, and he shakes tobacco out carefully on one of the thin butterfly papers, flicks it with his tongue, seals it and hands it to the tramp, who takes it and walks away. My father also rolls and lights and smokes one cigarette of his own.

He tells me how the Great Lakes came to be. All where Lake Huron is now, he says, used to be flat land, a wide flat plain. Then came the ice, creeping down from the North, pushing deep into the low places. Like *that* – and he shows me his hand with his spread fingers pressing the rock-hard ground where we are sitting. His fingers make hardly any impression at all and he says, 'Well, the old ice cap had a lot more power behind it than this hand has.' And then the ice went back, shrank back towards the North Pole where it came from, and left its fingers of ice in the deep places it had gouged, and ice turned to lakes and there they were today. They were *new*, as time went. I try to see that plain before me, dinosaurs walking on it, but I am not able even to imagine the shore of the Lake when the Indians were there, before Tuppertown. The tiny share we have of time appalls me, though my father seems to regard it with tranquillity. Even my father, who sometimes seems to me to have been at home in the world as long as it has lasted, has really lived on this earth only a little longer than I have, in terms of all the time there has been to live in. He has not known a time, any more than I, when automobiles and electric lights did not at least exist. He was not alive when this century started. I will be barely alive – old, old – when it ends. I do not like to think of it. I wish the Lake to be always just a lake, with the safe-swimming floats marking it, and the breakwater and the lights of Tuppertown.

My father has a job, selling for Walker Brothers. This is a firm that sells almost entirely in the country, the back country. Sunshine, Boylesbridge, Turnaround – that is all his territory. Not Dungannon where we used to live, Dungannon is too near town and my mother is grateful for that. He sells cough medicine, iron tonic, corn plasters, laxatives, pills for female disorders, mouthwash, shampoo, liniment, salves, lemon and orange and raspberry concentrate for making refreshing drinks, vanilla, food coloring, black and green tea, ginger, cloves, and other spices, rat poison. He has a song about it, with these two lines:

> *And have all liniments and oils,*
> *For everything from corns to boils . . .*

Not a very funny song, in my mother's opinion. A peddler's song, and that is what he is, a peddler knocking at backwoods kitchens. Up until last winter we had our own business, a fox farm. My father raised silver foxes and sold their pelts to the people who make them into capes and coats and muffs. Prices fell, my father hung on hoping they would get better next year, and they fell again, and he hung on one more year and one more and finally it was not possible to hang on anymore, we owed everything to the feed company. I have heard my mother explain this, several times, to Mrs Oliphant, who is the only neighbor she talks to. (Mrs Oliphant also has come down in the world, being a schoolteacher who married the janitor.) We poured all we had into it, my mother says, and we came out with nothing. Many people could say the same thing, these days, but my mother has no time for the national calamity, only ours. Fate has flung us onto a street of poor people (it does not matter that we were poor before; that was a different sort of poverty), and the only way to take this, as she sees it, is with dignity, with bitterness, with no reconciliation. No bathroom with a claw-footed tub and a flush toilet is going to comfort her, nor water on tap and sidewalks past the house and milk in bottles, not even the two movie theatres and the Venus Restaurant and Woolworths so marvellous it has live birds singing in its fan-cooled corners and fish as tiny as fingernails, as bright as moons, swimming in its green tanks. My mother does not care.

In the afternoons she often walks to Simon's Grocery and takes me with her to help carry things. She wears a good dress, navy blue with little flowers, sheer, worn over a navy-blue slip. Also a summer hat of white straw, pushed down on the side of the head, and white shoes I have just whitened on a newspaper on the back steps. I have my hair freshly done in long damp curls which the dry air will fortunately soon loosen, a stiff large hair ribbon on top of my head. This is entirely different from going out after supper with my father. We have not walked past two houses before I feel we have become objects of universal ridicule. Even the dirty words chalked on the sidewalk are laughing at us. My mother does not seem to notice. She walks serenely like a lady shopping, like a *lady* shopping, past the housewives in loose beltless dresses torn under the arms. With me her creation, wretched curls and flaunting hair bow, scrubbed knees and white socks – all I do not want to be. I loathe even my name when she says it in public, in a voice so high, proud, and ringing, deliberately different from the voice of any other mother on the street.

My mother will sometimes carry home, for a treat, a brick of ice cream – pale Neapolitan; and because we have no refrigerator in our house we wake my brother and eat it at once in the dining-room, always darkened by the wall of the house next door. I spoon it up tenderly, leaving the chocolate till last, hoping to have some still to eat when my brother's dish is empty. My mother tries then to imitate the conversations we used to have at Dungannon, going back to our earliest, most leisurely days before my brother was born, when she would give me a little tea and a lot of milk in a cup like hers and we would sit out on the step facing the pump, the lilac tree, the fox pens beyond. She is not able to keep from mentioning those days. 'Do you remember when we put you in your sled and Major pulled you?' (Major our dog, that we had to leave with neighbors when we moved.) 'Do you remember your sandbox outside the kitchen window?' I pretend to remember far less than I do, wary of being trapped into sympathy or any unwanted emotion.

My mother has headaches. She often has to lie down. She lies on my brother's narrow bed in the little screened porch, shaded by heavy branches. 'I look up at that tree and I think I am at home,' she says.

'What you need,' my father tells her, 'is some fresh air and a drive in the country.' He means for her to go with him, on his Walker Brothers route.

That is not my mother's idea of a drive in the country.

'Can I come?'

'Your mother might want you for trying on clothes.'

'I'm beyond sewing this afternoon,' my mother says.

'I'll take her then. Take both of them, give you a rest.'

What is there about us that people need to be given a rest from? Never mind. I am glad enough to find my brother and make him go to the toilet and get us both into the car, our knees unscrubbed, my hair unringleted. My father brings from the house his two heavy brown suitcases, full of bottles, and sets them on the back seat. He wears a white shirt, brilliant in the sunlight, a tie, light trousers belonging to his summer suit (his other suit is black, for funerals, and belonged to my uncle before he died), and a creamy straw hat. His salesman's outfit, with pencils clipped in the shirt pocket. He goes back once again, probably to say goodbye to my mother, to ask her if she is sure she doesn't want to come, and hear her say, 'No. No thanks, I'm better just to lie here with my eyes closed.' Then we are backing out of the driveway with the rising hope of adventure, just the little hope that takes you over the bump into the street, the hot air starting to move, turning into a breeze, the houses growing less and less familiar as we follow the shortcut my father knows, the quick way out of town. Yet what is there waiting for us all afternoon but hot hours in stricken farmyards, perhaps a stop at a country store and three ice-cream cones or bottles of pop, and my father singing? The one he made up about himself has a title – 'The Walker Brothers Cowboy' – and it starts out like this:

> *Old Ned Fields, he now is dead,*
> *So I am ridin' the route instead . . .*

Who is Ned Fields? The man he has replaced, surely, and if so he really is dead; yet my father's voice is mournful-jolly, making his death some kind of nonsense, a comic calamity. 'Wisht I was back on the Rio Grande, plungin' through the dusky sand.' My father sings most of the time while driving the car. Even now, heading out of town, crossing the bridge and taking the sharp turn onto the highway, he is humming something, mumbling a bit of a song to himself, just tuning up, really, getting ready to improvise, for out along the highway we pass the Baptist Camp, the Vacation Bible Camp, and he lets loose:

> *'Where are the Baptists, where are the Baptists,*
> *   where are all the Baptists today?*
> *They're down in the water, in Lake Huron water,*
> *   with their sins all a-gittin' washed away.'*

My brother takes this for straight truth and gets up on his knees trying to see down to the Lake. 'I don't see any Baptists,' he says accusingly. 'Neither do I, son,' says my father. 'I told you, they're down in the Lake.'

No roads paved when we left the highway. We have to roll up the windows because of dust. The land is flat, scorched, empty. Bush lots at the back of the farms hold shade, black pine-shade like pools nobody can ever get to. We bump up a long lane and at the end of it what could look more unwelcoming, more deserted than the tall unpainted farmhouse with grass growing uncut right up to the front door, green blinds down, and a door upstairs opening on nothing but air? Many houses have this door, and I have never yet been able to find out why. I ask my father and he says they are for walking in your sleep. *What*? Well, if you happen to be walking in your sleep and you want to step outside. I am offended, seeing too late that he is joking, as usual, but my brother says sturdily, 'If they did that they would break their necks.'

The 1930s. How much this kind of farmhouse, this kind of afternoon seem to me to belong to that one decade in time, just as my father's hat does, his bright flared tie, our car with its wide running board (an Essex, and long past its prime). Cars somewhat like it, many older, none dustier, sit in the farmyards. Some are past running and have their doors pulled off, their seats removed for use on porches. No living things to be seen, chickens or cattle. Except dogs. There are dogs lying in any kind of shade they can find, dreaming, their lean sides rising and sinking rapidly. They get up when my father opens the car door, he has to speak to them. 'Nice boy, there's a boy, nice old boy.' They quiet down, go back to their shade. He should know how to quiet animals, he has held desperate foxes with tongs around their necks. One gentling voice for the dogs and another, rousing, cheerful, for calling at doors. 'Hello there, missus, it's the Walker Brothers man and what are you out of today?' A door opens, he disappears. Forbidden to follow, forbidden even to leave the car, we can just wait and wonder what he says. Sometimes trying to make my mother laugh, he pretends to be himself in a farm kitchen, spreading out his sample case. 'Now then, missus, are you troubled with parasitic life? Your children's scalps, I mean. All those crawly little things we're too polite to mention that show up on the heads of the best of families? Soap alone is useless, kerosene is not too nice a perfume, but I have here –' Or else, 'Believe me, sitting and driving all day the way I do I *know* the value of these fine pills. Natural relief. A problem common to old folks too, once their days of activity are over – How about you, Grandma?' He would wave the imaginary box of pills under my mother's nose and she would laugh finally, unwillingly. 'He doesn't say that really, does he?' I said, and she said no of course not, he was too much of a gentleman.

One yard after another, then, the old cars, the pumps, dogs, views of gray barns and falling-down sheds and unturning windmills. The men, if they are working in the fields, are not in any fields that we can see. The children are far away, following dry creek beds or looking for blackberries, or else they are hidden in the house, spying at us through cracks in the blinds. The car seat has grown slick with our sweat. I dare my brother to sound the horn, wanting to do it myself but not wanting to get the blame. He knows better. We play I Spy, but it is hard to find many colors. Gray for the barns and sheds and toilets and houses, brown for the yard and fields, black or brown for the dogs. The rusting cars show rainbow patches, in which I strain to pick out purple or green; likewise I peer at doors for shreds of old peeling paint, maroon or yellow. We can't play with letters, which would be better, because my brother is too young to spell. The game disintegrates anyway. He claims my colors are not fair, and wants extra turns.

In one house no door opens, though the car is in the yard. My father knocks and whistles, calls, 'Hullo there! Walker Brothers man!' but there is not a stir of reply anywhere. This house has no porch, just a bare, slanting slab of cement on which my father stands. He turns around, searching the barnyard, the barn whose mow must be empty because you can see the sky through it, and finally he bends to pick up his suitcases. Just then a window is opened upstairs, a white pot appears on the sill, is tilted over and its contents splash down the outside wall. The window is not directly above my father's head, so only a stray splash would catch him. He picks up his suitcases with no particular hurry and walks, no longer whistling, to the car. 'Do you know what that was?' I say to my brother. '*Pee.*' He laughs and laughs.

My father rolls and lights a cigarette before he starts the car. The window has been slammed down, the blind drawn, we never did see a hand or face. 'Pee, pee,' sings my brother ecstatically. 'Somebody dumped down pee!' 'Just don't tell your mother that,' my father says. 'She isn't liable to see the joke.' 'Is it in your song?' my brother wants to know. My father says no but he will see what he can do to work it in.

I notice in a little while that we are not turning in any more lanes, though it does not seem to me that we are headed home. 'Is this the way to Sunshine?' I ask my father, and he answers, 'No, ma'am, it's not.' 'Are we still in your territory?' He shakes his head. 'We're going *fast*,' my brother says approvingly, and in fact we are bouncing along through dry puddle-holes so that all the bottles in the suitcases clink together and gurgle promisingly.

Another lane, a house, also unpainted, dried to silver in the sun.

'I thought we were out of your territory.'

'We are.'

'Then what are we going in here for?'

'You'll see.'

In front of the house a short, sturdy woman is picking up washing, which had been spread on the grass to bleach and dry. When the car stops she stares at it hard for a moment, bends to pick up a couple more towels to add to the bundle under her arm, comes across to us and says in a flat voice, neither welcoming nor unfriendly, 'Have you lost your way?'

My father takes his time getting out of the car. 'I don't think so,' he says. 'I'm the Walker Brothers man.'

'George Golley is our Walker Brothers man,' the woman says, 'and he was out here no more than a week ago. Oh, my Lord God,' she says harshly, 'it's you.'

'It was, the last time I looked in the mirror,' my father says.

The woman gathers all the towels in front of her and holds on to them tightly, pushing them against her stomach as if it hurt. 'Of all the people I never thought to see. And telling me you were the Walker Brothers man.'

'I'm sorry if you were looking forward to George Golley,' my father says humbly.

'And look at me, I was prepared to clean the henhouse. You'll think that's just an excuse but it's true. I don't go round looking like this every day.' She is wearing a farmer's straw hat, through which pricks of sunlight penetrate and float on her face, a loose, dirty print smock, and canvas shoes. 'Who are those in the car, Ben? They're not yours?'

'Well, I hope and believe they are,' my father says, and tells our names and ages. 'Come on, you can get out. This is Nora, Miss Cronin. Nora, you better tell me, is it still Miss, or have you got a husband hiding in the woodshed?'

'If I had a husband that's not where I'd keep him, Ben,' she says, and they both laugh, her laugh abrupt and somewhat angry. 'You'll think I got no manners, as well as being dressed like a tramp,' she says. 'Come on in out of the sun. It's cool in the house.'

We go across the yard ('Excuse me taking you in this way but I don't think the front door has been opened since Papa's funeral, I'm afraid the hinges might drop off'), up the porch steps, into the kitchen, which really is cool, high-ceilinged, the blinds of course down, a simple, clean, threadbare room with waxed worn linoleum, potted geraniums, drinking-pail and dipper, a round table with scrubbed oilcloth. In spite of the cleanness, the wiped and swept surfaces, there is a faint sour smell – maybe of the dishrag or the tin dipper or the oilcloth, or the old lady, because there is one, sitting in an easy chair under the clock shelf. She turns her head slightly in our direction and says, 'Nora? Is that company?'

'Blind,' says Nora in a quick explaining voice to my father. Then, 'You won't guess who it is, Momma. Hear his voice.'

My father goes to the front of her chair and bends and says hopefully, 'Afternoon, Mrs Cronin.'

'Ben Jordan,' says the old lady with no surprise. 'You haven't been to see us in the longest time. Have you been out of the country?'

My father and Nora look at each other.

'He's married, Momma,' says Nora cheerfully and aggressively. 'Married and got two children and here they are.' She pulls us forward, makes each of us touch the old lady's dry, cool hand while she says our names in turn. Blind! This is the first blind person I have ever seen close up. Her eyes are closed, the eyelids sunk away down, showing no shape of the eyeball, just hollows. From one hollow comes a drop of silver liquid, a medicine, or a miraculous tear.

'Let me get into a decent dress,' Nora says. 'Talk to Momma. It's a treat for her. We hardly ever see company, do we, Momma?'

'Not many makes it out this road,' says the old lady placidly. 'And the ones that used to be around here, our old neighbors, some of them have pulled out.'

'True everywhere,' my father says.

'Where's your wife then?'

'Home. She's not too fond of the hot weather, makes her feel poorly.'

'Well.' This is a habit of country people, old people, to say 'well,' meaning, 'Is that so?' with a little extra politeness and concern.

Nora's dress, when she appears again – stepping heavily on Cuban heels down the stairs in the hall – is flowered more lavishly than anything my mother owns, green and yellow on brown, some sort of floating sheer crêpe, leaving her arms bare. Her arms are heavy, and every bit of her skin you can see is covered with little dark freckles like measles. Her hair is short, black, coarse and curly, her teeth very white and strong. 'It's the first time I knew there was such a thing as green poppies,' my father says, looking at her dress.

'You would be surprised all the things you never knew,' says Nora, sending a smell of cologne far and wide when she moves and displaying a change of voice to go with the dress, something more sociable and youthful. 'They're not poppies anyway, they're just flowers. You go and pump me some good cold water and I'll make these children a drink.' She gets down from the cupboard a bottle of Walker Brothers Orange syrup.

'You telling me you were the Walker Brothers man!'

'It's the truth, Nora. You go and look at my sample cases in the car if you don't believe me. I got the territory directly south of here.'

'Walker Brothers? Is that a fact? You selling for Walker Brothers?'

'Yes, ma'am.'

'We always heard you were raising foxes over Dungannon way.'

'That's what I was doing, but I kind of run out of luck in that business.'

'So where are you living? How long've you been out selling?'

'We moved into Tuppertown. I been at it, oh, two, three months. It keeps the wolf from the door. Keeps him as far away as the back fence.'

Nora laughs. 'Well, I guess you count yourself lucky to have the work. Isabel's husband in Brantford, he was out of work the longest time. I thought if he didn't find something soon I was going to have them all land in here to feed, and I tell you I was hardly looking forward to it. It's all I can manage with me and Momma.'

'Isabel married,' my father says. 'Muriel married too?'

'No, she's teaching school out West. She hasn't been home for five years. I guess she finds something better to do with her holidays. I would if I was her.' She gets some snapshots out of the table drawer and starts showing him. 'That's Isabel's oldest boy, starting school. That's the baby sitting in her carriage. Isabel and her husband. Muriel. That's her roommate with her. That's a fellow she used to go around with, and his car. He was working in a bank out there. That's her school, it has eight rooms. She teaches Grade Five.' My father shakes his head. 'I can't think of her any way but when she was going to school, so shy I used to pick her up on the road – I'd be on my way to see you – and she would not say one word, not even to agree it was a nice day.'

'She's got over that.'

'Who are you talking about?' says the old lady.

'Muriel. I said she's got over being shy.'

'She was here last summer.'

'No, Momma, that was Isabel. Isabel and her family were here last summer. Muriel's out West.'

'I meant Isabel.'

Shortly after this the old lady falls asleep, her head on the side, her mouth open. 'Excuse her manners,' Nora says. 'It's old age.' She fixes an afghan over her mother and says we can all go into the front room where our talking won't disturb her.

'You two,' my father says. 'Do you want to go outside and amuse yourselves?'

Amuse ourselves how? Anyway, I want to stay. The front room is more interesting than the kitchen, though barer. There is a gramophone and a pump organ and a picture on the wall of Mary, Jesus' mother – I know that much – in shades of bright blue and pink with a spiked band of light around her head. I know that such pictures are found only in the homes of Roman Catholics and so Nora must be one. We have never known any Roman Catholics at all well, never well enough to visit in their houses. I think of what my grandmother and my Aunt Tena, over in Dungannon, used to always say to indicate that somebody was a Catholic. *So-and-so digs with the wrong foot*, they would say. *She digs with the wrong foot.* That was what they would say about Nora.

Nora takes a bottle, half full, out of the top of the organ and pours some of what is in it into the two glasses that she and my father have emptied of the orange drink.

'Keep it in case of sickness?' my father says.

'Not on your life,' says Nora. 'I'm never sick. I just keep it because I keep it. One bottle does me a fair time, though, because I don't care for drinking alone. Here's luck!' She and my father drink and I know what it is. Whisky. One of the things my mother has told me in our talks together is that my father never drinks whisky. But I see he does. He drinks whisky and he talks of people whose names I have never heard before. But after a while he turns to a familiar incident. He tells about the chamberpot that was emptied out the window. 'Picture me there,' he says, 'hollering my heartiest. *Oh, lady, it's your Walker Brothers man, anybody home?*' He does himself hollering, grinning absurdly, waiting, looking up in pleased expectation, and then – oh, ducking, covering his head with his arms, looking as if he begged for mercy (when he never did anything like that, I was watching), and Nora laughs, almost as hard as my brother did at the time.

'That isn't true! That's not a word true!'

'Oh, indeed it is, ma'am. We have our heroes in the ranks of Walker Brothers. I'm glad you think it's funny,' he says sombrely.

I ask him shyly, 'Sing the song.'

'What song? Have you turned into a singer on top of everything else?'

Embarrassed, my father says, 'Oh, just this song I made up while I was driving around, it gives me something to do, making up rhymes.'

But after some urging he does sing it, looking at Nora with a droll, apologetic expression, and she laughs so much that in places he has to stop and wait for her to get over laughing so he can go on, because she makes him laugh too. Then he does various parts of his salesman's spiel. Nora when she laughs squeezes her large bosom under her folded arms. 'You're crazy,' she says. 'That's all you are.' She sees my brother peering into the gramophone and she jumps up and goes over to him. 'Here's us sitting enjoying ourselves and not giving you a thought, isn't it terrible?' she says. 'You want me to put a record on, don't you? You want to hear a nice record? Can you dance? I bet your sister can, can't she?'

I say no. 'A big girl like you and so good-looking and can't dance!' says Nora. 'It's high time you learned. I bet you'd make a lovely dancer. Here, I'm going to put on a piece I used to dance to and even your daddy did, in his dancing days. You didn't know your daddy was a dancer, did you? Well, he is a talented man, your daddy!'

She puts down the lid and takes hold of me unexpectedly around the waist, picks up my other hand, and starts making me go backwards. 'This is the way, now, this is how they dance. Follow me. This foot, see. One and one-two. One and one-two. That's fine, that's lovely, don't look at your feet! Follow me, that's right, see how easy? You're going to be a lovely dancer! One and one-two. One and one-two. Ben, see your daughter dancing!' *Whispering while you cuddle near me, Whispering so no one can hear me . . .*

Round and round the linoleum, me proud, intent, Nora laughing and moving with great buoyancy, wrapping me in her strange gaiety, her smell of whisky, cologne, and sweat. Under the arms her dress is damp, and little drops form along her upper lip, hang in the soft black hairs at the corners of her mouth. She whirls me around in front of my father – causing me to stumble, for I am by no means so swift a pupil as she pretends – and lets me go, breathless.

'Dance with me, Ben.'

'I'm the world's worst dancer, Nora, and you know it.'

'I certainly never thought so.'

'You would now.'

She stands in front of him, arms hanging loose and hopeful, her breasts, which a moment ago embarrassed me with their warmth and bulk, rising and falling under her loose flowered dress, her face shining with the exercise, and delight.

'Ben.'

My father drops his head and says quietly, 'Not me, Nora.'

So she can only go and take the record off. 'I can drink alone but I can't dance alone,' she says. 'Unless I am a whole lot crazier than I think I am.'

'Nora,' says my father, smiling. 'You're not crazy.'

'Stay for supper.'

'Oh, no. We couldn't put you to the trouble.'

'It's no trouble. I'd be glad of it.'

'And their mother would worry. She'd think I'd turned us over in a ditch.'

'Oh, well. Yes.'

'We've taken a lot of your time now.'

'Time,' says Nora bitterly. 'Will you come by ever again?'

'I will if I can,' says my father.

'Bring the children. Bring your wife.'

'Yes, I will,' says my father. 'I will if I can.'

When she follows us to the car he says, 'You come to see us too, Nora. We're right on Grove Street, left-hand side going in, that's north, and two doors this side – east – of Baker Street.'

Nora does not repeat these directions. She stands close to the car in her soft, brilliant dress. She touches the fender, making an unintelligible mark in the dust there.

On the way home my father does not buy any ice cream or pop, but he does go into a country store and get a package of licorice, which he shares with us. She digs with the wrong foot, I think, and the words seem sad to me as never before, dark, perverse. My father does not say anything to me about not mentioning things at home, but I know, just from the thoughtfulness, the pause when he passes the licorice, that there are things not to be mentioned. The whisky, maybe the dancing. No worry about my brother, he does not notice enough. At most he might remember the blind lady, the picture of Mary.

'Sing,' my brother commands my father, but my father says gravely, 'I don't know, I seem to be fresh out of songs. You watch the road and let me know if you see any rabbits.'

So my father drives and my brother watches the road for rabbits and I feel my father's life flowing back from our car in the last of the afternoon, darkening and turning strange, like a landscape that has an enchantment on it, making it kindly, ordinary and familiar while you are looking at it, but changing it, once your back is turned, into something you will never know, with all kinds of weathers, and distances you cannot imagine.

When we get closer to Tuppertown the sky becomes gently overcast, as always, nearly always, on summer evenings by the Lake.

The Cantilever Principle

MARY MORRISSY

'Trussed-up', my father was saying, 'like a chicken. Oven-ready!' He beamed at me, grateful for my indulgence – I had heard the story several times over – then turned back to Sam.

'They daubed this stuff on me, like washing-up liquid. Rubbed it on neat – all over!'

'By the prettiest nurse, no doubt, Jack!' Uncle Sam winked extravagantly.

They were like boys again, gleeful with reprieve. Sam, snowy-haired, with a grizzled jaw, and my father, propped up on the pillows, his face ripe and waxy as a windfallen apple. The danger had passed. We were safely allowed our gaiety. Indeed, it was necessary because we had so nearly lost him. We lost my mother – early. For years he had measured time by her death. That was, he would say, puckering his brow, that was just before we lost your mother. That was his word for it. Lost.

I cannot remember her now except as a collection of sensations cut adrift – the smell of cold cream, the steady thump of another heart, a benign shape leaning over me as a prelude to embrace. He was generous with details of her. They had met at a tea dance at the Metropole. She was a good deal younger than him. He had been accused of cradle-snatching. They had walked out together for eight months. Her family did not approve. After they were married his landlady let her move in. Then there was the flat by the canal before they bought a home – here. This other world that they belonged to, grey and grainy, the one before I was born, this was where I was convinced my mother was lost. I identified the year as 1947, the worst winter on record, and pictured her wandering in a blizzard in the wrap-around coat and angora beret she wore in those long-ago holiday snaps. These seemed always to be taken in winter, at the edge of cliffs, my mother's hair wild around her face, her teeth chattering with cold through a brave smile. My father, it has to be said, looks pretty goofy in these pictures. The short-back-and-sides haircut, his large ears, a gormless sort of smile. He has improved with age. Whereas she seems perfect then, for then, as if she somehow knew . . . but, no, that's ascribing premonition to mere candour for the camera.

Of her death he would not speak. A brain haemorrhage. My only guide is Mrs Parfitt. He had left for work. And where was I? Somewhere out of the picture. My mother is sitting over the debris of breakfast things. It is a wan April morning aching to be spring. She is gazing out the kitchen window, elbows propped on the table, one hand clasping a cup of lukewarm tea. Suddenly there is an intruder who strikes her one blow on the temple sending everything spinning. The cup leaps from her hand, a plate slides off the edge of the table. She tries to rise but her arm buckles beneath her, crumpling the waxed folds of the oiled cloth and rattling the teapot. Her last view is of the mocking darkness of its spout. My father finds her at lunchtime, face bathed in milk, crumbs in her hair, dried blood around her ear. He thinks she has passed out or, comically, has fallen asleep. He leaves her be and calls a neighbour – the inner workings of women are no business of his. *She* knows.

'She's dead, Mr Eustace,' Mrs Parfitt says, 'your wife is dead.' Here, she says, here at this very table.

Without a mother, not only death, but birth, too, was a mystery. We found you in a basket on the canal, my father used to say. I liked the 'we' in this; for the first time it included me. And it beat those stories about cabbage leaves. I could imagine this. The pair of them walking along the towpath near the gasworks and finding a Moses basket in the green, scummy water by the bank. My mother (wearing the same hat and coat; there are no costume changes for her) lifts me out carefully.

'Ah look,' she says, 'look at the wee mite.'

I am wearing a long white christening robe.

'John, just look.'

She hoists me up on her shoulder and turns around so that he is looking directly into my eyes. Was it then it started – this fierce, reluctant attachment?

She swings around, her voice brimming with excitement and says: 'Shall we keep her?' as if it's the most reckless, daring adventure they have ever considered.

My father says yes.

Hospital time is different. Elongated. It was – is – high summer but already the recent gusty, blue-bright days and cool, lilac evenings belong to a carefully delineated past. Even the heartbreaking sunsets, melancholy and grand, which accompanied my vigil, now seem like the fevered reproduction of some long distant memory. A bypass. Appropriate surgery for the man. My father, the engineer. Bridges were his thing. During school holidays we made pilgrimages to them. I remember a misty January evening standing reverentially by the Forth Bridge which rose like a giant brontosaurus out of the still waters.

'The cantilever principle,' my father said importantly. 'See, the three spans.' He pointed, one hand on my shoulder. 'They each stand separately but when projected towards each other they form a bridge. Stress against stress.'

I was terrified that he would die.

'Don't worry,' Sam had said, 'he's a hardy one.' But the warning signs, once glimpsed, will never go away. His breathlessness, the alarming puce of his cheeks, the panic in his eye. I had seen them all and knew the cold, hard dread they induced in me. I grew to hate him for his frailty. I despised him when he gasped for air. I turned away, ashamed, when he clutched his chest in pain. I told myself he was pretending, doing it for effect, and that sympathy would only make him weaker. He had deceived me. His robust good health all these years had been a sham. He had secretly been cultivating the germ of his own death.

Intensive Care. My father adrift somewhere while all around him gadgets did his struggling for him. There was a bleeping green monitor and the noisy shuffling of a ventilator. Narrow tubes snaked in under the bedclothes and a bulbous bag of intravenous drip stood sentry at the bedhead. It reminded me of the pictures of bridges he collected, all huge beams and girders and in between the steel and metal latticework, a tiny train trapped.

The hardware hid him from me; all his fear and helplessness put on hold.

'It's quite normal,' one of the nurses assured me, 'we keep them heavily sedated. Lessens the likelihood of rejection.'

For days I sat by his bedside or paced up and down the phlegm-coloured corridors. The light there was dull and dead as if it, too, had been etherized. And the noise – like the muted clamour of a penitentiary. The wheeling and droning of cleaners, the rattle of trolleys shivering with instruments, the clangour of bed pans, gave way to periods of forsaken quiet. At night, after visiting hour, it seemed as if we were on board a ghostly liner, abandoned and adrift. Sometimes I would go to the Day Room. A television with the sound turned down was perched high on a ledge. Animated faces on the screen mouthed messages to the silent room. Several patients would be slumped in the leatherette armchairs which broke wind when they sat down. Their slippers chafed the shiny lino. Some of them had crude crosses in gentian violet daubed on their faces to mark where they'd been treated. It was also a cancer hospital.

That must have been what he had. My friend. That's what I thought of him as, although we never spoke. He was in the ward opposite the intensive care unit, his bed just inside the door. He was a young man, the same age as me, perhaps. He lay on the bed in pyjama bottoms and a dressing gown, open and stranded around his waist. There was, to look at him, no sign of illness except for the shaved rectangle at his temple. Beneath the hurtful ridge of his brow his eyes were sunken, fogged-looking, slow to register, and yet, I had the feeling that I was being watched intensely. He was stricken on one side. Above his head like a noose, a tubular triangle hung. With one arm he used this to manoeuvre himself in the bed. He moved his good leg constantly, grinding his heel against the bedclothes like the restless kicking of a baby. Everything about him was like a baby. The awful trustfulness of his gaze. The little identity tag around his wrist with those bare details with which he had come into the world – his name, his date of birth. He seemed utterly defenceless and alone.

And yet, he was not alone. A woman, Miriam (I gave her a name, but never him), came daily, kissing him on the forehead before settling down in a chair beside his bed. She moved with what seemed like exaggerated care as if any sudden gesture might startle him. He watched her silently, following her about wonderingly with his eyes. He would grasp her hand, rubbing his fingers on her knuckles as if touch were new to him. I could hear her speak soothingly to him.

Intimacy is shocking in a hospital, absurd amidst the starch and clatter, and *their* tenderness, especially, seemed alien. But I couldn't take my eyes off them. She drew things from a crowded tote bag like a conjurer desperate to please. She brought flowers which she carefully arranged in a jug beside the bed. Once she sellotaped a child's drawing to the side of his locker. She fed him, handing him a cup with a straw in it to drink from. She wiped his mouth. She peeled fruit for him – oranges, bananas – holding them up in front of him before clamping his fingers firmly around them. It was like watching a mother and child. I felt as I do when women breastfeed in public. The fear of other people's nakedness.

I never wanted to know any more about him except what I could learn from watching. Perhaps I knew the bargain I was about to make. His life for one I valued more.

'And at last Pharaoh made a proclamation to the whole of his people: Whenever a male child is born, cast it into the river, keep only the girls alive. And now one of the descendants of Levi wooed and married a woman of his own clan, who conceived and bore him a son. So winning were the child's looks that for three months she kept him hidden away; then, unable to conceal him any longer, she took a little basket of reeds, which she smeared with clay and pitch, and in this put her baby son down among the bulrushes on the river bank . . .'

On the third day there was a change in my father's condition. I detected this only by a certain change in the atmosphere, an added grim bustle in the room. The nurses, usually chatty and given to small talk, instead conferred with one another at the door casting anxious glances in my direction. They made what seemed to be futile adjustments to the equipment, picked up my father's lumpen hand to get a pulse with an air of resignation, leafed through his charts as if searching for some clue to his condition they'd overlooked. I didn't ask them, of course, what they thought was wrong. I was too afraid. 'Not responding,' was a phrase I overheard.

Meanwhile in the ward opposite, my friend was celebrating. He was in a wheelchair by the bed, a rug thrown over his legs. Above him, hanging from the curtain rails was an array of balloons and streamers, and Miriam was stringing together a loop of cards behind his bed. It was his birthday. In the afternoon visiting hour, a gang of people arrived. They drew up in a circle around him. Some perched on the bed, others stood. There was the popping of corks and a rush of paper cups to catch the foaming champagne. There were bursts of raucous laughter, an air of triumph.

'Come on,' someone called out to one of the nurses, 'join the party!'

'Ye'll all be thrown out,' she warned mockingly.

A loud 'awh' from the group.

I couldn't see him in the midst of them but I imagined him there smiling jaggedly, drunk with memory. When the visitors' bell rang at four they wheeled him recklessly out of the ward and down the corridor towards the Day Room, whooping and singing – 'Happy birthday to you, happy birthday to you, happy birthday dear . . .' The swing doors closed behind them.

★

Three a.m. Condition, stable. They had told me to go home but I wouldn't. I didn't trust them. I was a nuisance, I knew that, prowling around, nervously alert from lack of sleep and haunted by unspoken fears. Even Sam had got irritated.

'Don't do the martyr on us. For God's sake, go home. There's nothing you can do here,' he had said when he left at midnight. He was right; there was nothing I could do – there or anywhere else. But I thought that any sudden movement of mine might precipitate disaster. As long as I was there, nothing could happen to him.

There is something sacred about those early hours of the morning. A hush. It isn't difficult to see why death comes then, how it gains easeful entry when the defences of the world are down. The graveyard hours. If Dad makes it through these, I thought, he will make it through another day. It was then I remembered my friend. I slipped out of Intensive Care and crossed the corridor. He too was sleeping. It was a warm night and he had thrown off all the bedclothes except for a sheet swaddled around his groin. In the blue light his limbs looked startlingly beautiful; there were perfect half-moons on all his fingernails.

A breeze sighed softly at the open window. I thought of wind among rushes. It would be easy now to push him forth out into the calm waters of the night in this, the easeful hour. I laid my hand on his pillow. There would be no struggle. In his slumber he would barely notice the gentle rocking of the basket. He was the boy-child, the one who must be sacrificed. And, in return, my father would be saved. Take him, I urged the darkness, take *him*.

By the next morning my father was awake, in a different ward, the hardware all removed. He smiled sheepishly at me as I came in, as if he'd been away on a drunken binge.

'I'm sorry,' he said weakly, 'for giving you a fright.'

'You had us worried, you old dog,' Sam said, 'we'd thought you'd given up the ghost. Isn't that right, Kate?'

For days, almost a week, I dared not see my friend. It was easy to avoid him. His ward was on the floor below and I did not have to pass it now. Only when my father could leave his bed did I have the courage to venture down. I walked along the familiar corridor, halting at his doorway. The bed was empty, the locker cleared. The child's drawing had been torn roughly from its spot leaving only a corner scrap. The coverlet on the bed did not even bear the outline of his body.

'Gone, my dear,' a nurse said as she bustled past.

I did not – could not – ask what she meant by gone.

I watch out for him on the street now. Certain men remind me of him. I see them in pubs, on trains, in buses, and my heart leaps. I am about to rush up to them when they turn around and reveal themselves as imposters. Anyway, I know it's all in vain. I know the price that's been exacted. I *know* that I will never see him again.

North Sea Crossing

HELEN DUNMORE

Carl wakes at six. There are shadows on the ceiling, bright sloppings of sea. Or do you call it a ceiling, when it's a boat? He lies tight under the quilt and watches the room heave. His throat aches, but he knows it's not seasickness.

'You can't be seasick. I've never known it so calm.'

The boat gives a lunge like a selfish sleeper turning over in bed, dragging the quilt with it. His father is buried in the opposite bunk. He never twitches or snores. Once Carl talked about a dream he'd had, and his father said, 'I never dream.' The second his father wakes he starts doing things.

On one elbow, leaning, twisting, Carl watches the water. It's navy, like school uniform, with foam frisking about on top of the slabs of sea. Even through the oblong misted window the sea is much bigger than the boat. He'll get up. He'll go and explore. He'll walk right round the decks and come back knowing more about the boat than his father.

'Hey Dad,' he'll say, 'guess what I saw up on deck!' and then his father's waking face will crease into a smile of approval.

No. Much better to go out, come back, say nothing. Later, maybe, if his father asks, he could say, 'Oh, I thought I'd have a look up on deck.' That way it won't be like running to him saying, 'Look at me! Look what I've been doing.' His father doesn't like that.

'Just do it, Carl. Don't tell the world about it.'

Remember when he'd thought it was a good idea to go out and chop logs. He'd haul in a basket of clean-cut logs, all the same size, enough to keep the fire going for two days. '*Did you do those, Carl?*' '*Yes, Dad. Thought we were getting low.*' '*Good. Well done.*' But the wood was damp and slippery. When Carl brought down the axe it skidded on the bark and the lump of wood bounced away off the chopping block. And then his father was suddenly there, watching.

'What the hell are you supposed to be doing?'

'I'm chopping some logs, Dad – I just thought –'

'That wood's green. It won't be ready to burn for another year.'

Carl saw his father looking at the mangled wood. 'Next time, ask,' he said.

A small thought wriggles across the ceiling where the sea patterns had played. Why won't his father have central heating like everyone else? Like Mum? No, it has to be a real fire. '*Warm soup swilling round metal pipes – who wants that when they could have a real fire.*' The quilt has slipped off his feet. They're long and bony and they look as if they belong to someone else. The feet Carl used to have don't exist any more. Someone has taken away their firm, compact shape. Now he trips over things and stubs his toes. Last night he hit his big toe so hard against the step to the cabin bathroom that he thought it was broken. He sat on the bunk, nursing it. His toe was red and there was a lump on it that hadn't been there before. The kind of lump a broken bone makes, poking out. If he sucked it . . . He leaned forward, screwed his face round and hoisted up his knee, but he couldn't get his foot in his mouth any more. And it used to be so nice doing that, sending little shivers up the sole of his foot into his spine as he sucked and licked. What if he twisted round a bit more and braced his back against the end of the bunk . . . And there he was, knotted, when Dad came back to the cabin. He didn't say anything, just looked while Carl untangled himself like a badly tied shoelace.

There's no more sun on the ceiling. Everything has turned grey, and the sea is quieter, but as close at the window as a bully calling round after school. Its folds look greasy. It's settling down just like Dad said it would. Carl swings his legs and feels for the floor, which thrusts up at his feet like someone pretending to punch you and then pulling back: '*You really thought I was going to hit you, didn't you? You were scared!*'

Anyway, he'll be first washed and dressed. The shower is quite nice, then its trickle of water suddenly burns and makes Carl yelp. But it's all right. Dad can't have heard through the door. Carl comes out, hair slicked back, teeth immaculate. Dad can't stand mossy teeth. Now a thick whiteness is flattening the water. Fog. A second later the boat gives a long scared *Mooo*. 'Fog,' says Carl to himself. 'Fog at sea.' He looks round at the neatness of the cabin. Everything is stacked and folded; even his father is folded away under the quilt, sleeping so well you wouldn't guess he was breathing. 'It's just like being in a ship's cabin,' thinks Carl, delighted. He loves things to be exactly as they should be, no more and no less. But his father has woken up. It wasn't me, it was the foghorn, thinks Carl. He finds he is saying it aloud.

'I know a foghorn when I hear one,' says his father. Then he is out of bed, standing naked at the window. He always sleeps naked. Carl watches the shadow of his father's genitals as he stands there, legs braced, staring knowledgeably into the fog. He reaches round a hand to scratch his buttock. His arms are long. In a minute he'll turn round. Carl looks down. He fusses with the pillow, buffing it up, but as he does so he catches the snake of his father's backward glance.

'What are you doing that for? Can't you leave things alone?' This time his father doesn't say it, but by now the words say themselves anyway, inside Carl's head.

His father wears a watch on his naked body. Now he looks at it.

'They start serving breakfast in quarter of an hour. Stoke up and it'll keep you going. You can eat as much as you want – it's all in the price.'

Carl has read the breakfast list outside the restaurant. Eggs, cheese, ham, bacon, cereals, toast, rolls, jams, marmalade, as many refills of coffee and tea as you want. 'It's a real bargain,' said the woman reading it beside him. 'But only worth it if you eat a big breakfast.' Then she smiled at him 'I'm sure that won't be a problem.' Why can't they go to the cafeteria? There you can buy a mini box of cornflakes and a giant Coke. In the restaurant he'll have to eat and eat until he feels sick to make it worth the money.

'What's the matter? Feeling queasy?'

There are tufts of hair coming out of his father's belly. Carl doesn't want to have to look at his father's penis, but he can't help it. He just can't look anywhere else. His father's penis is so big and dark and it's the same colour as a bruise. And it stirs. Perhaps it's the movement of the boat.

'No,' says Carl, 'I'm not seasick at all.' But he says it wrong. It comes out as a boast.

'I should bloody well hope not. That sea's as flat as a cow's backside. But visibility's going down,' his father adds critically, professionally, glancing back over his shoulder at the sea as if he owns it.

They walk up the staircase to the restaurant. All that is left of the boat's rocking is a long oily sway from side to side. Carl feels tired inside his head. There are plenty of people about, playing video games and slotting coins into snack machines, but nobody talks much. The fog presses down on them all. In the restaurant his father pays for two breakfasts and it costs nearly ten pounds. Carl starts to work out how much breakfast they must eat to justify the ten pounds. As they go past a table a baby is suddenly, silently sick, pumping out a current of red jam and wet wads of bread. Both parents lean forward at once and drop tissues over the vomit. The father takes another tissue and wipes strings of vomit from round the baby's mouth. The baby cries weakly and the father says something, stands, scoops him out of his high-chair and carries him off, held close against his chest.

'Have bacon and eggs,' says Carl's father as Carl puts rice krispies, an orange and an apple on his tray.

'I'm going to come back again,' says Carl quickly. He pours orange juice in a long stream from the dispenser into a half-litre glass.

'You don't need all that,' says his father.

They take seats by the window, looking out at nothing. The noise of the engines is swollen by the fog, as if the boat is sailing inside a box. Carl pours the milk over his rice krispies and raises his spoon to his mouth. His father loads a fork with strips of bacon and cut-up egg. Carl's stomach clenches. His spoon hangs in mid-air, doing nothing. His father stabs the forkful of bacon and egg towards Carl, but at that moment there is a soft 'thuck', a slight, infinitely dangerous noise which silences the restaurant. Its echo is louder than the echo of the huge engines. People look at one another, then quickly away. Carl notices a shiver run down the pale orange curtains. His spoon hangs, his father's fork stays poised in its stab. The boat swings forward like a man gathering himself on a high diving-board. Carl feels his heart tip inside him, a huge tip which will overbalance him and leave him helpless on the floor at his father's feet. Or is it the boat tipping? Someone is putting on the brakes, much too hard. Carl's orange juice glass goes *hop hip hop* along the table, reaches the edge where there is a ridge to stop things sliding, and then falls on to the floor.

'It's all right,' says Carl to himself, 'it doesn't matter. You can go back and have as much as you want once you've paid.'

But his father isn't even looking at the orange juice. He is staring out of the window, listening.

'They've put the engines into reverse,' he says, but not to Carl. A man looks over from the next table. Carl's father is a man people turn to. He always knows what's going on. A small flush of pride warms Carl. 'Into reverse,' he thinks, 'into reverse.' The boat pushes against itself, back-pedalling. Long lumpy shivers run through it, bump bump bump as if it is riding over a cattle-grid.

'Let's get up on deck,' says his father. But there's all this breakfast on the table. Eggs, bacon, rolls, little sealed packets of cheese. His father's coffee has sloped right over the top of his cup and run away in a thin brown stream over the table. Often Carl has thought that his father could pee black pee out of his big bruised penis.

'Carl,' says his father, not angrily. He is right by the boy, standing over the chair where Carl just sits and watches the stream of coffee. He puts his hands on Carl's upper arms. He could easily lift him but he doesn't. His hands tell Carl what he has to do, and Carl rises and leaves the table without giving the breakfast another thought. Everybody else remains at their tables, their eyes following Carl and his father, and at that moment the ship's loudspeaker system begins to honk in a language Carl doesn't understand.

'We've had a collision,' says his father.

Carl looks up at him without speaking.

'It's all right. We'll find out what's happening.'

Behind them people are beginning to struggle up, fumbling for bags and children. There is a lady with baby twins. Carl was watching her last night. Now she staggers as she tucks one twin under her arm and wrestles the second out of his car seat.

'Dad –' begins Carl, but suddenly they're moving fast, out of the restaurant and nearly at the second staircase which leads up to the deck. People are crowding up the steps. They're not really pushing but Carl thinks that if he stopped they would keep walking over him. But his father is ahead of him and his body is wider than Carl's, making way.

'Hold on to my jacket,' says his father, and Carl gets hold of it with both hands. People dig into him on both sides but he keeps moving, carried up the narrow stairs holding on to his father's jacket. No one would be able to walk over his father. The heavy doors to the deck have been wedged back and they squeeze through, grabbing at the white space beyond.

They are up on deck. An edgy mass of people flows to the rails, but there is nothing to be seen. Only fog, licking right up to the edge of the boat. None of the people round him are speaking English. More sound spurts out of the speakers, but it is twisted up like bad handwriting and Carl can't understand a word.

'It's OK,' says Carl's father. 'We ran down a yacht in the fog. They've put a boat out from the other side.'

The crowd ripples as the news passes over it. It's all right.

No danger to passengers. We've stopped to pick up the crew, that's all. And the hot panicky feeling rolls away into the fog. The lady with her twins is up on deck, and now people are eager to help her.

Another lady holds out her hands to take one of the babies, hoists him into her arms and joggles him to make him smile. People find they have still got bits of breakfast in their hands, and those who have picked up life-jackets let them dangle as if they're of no importance at all.

'Run down a yacht,' thinks Carl. 'Splintered to matchwood.'

The big ferry thrums and rocks on its own weight.

'How will they find them in the fog?' he asks his father.

'They'll have flares. Let's go to the other side.'

Is the fog clearing? It is whiter than ever, and it hurts Carl's eyes. Maybe that's the sun behind it, trying to break out. There is a sharp smell of sea and oil. Announcements come jerkily, in the same voice they used to announce breakfast and the bingo session last night. It's very cold, and to Carl's amazement quite a few people are going down below, rubbing their arms, making way for one another.

'You first.'

'No, please, after you.'

A man comes up with his camcorder. Its blunt nose butts around in the fog and finds nothing.

His father leans on the rail, looking down. The rail is wet with spray or fog, and it makes a dark bar on his father's jacket. He's looking downward and backward, behind the ship. The speakers sound again.

'They've picked up the dinghy,' says Carl's father.

It all takes so long. Carl is cold and shivering and he can't see much because a wall of adults has crowded to the rail. Suddenly his father says sharply, 'There they are!' He is leaning out over the rail, grasped by two men. A pair of binoculars is handed to him over the heads of the crowd. People shove against Carl from all sides. He can't see anything at all.

'They're bringing the boat alongside,' he hears his father say. 'There's the dinghy.'

His father is the leader. Everyone is asking questions.

'Are they all right?'

'How many are there – can you see?'

And a woman beside him says, 'At least they had time to launch the dinghy. Must've been terrifying. Imagine being hit by this thing.'

Then his father's voice. 'There's two of them. A man and a boy.' Carl hears the charge in his voice. A man and a boy. What sort of boy?

'They're alongside. They'll be bringing them up. Can't see any more from this angle.'

The pressure of the crowd relaxes. Carl wriggles through to his father, who is down from the rail and talking to another Englishman.

'– any more of them?'

'– sailing alone with the boy . . .'

'– bloody awful thing to lose your boat like that –'

Carl stands and watches and listens. A man and a boy, sailing alone in the North Sea. The big ferry like a clumsy cliff bulging out of the fog to sink their boat. He tries to catch his father's eye. He tries a joke. 'Well, at least it wasn't the bow doors! We were lucky.' But his father looks at him.

'*We* weren't in any danger,' he points out coldly.

Not like that other boy. His father's criticism hangs in the air. His father had the binoculars. He'd have seen the boy's face. And the man's, too.

The fog is clearing now. Suddenly, when Carl looks, holes open in it and he can see right along the grey water. It's very calm. He can't help saying, 'It wasn't rough, anyway,' but his father has an answer for that, too.

'That's why it happened. If there'd been a wind it would have blown the fog away. They'd have seen our lights.'

But by lunch-time the whole thing might as well never have happened. They'll be in port in three hours' time. The cafeteria and restaurant are crowded and there is a pub quiz in the Marco Polo bar. Carl has been playing the video games at the bottom of the second staircase. He's done really well on *Rally Rider*. But it's so expensive and there's no one to turn to and say, 'Hey, did you see that? Level fourteen!' His father can't stand video games.

'I might have known you'd be here,' says his father's voice just as Carl gets farther than he has ever got before. 'Come on, we're going to eat.'

They find a table. 'Wait here while I pay for our tickets,' says his father. You have to buy a ticket and then you can eat as much as you want from the buffet. People go past with their trays loaded. There are two empty chairs opposite, and he must keep that one for his father. His father has touched it, indicating that it is his. But then a man puts his hand on Carl's father's chair. He is a big, stooping man with a worried face. Carl blushes and says, 'I'm sorry. My father is sitting there,' but the man just smiles and pulls out the chair, then beckons to someone else. Carl looks. It's a boy, a thin, fair-haired boy about his age. His hair is so pale it's nearly the colour of the salt spilt on the table. The man smiles again at Carl as he sits down, while the boy pushes his way politely down the rows of other people's chairs, and squeezes into his place. The father pats the boy's arm as he sits down. They both have meal tickets but they don't seem to know what to do with them. They talk briefly, seriously, heads close together.

Suddenly, Carl sees that the boy is crying, without sound, pushing big tears away from his eyes with his fingers. His father talks to him all the time in a murmuring, up and down voice, as if he doesn't mind, as if the tears are something he had expected. They're sitting close together anyway, but then the father puts his arm around the boy. Carl ducks his head down and flushes. What if his father sees? What if his father says something in that voice of his that can cut worse than a knife? Even if the boy doesn't understand he'll recognize the tone of voice. And his father is coming back, weaving his way across the room with a full tray in his hand, not holding on to anything because he's got a perfect sense of balance and the sea is as flat as a cow's backside. Carl darts a miserably apologetic smile at his father.

'I'm sorry,' he says, as soon as his father is close enough to hear, 'I couldn't keep your place –'

'No, of course not,' says his father. Carl stares, but can't hear any sarcasm, can't see any cold disgust on his father's face. 'Come on, there are some more seats over here,' continues his father, and leads the way to a nearby table where a family has just got up from its meal. There's rubbish all over the table. Normally his father would hate it, but he doesn't seem to mind.

'Did you talk to them?' he asks Carl, with a little backward nod of his head towards the table Carl has just left.

'No, I – they weren't speaking English.'

'Norwegians,' says his father confidently. 'But I don't suppose they were in the mood for conversation.'

Carl stares at his father, bewildered. Then there is a click in his mind like something loading on to a computer screen.

'Oh,' he breathes, 'it's *them*.'

'Yes, of course. What did you think?'

'I don't know, I –'

'I just hope the ferry company's given them a free lunch, that's all,' says his father.

'But it might not have been – I mean, we don't know whose fault it was,' says Carl.

'Sail takes priority over steam,' says his father, stubbing Carl out. But something's got into Carl. He opens his mouth again.

'That boy,' he says, 'that boy was crying.'

He follows his father's glance at the man, the boy. They are sitting still, close together, weary, their meal tickets crumpled on the table in front of them. Then the man reaches forward and touches, very lightly, his son's hand.

'Reaction,' says Carl's father, 'a perfectly natural reaction once danger's over. They were sailing back from England – managing perfectly well till our bloody ferry went across their bows.'

Across their bows, thinks Carl. What does it mean? He feels his shoulders bow down too, crushed by the phrase, by the cliff of what his father knows and he does not. The engine of his father's scorn churns and cuts into him. Then a small, treacherous thought slips into Carl's mind. He looks across at the father and son at the other table. He's seen something his father hasn't seen. The boy's sliding tears, the father's face bent down to his. That language the man was murmuring. Carl's father speaks a bit of Norwegian, like he speaks a bit of everything. But does he really know what it means, that language the Norwegian father spoke to his son?

Stopping at the Lights

DEBORAH MOGGACH

I saw Scottie today. I was stopped at some traffic lights and I saw his little face, quite clearly. When he grinned, that's when I knew. But there were cars behind me, honking.

I've still got the bit of paper from his Dad. It's somewhere, I know it is. Tonight I'm going to have a really good look. Wigan, I think he's gone. I'm meeting this bloke tonight, 7 p.m. outside Garfunkel's. He's from Computer Dateline, so I bet I'll be home early. I'll look then.

Off and on all day I've been thinking about him. Scottie, I mean. He was such a gorgeous kid. Ginger hair, freckly nose. Racing around going vroom-vroom. He arrived with his mum four years ago and they moved into Trailer Four. They didn't have a car; they must have walked from the bus stop with their suitcases, the wind blowing off the fens like knives. His mum, Janine, was very young but she always wore high heels. Mottled, bare legs, but always a pair of slingbacks. Ankle-chain, too. Looking at her face, you wouldn't think she was a goer. Mousy little thing, undernourished. It was like all the vibrancy had drained into her footwear. And into her son; he was bouncing with life.

I never knew where they came from, but that wasn't so unusual in those days. My husband, Jim, asked no questions. He didn't ask *me* many questions, either. To tell the truth, he didn't talk much at all, except to his budgies. He bred pieds and opalines; he played them Radio One. He stood in their aviary for hours, squirting his champion hens with plume spray.

Graceland, that's what our place was called. After The King, of course. It was a little bungalow outside Spalding. There were ploughed fields either side, as far as you could see. It was dead flat. The road outside ran straight as a ruler. We had half an acre out the back, conifers fencing it in, and it was there that the trailers were parked. Seven of them. At night you could see the seven blue glows from their TVs. Sometimes, when I was feeling fidgety, I'd walk around at night; I could follow the story in *Miami Vice*, the actors mouthing at me.

I could hear the sneezes, too; the walls were that thin. And the rows, of course. There were always people coming and going, cars starting up in the middle of the night. That's why Jim insisted on rent in advance, and deposits on the calor-gas cylinders. Our tenants told me such stories about their lives and I always believed them. Mr Pilcher, who said he was just stopping for a week or so while a loan came through from the Chase Manhattan Bank. Mr Carling, who said the girl he was living with was his wife, though I heard her, quite clearly once, call him 'Dad'. The bloke who said he was a Yemeni prince before they took him back to the hospital. Sometimes the police arrived, Sheba barking, blue lights flashing around our lounge. When Mr Mason did a flit, for instance. He told me he owned a copper mine in the Cameroons but when they opened up his trailer it was full of these videos. I nicked one; I thought it might re-activate our sex life, but I just got the giggles and Jim was shocked. He was much older than me, you see; he liked to believe I was innocent. He wouldn't listen to those stories of Elvis getting bloated either. Who was I, to tell him the truth? I was in a real mess when he took me in, he was ever so good to me. I loved Jim, I really did, though I did behave badly on occasions. But he always took me back, no questions asked. He didn't want to hear.

Janine was running away from something, I could tell, because she never got any letters. Nobody knew she was there. But then nobody knew that most of our tenants were there. It was as if we didn't exist.

'Know what we are?' I said to Jim one night. 'Lincolnshire's answer to the Bermuda Triangle. We're the place people disappear to.'

We were playing Travel Scrabble; he was trying to enlarge his vocabulary. 'FYRED', he put down, smoke wreathing up between his fingers. He had been a heavy smoker since he was fourteen, and ran away to join the Wall of Death.

'It's not Y,' I chortled, 'it's I!'

'I know it's you,' he said, stroking my cheek with his nicotine-stained finger. 'Every morning, I can't believe my luck.'

After that, I hadn't the heart to correct him.

Janine was a hopeless mother. At that period there happened to be no other kids around; Scottie was bored, but I never saw her playing with him. She sat on the steps of her trailer, painting her toenails and reading the fiction pull-outs in women's magazines. Sometimes she tottered up the road in her high heels and stopped at the phone box. Once she dyed a whole load of clothes mulberry and hung them up to dry; they flapped in the wind like whale skins. She hadn't a clue about cooking; then neither had I. Sometimes, suddenly, she decided to make something impossible like angel cakes. 'Can I borrow a recipe book?' she'd say, but I only had the manual that came with my microwave. Domesticity wasn't our *forte*. But surely, I thought, if *I* had a kid I'd be better at it?

Scottie liked wandering into our bungalow. He liked tapping on the aquarium and making the guppies jump. He liked inspecting Jim's trophies from the Cage Bird Society. He liked sitting on my knee, pulling bits of fluff out of my sweater and telling me stories. 'My Dad's an airline pilot,' he said one day. The next time his Dad would be a champion boxer. I'd be lying under my sun lamp and there he would be, staring at me with that clear, frank look kids have.

'Why're you doing that?' he said.

'Got to be ready for when the limo arrives,' I said, my eyes closed behind my goggles. 'It's a stretch, see. Cocktail cabinet and all. Got to be ready for Tom Cruise.'

One day he came in when Jim had got dressed up in his Elvis gear. It was the white satin outfit – slashed shirt, rhinestones, the works. Jim was going to the Elvis Convention in Coventry. I was embarrassed – I was always embarrassed when Jim looked like that – but Scottie didn't mind. Besides, he was togged up too, in his cowboy suit. I looked at them in their fancy dress: the six-year-old Lone Ranger and the fifty-year-old Elvis with his wizened, gypsy face and bowed legs.

'My Dad's a famous pop singer,' said Scottie.

'Is he now?' asked Jim, inspecting himself in the mirror. He combed back his hair to cover his bald patch.

'He's so famous I'm not allowed to say his name,' said Scottie. 'My Dad's got a Gold Disc.'

'Know how many he's got?' Jim pointed to the Elvis medallion on the wall. 'Fifty-one. The most awards to an individual in history. Fifty-one Gold Discs.'

I laughed. 'Know what Jim's got? A slipped disc.'

They both swung round and stared at me. I blushed. I hadn't meant to say that; it had just popped out. Jim turned away. He knelt down and adjusted Scottie's bootlace tie.

I tried to make it better. 'He got it on the Wall of Death,' I said. 'Riding the motorbikes. You know he worked on it? He was the champion for years. They went all over – Strathclyde, Farnham. Till he did his back in.'

Neither of them replied. Jim was kneeling beside Scottie, re-buckling his holster belt. 'Wrong way round, mate,' he said.

Eight months passed. Scottie didn't go to school. Sooner or later, I thought, somebody in authority was going to catch up with him and his mother. She looked restless, laying out Tarot cards on her steps and then suddenly sweeping them all into a pile. Sometimes she tottered up the road and just stood there at the bus stop, looking at the timetable. I dreaded Scottie going. I loved having him around, even though he got up to all sorts of mischief. One day I caught him opening the aviary door. Luckily the budgies just sat there on their perches, the dozy buggers. They were that dim. God knows what Jim used to find to say to them.

At our place, see, people came and went; they never stayed for long. Eight months was about the limit, for us. I remember one evening, when I was waiting for my highlights to take – I was wearing one of those hedgehog caps – I remember saying to Jim: 'It's like, this place, we're like traffic lights. People just stop here for a while, you never know where they've been or where they're going. The lights turn green and whoosh! They fuck off.'

I think he replied but I couldn't hear, the rubber cap was over my ears, but it was true. We were just a stopping place at some dodgy moment in people's lives, people who were trying to make it to London one day, when their luck changed. Or maybe they were escaping from London, from something in their past, and they fetched up with us. I had a friend in London, Mandie; she and I had this dream of setting up our own little hairdressing business one day.

People came and went, and there Jim and I were, grounded on East Fen Road with our broken cars. Jim had these cars out in the front yard, you see – Cadillacs and things, Pontiacs, American cars, the sort you saw in films with Sandra Dee in them, and despite his arthritis he spent all day underneath them, tinkering with their innards, while his beloved Country and Western songs played on his portable cassette recorder.

Scottie liked to sit in the cars too. He would sit there for hours, waggling the steering wheel and making humming noises through his lips. He was in a world of his own, he was going anywhere in the world. When he climbed out he wiped his hands on his jeans, like Jim wiped his hands on his overalls when they were greasy; his face had that set, important look blokes have when it's a job well done, that nobody else would understand.

In July there was a heatwave. Janine grew jittery, like a horse smelling a thunderstorm. I woke up one night and saw her standing in the dark, ghostly in her white nightie against the solid black of the cypress trees. The moon shone on her upturned face.

The next morning it was very hot. There was a tap on my back door and there she stood, thin and pale in her halter-neck top. She never got tanned, even in that heat, and even though I had offered her unlimited sessions under my lamp. Her face was tight; just for a moment I thought that something terrible had happened.

She said: 'It's Scottie's birthday today and he's set his little heart on meringues.'

'Why didn't you tell me? I want to get him a present!'

'Is Jim going into Spalding? He could give me a lift and I'll buy some.'

But Jim had removed the carburettor from the Capri, our only roadworthy car; bits of dismembered metal lay all over the yard. We were marooned.

So we decided to have a go at cooking the meringues ourselves. I phoned up my friend Gloria, who was trained in catering, she did the lunches at the King's Head, and she told me the recipe. Egg whites, icing sugar, easy-peasy but keep the oven really low, Mark One.

Easy-peasy it wasn't. Janine had run out of calor gas, see, so we whisked up the egg whites and put them on a baking tray in my own oven. Just then we heard a bellow from Trailer One. Mr Parker's TV had gone dead. He used to sit in there all day watching TV, and it was in the middle of Gloria Hunniford when the electricity went off. We were always having power cuts.

Nobody else was home that day except Mr Parker. We couldn't use his calor-gas cooker. I'd only been in his trailer the once and, to put it mildly, hygienic wasn't the first word that sprang to mind. Besides, he was always trying to lift my skirt with his walking stick.

So know what I did? I put the tray of meringues into the Ford Capri. It was at least 120 degrees in there. I put the baking tray on the back seat and closed the door. 'Aren't I a genius?' I said, polishing an imaginary lapel. 'I'm wasted here.'

We suddenly got the giggles. Even Jim joined in.

'One oven, fully MOT'd,' I said.

'It's Meals on Wheels,' said Jim.

'Change into fourth,' said Janine, 'to brown it nicely on top.'

Jim was chuckling so much that he started one of his coughing fits. Scottie jumped up and down. Sheba's chain rattled as she ran this way and that, suddenly sitting down and thumping her tail.

While the meringues were cooking in the car I went indoors, to find Scottie a present. I went into the bedroom. All my soft toys were there, heaped up on the bed – teddies, rabbits, the giraffe from my twenty-first. I liked to cuddle them at night. I picked up Blinge, my koala bear, and paused. It was as if I was seeing them for the first time. They made me feel awkward, as if I was intruding on myself. They were too babyish for Scottie.

Just then Jim came in. He had recovered from his coughing fit and he was mopping his forehead. He opened the wardrobe and looked in. He always took his time. Then he took out his cowboy hat.

It was still wrapped in plastic. You should have seen it: palest tan, with a woven suede band around the brim. The genuine article. He had bought it at a country and western event in Huddersfield and it had cost a fortune.

'Oh Jim,' I breathed.

'Got any wrapping paper?' he asked.

We had a wonderful party, the four of us. Looking back, maybe we all felt that something was about to happen. At the time I just thought it was the rush you get with a birthday, the jolt it gives you. The fridge had rumbled back to life and we drank cans of Budweiser and a bottle of German wine. Janine and Jim, who had hardly spoken all those months, even danced together to Tammy Wynette, crooning the soppy lyrics. Jim was supposed to be off the booze, but to tell the truth it improved him. Janine's sallow face was flushed. I danced with Scottie, the cowboy hat slipping over his nose. In the middle we suddenly remembered our meringues. We rushed out and opened the back door of the Capri. They hadn't cooked; they had just sort of subsided. It didn't matter. We gave them to Sheba, our canine dustbin.

When the sun went down we sat on the back porch. Janine put

her arm around her son and squeezed him. She wasn't usually demonstrative.

'You're a big boy now,' she said, 'you're the man of the family.'

'He's not big,' I said. 'He's only a kid.'

She squeezed him tighter. 'You'll look after me. You'll see it's all OK.'

'At seven?' I asked. 'Give him a chance!'

There was a silence. From the trailers came the murmur of TVs, the rising laughter of a canned audience. Beyond the bungalow, we heard cars whizzing past on the road. Where were they going?

Jim spoke. He said: 'I wish to God I'd had a son.'

That was the first and last time he ever spoke of it.

The next morning I was standing in the kitchen, looking at the bowl of egg yolks. Six egg yolks; what was I supposed to do with them? I was standing there when the phone rang.

A woman's voice asked: 'Is there a J. Maddox at that address please?'

'Nobody of that name,' I replied. It was so hot that the receiver stuck to my hand.

'Are you sure about that? Janine Maddox?'

I paused. Janine's surname was Smith. That's what she had told us, anyway. We got a lot of Smiths.

Something in the woman's voice made me wary. 'Sorry,' I said, 'nobody of that name here.'

A fly buzzed against the window pane. Outside, in the yard, Scottie was sitting in the Chevrolet. It was his favourite. I could just see the top of his head, at the wheel. Jim had managed to get the electrics working and Scottie was trying out the indicators. First the left one winked: that way it was London. Then the right one: that meant somewhere else, somewhere beyond my calculations. Somewhere only Scottie knew.

I suddenly felt sad. I went out the back. Janine had washed her hair. She sat on the steps of her trailer, her hair wrapped in a towelling turban, smoking. For once there was no sign of a magazine. I realized for the first time that she was ever so young – twenty-two, maybe.

Twenty-three. Younger than me. I realized that I hardly knew anything about her.

'Someone just phoned,' I said, 'asking about you.'

Her head jerked up. 'Who was it?'

'A woman,' I replied. 'It's all right. I said I didn't know you.'

She looked down at her feet. They were bare today, but her scuffed white slingbacks were lying on the grass nearby. When her toes were squashed into them, Scottie said they looked like little maggots.

She blew out smoke, shrugging her bony shoulders. 'Thanks,' she said.

There was a thunderstorm that night. I lay next to Jim, listening to his wheezing breaths. His lungs creaked like a door, opening and closing. My koala, Blinge, was pressed between us; my giraffe, Estelle, lay on the other side. She took up as much room as another person. I could feel her plush hoof resting against my thigh.

Outside, the sky rumbled. It sounded like furniture being shifted. It sounded like bulky objects being dragged across tarmac. I lay there drowsily. I've always loved thunderstorms; when I was little I used to crawl into bed with my mum and smell her warm body smells.

Maybe, in fact, that noise *was* something being moved. At our place, things were often shifted at night. The thunder cracked. I touched Blinge's leather nose. 'It's all right,' I whispered, 'it's nothing.' I ran my finger over his glass eye; there was only one left. 'I'm here.'

Jim stirred in his sleep. He wheezed, and then there was a silence. It went on for an alarmingly long time. I held my breath, willing the noises to start again.

Finally they did; the creaking wheezes. I wrapped my arm around his gaunt chest. He muttered something in his sleep; I couldn't catch the words. Then he said, quite distinctly: 'You've got your life waiting.'

★

The next morning Janine and Scottie had gone. Cleared out. Their trailer was empty. We never knew who had come to collect them, moving their belongings in the night, or where they had gone. All that remained were small mementoes of Scottie: his sweet wrappers, swept into a corner of the trailer – Janine was surprisingly tidy, she wasn't like me in that respect. A criss-cross of knife marks in the trunk of one of the cypress trees, as if he were going to start a game of noughts and crosses, and hadn't found anybody to play them with.

Not long after that, a few months in fact, they demolished our place to build an out-of-town shopping mall. A socking great thing, with an atrium – they're all the rage. It was called the Rushy Dyke Shopping Experience. Rushy Dyke made me giggle; it sounded like a lesbian in a hurry. Despite my sojourn in the fens I hardly knew that dyke meant ditch. To tell the truth, I'd hardly stepped a hundred yards up the road. If you had seen our locality you would understand. No point walking somewhere when you can see exactly where you're going, is there?

Our property, where we lived, that's where the access road is now. They've put up traffic lights, too, it's that congested. So I was proved right. Graceland, and its accompanying trailer park, was just a brief stopping place for all concerned.

I got a job at the Rushy Dyke Shopping Experience. Jim was in hospital by then, and I visited him in the evenings, en route to my flat above one of Spalding's hot spots, Paradise Video Rentals. Sitting beside my storage heater I grieved for my husband, whilst the local ravers visited the premises below, hiring videos with Bruce Willis in them. The manager, Keith, watched the latest releases all evening, gunfire erupting through my carpet. It was as if Scottie was downstairs, shooting everything in sight. Then the shop went quiet, and I was alone. I thought of Jim, wheezing beside me in the night. I thought of him more than he ever believed.

I'll tell you about my job. I stood under the atrium bit, glass arches above me as high as a cathedral. One side of me there was a Next; the other side there was a Body Shop. It was nice and warm, that was something. Canned music played, to put people into the mood. It never rained there, and the wind never blew like knives. They had invented new street names and put up the signs: Tulip Walk, Daffodil Way. That was because Spalding is famous for bulbs.

I had to wear: Item One – a mob cap. Item Two – a gingham apron. The first day I felt a right prat. I stood at a farm cart in the middle of the mall, selling Old Ma Hodge's Butterscotch Bonbons. They were packaged in little cardboard cottages, with flowers printed on them. Actually the bonbons were made in a factory in Walsall but who was I to tell? Maureen, who became my friend, she stood at an adjacent cart selling Country Fayre Pot Pourris. Know them? Those things full of dead petals nobody knows what to do with. Both enterprises were leased on a franchise basis to a man we never saw, called Mr Ranesh.

I only worked there for a year, while Jim was holding on for longer than anyone had expected. He had always been stubborn. Now he couldn't speak so well, he suddenly seemed to have a lot to say. On my visits he told me more than I had heard in five years of marriage to him. It was mostly about his early days in children's homes. He spoke in a rush, kneading my fingers.

At work I re-arranged my wares, stacking up my toffee cottages and signalling by semaphore to Maureen, who was going through a divorce. She crouched behind her cart reading a book called *Life Changes – a User's Guide*. She said we were in the same boat, but I didn't agree.

I never knew what the weather was like outside, so I can't recall what season it was when the man came in. He wore a two-tone turquoise anorak, so maybe it was winter. He looked lost; he didn't look as if he had come in to do any shopping. We didn't get many single blokes there, except at Discount Digital Tectonics; most blokes were simply being towed along by their wife and kids.

I saw him approaching Maureen, at the next cart. She flirted with him and flashed me a glance. A man! He spoke to her for a moment, then she pointed to me. He came over.

'Douglas McLaughlan,' he said, extending his hand. He was a

beefy bloke, not unattractive. Ginger hair and twinkly eyes. Sort of jaunty. Despite the name, he had a London accent. 'The charming young lady over there thought you might be able to help me.' He cleared his throat. 'I believe you have connections with a caravan park hereabouts.'

'Me and my husband ran it,' I said. 'It was right here, where you're standing. But they knocked it down to build this.'

He paused, taking this in. 'Ah,' he said. He offered me a small cigar. A woman passed, pushing a pair of twins in a double buggy. A group of schoolgirls came out of the Body Shop, linking arms. 'I'm looking for a young lady called Janine,' he said. Then he added casually: 'And her little lad.'

It was then that I realized. I looked at him, recognizing the likeness. The ginger hair, of course. He had Scottie's freckles, too, and his jutting lower lip. Scottie's lip had that determined look when he was concentrating on his driving.

'I'm sorry,' I said, 'I haven't a clue where they've gone.'

He smoked in silence for a moment.

'I'm sorry,' I said again. I felt awkward, and re-arranged the cottages.

'Had to do a bit of travelling,' he said, 'what with one thing and another. Thought I'd found them this time. Thought I'd hit the jackpot.'

I looked up. 'He was a gorgeous kid.'

'He was?'

I nodded. The man took out a piece of paper and wrote something down. 'If you hear anything . . .' He said something about going to Wigan. Then he handed the paper to me. 'Funny old business, isn't it.'

We stood there for a moment. Then he pointed, with his thumb, at the little cardboard cottages. Sometimes, when I was bored, I arranged them into streets like a real village. He pointed at the display trays featuring the smiling face of Old Ma Hodge in her broderie anglaise bonnet.

'Don't believe a word of it myself,' he said. 'Do you?'

★

I drive a Sunbeam Alpine now; it's a collector's item. First thing I did, when I came to London, was learn to drive. I whizz all over London, fixing people's hair in their own homes. I started on my friend Mandie's hair, and some of the blokes at the club where she works, and the word got round. I'm quite good, you see. I tell my new clients that I trained at Michaeljohn's and I believe it myself now. Jim believed he worked on the Wall of Death even though he only drove the equipment lorry. His real name was Arnold, in fact, but he re-christened himself after Jim Reeves, another of his heroes. I only learnt this near the end. With all the harm in the world, what's the harm in that? Scottie never knew his father; he can believe anything.

I was thinking this today, because I saw him. I told you, didn't I? I saw Scottie when I was sitting at the lights.

It was at a junction leading into the Euston Road. These two boys were there, teenagers really, washing windscreens. They started on mine before I could stop them. There was a lot of splashing and lather. I think they liked the car; you don't see many Sunbeams around nowadays. Anyway I sat there, flustered, rooting around for a 50p piece.

They did it really thoroughly, there was foam all over the place. Then suddenly, as the lights changed, the windscreen was wiped clear and I saw his face. He was wearing a denim jacket and a red T-shirt; there were pimples on his chin, as well as freckles. I only realized who he was after I had wound down the window and passed him the coin. 'Cheers,' he said. His piping voice had broken.

The cars behind me were blaring their horns. I had to move on. I was helpless in the three lanes of traffic, like a stick in a rushing current, there was a socking great lorry thundering behind me.

It took me a while to get back to where I'd begun. It was the same place, I know it was – big office block one side, church the other, covered with plastic sheets and scaffolding. It was the same place, all right. But the boys had gone.

Not a trace. They must have picked up their bucket and gone. There was nothing left except some damp patches on the tarmac.

Gentlemen always sleep on the damp patch. I suddenly thought of

Jim, and how he winced when I said something crude like that. I thought of how he had been a gentleman all his life, with nobody to tell him how.

The lights changed to green. I thought of how he never blamed me for the one thing I couldn't give him. Then the chorus of horns started up behind me, and I had to move on.

A SELECTION OF BOOKS FROM BBC/PENGUIN

Absolutely Fabulous Jennifer Saunders

Wicked and funny, *Absolutely Fabulous* is the hit television comedy series that blows the lid off the fashion industry. The cast includes PR mogul Edina, slave to every media-induced fad from designer diets to flotation tanks; her alcoholic and sponging best friend Patsy, addicted to everything that's harmful (and probably illegal); and Saffron, Edina's long-suffering, sensible daughter who struggles to stay sane in the midst of the chaos which erupts around her.

A brilliant send-up of all the trends and neuroses that afflict life in the nineties, *Absolutely Fabulous* contains all the episodes from the first series including some scenes and dialogue not eventually transmitted. Written by Jennifer Saunders in her uniquely acerbic style, this book of scripts demonstrates just how fabulous *Absolutely Fabulous* really is!

Absolutely Fabulous 2 Jennifer Saunders

Edina and Patsy, television's most outrageous duo, offer a riotous second helping of the award-winning *Absolutely Fabulous*.

Blazing their way through the world of fashion PR, all their adventures from the second series can be found in this explosive collection of scripts, including the photo-shoot in Marrakesh where Saffy is exchanged for a small amount of dirhams, and disturbing revelations about Patsy in *Hello!* magazine.

A SELECTION OF BOOKS FROM BBC/PENGUIN

EastEnders: A Celebration   Colin Brake

The full, inside story of the BBC's most popular programme.

No television serial has ever offered viewers as much drama, excitement and gritty realism as *EastEnders*. From its first episode over ten years ago it gripped the nation, and it has kept us enthralled with some of the most compelling story-lines and controversial issues – from kidnapping to teenage pregnancies – yet seen on prime-time television. This is the real story – including the tenth anniversary and beyond – of Britain's favourite soap, and it gives the low-down on the who, what, where and when of more than a decade of *EastEnders*.

Jimmy McGovern's **The Lakes**   K. M. Lock

Danny Kavanagh may be bright but he's idle. The money from his giro disappears in the betting shop on the day it arrives, and he's driving his parents round the bend. So Danny leaves Liverpool behind him and takes off for the Lakes. On the way he meets Emma Quinlan. But before their destinies – and their bodies – become entangled, Danny finds himself a job as a porter in the frantic bustle of a hotel kitchen. Run by the domineering, oversexed chef, the kitchen is the hub of Danny's life, although Emma is to play an increasingly large role in it . . . whether her family likes it or not.

To their way of thinking, Danny is a good-for-nothing money waster. And they could be right. But there is another side to Danny: a selfless, heroic side, which emerges when tragedy strikes at the heart of a small Lakeland community.

A SELECTION OF BOOKS FROM BBC/PENGUIN

Mediterranean Cooking Claudia Roden

From the colourful and aromatic fruit and vegetable dishes to the simple tastes of chargrilled fish and meat, Claudia Roden captures the essence of the Mediterranean in this newly revised edition of her classic work.

Among the 250 recipes included in the book, twenty-five of which are entirely new, Claudia Roden includes both the classics and the more unusual specialities of particular countries and regions: the *tapas* of Spain and the *mezze* of the Middle East; the vegetable *tians* of Provence and the fruit and meat *tagines* of Morocco. In addition, she also provides a fascinating historical introduction to the gastronomy of the area together with advice on traditional techniques and utensils.

'Claudia Roden's writing has the fascination of her conversation. Her books are treasure-houses of information and mines of literary pleasures' *Observer*

The Complete BBC Diet Dr Barry Lynch

If you enjoy food and dread the thought of dieting, think again. Now you can lose weight without the misery of hunger with *The Complete BBC Diet*. By reducing fat and sugar and increasing fibre you can transform your diet – and your figure – and keep weight off for good. Medically approved, easy to follow and tremendously successful, this book has helped hundreds of thousands of people become fitter and slimmer.

A SELECTION OF BOOKS FROM BBC/PENGUIN

The Making of Pride and Prejudice Sue Birtwistle and Susie Conklin

Filmed on location in Wiltshire and Derbyshire, *Pride and Prejudice* was watched and enjoyed by millions. Chronicling eighteen months of work – from the original concept to the first broadcast – *The Making of Pride and Prejudice* brings vividly to life the challenges and triumphs involved in the production of this sumptuous television series.

Follow a typical day's filming, including the transformation of Lacock village into the minutely detailed setting of Jane Austen's Meryton. Discover how an actor approaches the character, how costumes and wigs are designed, and how the roles of casting directors, researchers, and even experts in period cookery and gardening, contribute to the series. Including many full-colour photographs, interviews and lavish illustrations, *The Making of Pride and Prejudice* is a fascinating insight into all aspects of a major television enterprise.

Pride and Prejudice Jane Austen

'I must confess I think her as delightful a creature as ever appeared in print,' wrote Jane Austen of Elizabeth Bennet, the heroine of *Pride and Prejudice*. Few readers have disagreed. Yet Elizabeth's vivacity, beauty and wit leave Jane Austen's hero Mr Darcy unmoved on their first meeting, and his aloof superiority is more than matched by Elizabeth's cool disdain. Darcy is peremptorily dismissed – 'the last man in the world I could be prevailed upon to marry' – whereupon, in one of English literature's sublime volte-faces, Elizabeth is compelled to realize that first impressions are not always the truest.

Pride and Prejudice is probably Jane Austen's best-loved work. In its sparkling comedy of love and marriage, wit, form and feeling achieve a perfect balance.